P9-CAO-173

CultureShock!
A Survival Guide to Customs and Etiquette

HAWAI'I

Brent Massey

Marshall Cavendish
Editions

This 2nd edition published in 2009 by:
Marshall Cavendish Corporation
99 White Plains Road
Tarrytown NY 10591-9001
www.marshallcavendish.us

First published in 2006 by Marshall Cavendish International (Asia) Private
Limited, reprinted 2007.
© 2009 Marshall Cavendish International (Asia) Private Limited
Other Marshall Cavendish Offices:
Marshall Cavendish International (Asia) Pte Ltd. 1 New Industrial Road,
Singapore 536196 ■ Marshall Cavendish Ltd. 5th Floor, 32-38 Saffron Hill,
London EC1N 8FH, UK ■ Marshall Cavendish International (Thailand) Co Ltd.
253 Asoke, 12th Flr, Sukhumvit 21 Road, Klongtoey Nua, Wattana, Bangkok
10110, Thailand ■ Marshall Cavendish (Malaysia) Sdn Bhd, Times Subang,
Lot 46, Subang Hi-Tech Industrial Park, Batu Tiga, 40000 Shah Alam, Selangor
Darul Ehsan, Malaysia

Marshall Cavendish is a trademark of Times Publishing Limited

ISBN: 978-0-7614-5666-7

Please contact the publisher for the Library of Congress catalogue number

Printed in Singapore by Times Printers Pte Ltd

Photo Credits:
All black and white photos from the author except page xii (Photolibrary).
Colour photos from Photolibrary pages a, d–e, i, j–k, l–m, n–o, p; the author
pages b–c, f–g; Juan-Diego Garcia page h ■ Cover photo: Photolibrary

All illustrations by TRIGG

ABOUT THE SERIES

Culture shock is a state of disorientation that can come over anyone who has been thrust into unknown surroundings, away from one's comfort zone. *CultureShock!* is a series of trusted and reputed guides which has, for decades, been helping expatriates and long-term visitors to cushion the impact of culture shock whenever they move to a new country.

Written by people who have lived in the country and experienced culture shock themselves, the authors share all the information necessary for anyone to cope with these feelings of disorientation more effectively. The guides are written in a style that is easy to read and covers a range of topics that will arm readers with enough advice, hints and tips to make their lives as normal as possible again.

Each book is structured in the same manner. It begins with the first impressions that visitors will have of that city or country. To understand a culture, one must first understand the people—where they came from, who they are, the values and traditions they live by, as well as their customs and etiquette. This is covered in the first half of the book.

Then on with the practical aspects—how to settle in with the greatest of ease. Authors walk readers through topics such as how to find accommodation, get the utilities and telecommunications up and running, enrol the children in school and keep in the pink of health. But that's not all. Once the essentials are out of the way, venture out and try the food, enjoy more of the culture and travel to other areas. Then be immersed in the language of the country before discovering more about the business side of things.

To round off, snippets of basic information are offered before readers are 'tested' on customs and etiquette of the country. Useful words and phrases, a comprehensive resource guide and list of books for further research are also included for easy reference.

CONTENTS

FOREWORD

Mark Twain loved Hawai'i, and in his *Letters from Hawai'i*, he called it the 'Rainbow Islands' because of the frequent rainbows in the sky. Twain visited Hawai'i 88 years after Captain Cook, and in his letters he told how the missionaries had regrettably supplanted the local Hawaiian culture with Western culture and Christian values.

In the 140 years since Twain's visit, Hawai'i continues to change rapidly. Honolulu and even O'ahu may look and act more like Los Angeles than other Polynesian islands like Tahiti. New skyscrapers and shopping centres are being built. The island pace of life is lost in the crowding, traffic jams, high prices and competition for jobs. On the road to work, sirens wail, hip-hop pounds in low-rider Hondas and people yell into mobile phones. Tourist planes take off and land every minute, and military jet fighters and helicopters rumble through the skies.

On the other hand, on your first day here, you may go out to your car and find that there are flowers covering it, as if someone has left a romantic note. Everyday, white and yellow flowers fall from a tree onto the windshield. In the morning dew, the flowers are strung together like a *lei*. You brush them onto the ground because you have learned that flowers get smeared on the window by the windscreen wipers. Nearby, the landscapers sweep and fill their pails. The trash of paradise is flowers. Despite it all, you may find a spot in your heart for the Rainbow Islands.

OUR PERCEPTION

For first timers to Hawai'i, it is important to buy a *lei* with a flower that has a fragrance. The fragrance of the flower mixed with the balmy ocean breeze makes you know without a doubt that you have arrived in Hawai'i. As a newcomer to O'ahu, you are filled with Polynesian dreams and visions of a multiracial paradise, but living in Hawai'i will change these perceptions. Many customs, behaviours, attitudes and values are different from mainland USA and it can feel like you are living in a foreign country. You wonder at their odd behaviour, and them at yours, until you learn the ways of the people of Hawai'i.

You may know Hawai'i's travel industry's advertising, but most don't know the history of Hawai'i or even Polynesia. You are at a disadvantage, having so much misinformation and lack of information. It is common to assume that moving to Hawai'i is like moving to any other state in America; after all, how different could it be?

Hawai'i has a long history that is different from mainland USA. For more than a millennium, it was a Polynesian paradise, but the last few hundred years are a picture of struggle against exploitation. The pidgin English, spoken locally, grew out of this struggle as a way to communicate among the many non-native English speakers. The local accent and pidgin English can sometimes make it difficult for mainlanders to understand and communicate with the people of Hawai'i.

HAWAI'I'S PEOPLE

Hawai'i is a mix of Polynesian, Asian and Caucasian cultures. The Polynesians have been in Hawai'i since around 400–500 AD. Captain Cook arrived in 1778 and the missionaries later in 1820. The 1800s saw the arrival of Chinese, Japanese and Portuguese immigrant plantation workers, and in the beginning of the 1900s, Okinawan, Korean and Filipinos.

Through massive migration, Hawai'i became a mix of races and cultures. In Hawai'i, everyone is a minority; there is no dominant race. There is an influence of American mainland culture, but that isn't the dominant culture in Hawai'i. Even today, the heritage cultures of many ethnic groups remain strong, and can be seen in their food, festivals, TV, radio, religions, etc.

In addition to the individual ethnic cultures, there is also the local culture of Hawai'i. When mixing with people from other groups, Hawai'i's residents tend to default to the customs and behaviours of the local culture. The local culture developed through the unique history of Hawai'i and has contributions from all the ethnic groups. One example is the pidgin English which borrows words from the Hawaiian and Asian languages.

So what are the ethnic and local cultures? What are the customs and behaviour we need to be aware of? Just as there are different shades of people in Hawai'i, there are different shades of culture and therefore many exceptions to any conclusion we make in trying to understand the culture of Hawai'i. For the newcomer, this can be confusing and difficult to understand because Hawai'i's cultures are complex and changing. This book explains the major ethnic cultures— Hawaiian, Japanese, Filipino, Caucasian and Chinese—which provides a foundation for understanding the local culture. And then it explains the local culture and how newcomers from the mainland and foreign countries fit in.

CROSSING CULTURES

The cost of living, homes for sale, employment opportunities and local news information are important because it helps newcomers get physically oriented, but the real adventure begins when they start to interact with the people of Hawai'i. This book has information on physical orientation but more importantly, it tells you about the people: what they value, why they act the way they do and how their unique history affects their philosophy and way of life. This book will help you cope with the volcano of unexpected issues when living in Hawai'i.

The next best thing to living in a strange land is reading about it. Many of us love travel stories like Mark Twain's *Letters from Hawai'i* because it shows someone stumbling about in a different society, and we laugh at the inevitable mishaps that occur. As a newcomer, we can have some wonderful new experiences in Hawai'i, but sometimes we can have some unpleasant culture shocks that aren't easy to laugh about.

The American mainlander may feel like the outsider in Hawai'i for various reasons. There is a history of Westerners exploiting and changing Hawai'i that some residents may hold mainlanders accountable for. However, the most likely reason is a fear of security. The people of Hawai'i do not want to lose their jobs or anything else to mainlanders or foreign immigrants. They also do not want to return to the days when the Caucasian was in the majority and held political control over Hawai'i's people.

Moving to a new place is stressful enough, and adding culture shock doesn't make it any easier. In everyday life, we can only see the tip of the iceberg; underneath the surface is a mass of unspoken and unseen behaviour, customs and values. Understanding this mass helps make sense of our daily interactions with the people of Hawai'i.

Culture shock has a learning curve with stages of frustration, isolation, and eventually adaptation. This book conveys the experience of many newcomers and old-timers, and it provides you with some sample scenarios to test your cultural readiness. This may save you and the people you encounter the discomfort of a cultural collision, while you adapt to living in Hawai'i.

There are thousands of people who move to Hawai'i each year and then move back to the mainland a year later. This book will help you avoid being another short-timer statistic by dispelling the misinformation, myths and stereotypes you may have already learned about Hawai'i; and then give you a better understanding of the people and their customs so that you and your family will be successful living among the people of Hawai'i.

Lastly, James A Michener in his book *Hawaii* wrote of a 'golden man' of Hawai'i. The golden man is not a mixing of races, or even the mingling of cultures; it is a product of the mind. It refers to someone knowledgeable of the ways of the East and the West and bearing fruit on both sides. Through our crossing of cultures, we become a golden man or woman.

ACKNOWLEDGEMENTS

I would like to say a big thank you to Rheba Massey, Mark and Shari Massey, Drew Massey and the rest of my family for their support. I would also like to thank Bernie Ostrowski and his developmental psychology class at Leeward Community College, Ray Moody and the members of the Honolulu MBTI group, Spring and the staff at the Leeward Community College Children's Center, Richard Brislin and the members of his intercultural group at the University of Hawai'i, Monica Okido for all her support and information when we first moved here, Rosemarie Woodruff, Clement Bautista and Farzana Nayani for their feedback, Norman Gibson and Mike Giglio for their emotional support and Hideo Asano for inspiration.

This is dedicated to the Lord and my family;
to my children who shared their father with his work;
and to my readers,
who I hope to have served to the best of my ability.

Be welcomed by the warm hospitality and rich diversity of the people of Hawai'i.

MAP OF USA

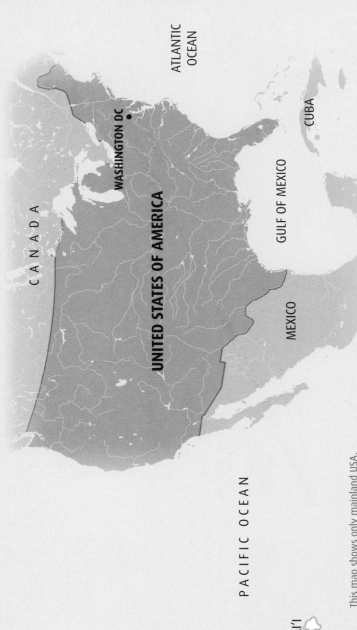

ATLANTIC
OCEAN

CUBA

GULF OF MEXICO

WASHINGTON DC

UNITED STATES OF AMERICA

CANADA

MEXICO

PACIFIC OCEAN

HAWAI'I

This map shows only mainland USA.
It does not include the state of Alaska
and the islands of San Juan.

MAP OF THE HAWAIIAN ISLANDS

FIRST IMPRESSIONS

CHAPTER 1

'The people of Hawai'i are more friendly and
welcoming than residents of the other 49 states.
'*E komo mai*' is not just a phrase;
it is a way of life.'
—Lenny Klompus, *Honolulu Star Bulletin*

ALOHA

E komo mai means welcome in Hawaiian. It is part of the *aloha* spirit and hospitality that everyone feels when visiting the islands.

University of Hawai'i professor Richard L Rapson, in his book *Fairly Lucky You Live in Hawai'i: Cultural Pluralism in the Fiftieth State*, states: 'In my opinion, *aloha* spirit, like 'southern hospitality', is alive for some people and has died for others. It represents a most worthy goal for the state... I don't think the people of Hawai'i are more friendly or less friendly, more loving or less loving, than those of comparable regions.'

Experiencing the Hawaiian Spirit

My first experience with *e komo mai*, *aloha* and *maikai* (excellence) was when the movers and furniture delivery people took off their shoes when carrying in new furniture and household items. The movers were shocked when they saw how poorly the movers in Colorado had loaded our van. Things were falling out of crunched boxes. Here, the movers wrap everything up with lots of paper and blankets. They go the extra mile. I could see the differences of culture by comparing Colorado to Hawaiian movers.

MELTING WOK?

Hawai'i is a huge kaleidoscope—a colourful collage of ethnic people with different behaviour. Talking about race in Hawai'i is OK, and that may surprise some people. In certain parts of the US, like the east coast, you are taught that it isn't politically correct to talk about race. You avoid saying 'Japanese guy' or 'Black guy'. You jump around the subject like it is a landmine. People here throw around racial tags without any hang-ups. They also make frequent racial jokes. It's a level playing field—jokes are made about every race.

Talking about racial differences is a common, accepted topic of conversation. They have no problem asking each other "What are you?" Chinese, Hawaiian, Portuguese or what? If you are a newcomer, locals aren't sure where you are coming from or what your beliefs are so they are cautious. Build a rapport, establish a relationship with them and they will feel at ease with you and make jokes about you and your race as much as their race and other races. This is a different paradigm for people who haven't lived in a multi-ethnic community before. The common language is race and talking about racial differences is part of the experience.

The population of Hawai'i is mixed and people claim to be all or part of the following: 58 per cent have Asian blood, 39.3 per cent have Caucasian and 23.3 per cent part Native Hawaiian or Pacific Islander. This is the population of the largest ethnic groups: White (294,102), Japanese (201,764) Filipino (170,635), Native Hawaiian (80,137), Chinese (56,600) and Korean (23,537). Three-quarters of the population is Christian and one-quarter is Buddhist. 25 per cent of the people of Hawai'i do not speak English at home. The top three non-official languages spoken in Hawai'i are Filipino (Tagalog and Ilicano), Japanese and Chinese. Less than 1 per cent of the population speak Hawaiian at home.

> By 2050, Caucasians will no longer be the majority in the US with projected Spanish and Asian population growth. In Hawai'i, all races and ethnic groups are minorities—including Caucasians. Good or bad, Hawai'i will be looked to for examples of how different races will integrate or separate.

According to the US Census Bureau, about 38,000 people migrate from other parts of the US to Hawai'i every year. More people migrate from California than any other state. In contrast, there are more people leaving Hawai'i; about 40,000 a year move to other states. Nevada has a huge population of people that originally lived in Hawai'i.

There are also people coming from other countries. About 5,000 foreign immigrants arrive in Hawai'i each year. The top country to emigrate from is the Philippines, followed by China, Japan, Korea and Vietnam. In addition to mainland and foreign immigrants, there is a high turnover of military personnel and their families. They number around 80,000 in Hawai'i and are all stationed on O'ahu, with the exception of about one thousand who are on the other islands. On O'ahu, this segment alone accounts for 10 per cent of the island's population.

Immigrants Admitted by Country of Birth 1998–2002 (US Census Bureau)					
Country of birth	1998	1999	2000	2001	2002
All Countries	5,465	4,299	6,056	6,313	5,503
Canada	49	58	106	120	120
Hong Kong	(NA)	(NA)	(NA)	(NA)	106
Japan	(NA)	(NA)	(NA)	585	480
Korea	286	186	305	286	263
Mexico	75	70	62	116	67
People's Republic of China	482	368	551	530	538
Philippines	3,140	2,472	3,053	3,341	2,800
Taiwan	48	43	72	65	73
Vietnam	101	148	196	228	210
Other Countries	1,284	954	1,711	1,042	846

People Moving From Other US States to Hawai'i 1995–2000 (US Census Bureau)	
State	Number of Immigrants
Total	125,160
California	32,321

People Moving From Other US States to Hawai'i 1995–2000 (US Census Bureau)	
Washington	8,128
Texas	7,792
Virginia	5,801
Florida	5,639
New York	5,030
Georgia	3,541
North Carolina	3,529
Oregon	3,486
Arizona	3,186
Colorado	3,173
Maryland	2,900
Illinois	2,892
Ohio	2,159
Pennsylvania	2,116
Michigan	2,021
Nevada	1,853
New Jersey	1,707
Massachusetts	1,695
Alaska	1,671
South Carolina	1,649
Tennessee	1,623
Utah	1,615
All Others	19,633

People Moving From Hawai'i to Other US States 1995–2000 (US Census Bureau)	
State	Number of Emigrants
Total	201,293
California	44,192
Washington	17,491

People Moving From Hawai'i to Other US States 1995–2000 (US Census Bureau)	
Texas	13,127
Nevada	12,079
Virginia	10,593
Florida	9,820
Oregon	6,812
Arizona	6,700
Georgia	6,313
Colorado	6,110
North Carolina	6,085
Maryland	4,140
New York	3,988
Illinois	3,519
Utah	3,218
Tennessee	2,908
Ohio	2,684
Missouri	2,639
Oklahoma	2,444
Pennsylvania	2,314
South Carolina	2,290
Alaska	2,287
Michigan	2,272
All Others	27,268

MULTI-ETHNIC COMMUNITY

Waikele is the perfect example of a multi-ethnic community. Waikele is 37 per cent Japanese, 30 per cent Filipino, 28 per cent Caucasian, and 5 per cent Korean. The Japanese and Filipino population isn't surprising because Waikele is wedged in between the two ethnic enclaves of Waipahu (Filipino) and Pearl City (Japanese). According to one Waipi'o Century 21 realtor, Waikele is popular with the military because it is central to several military installations. Schofield Barracks is just up the hill past Mililani in Wahiawa. Pearl

Harbour is down the hill past Pearl City; and out towards leeward coast is the Coast Guard in Kapolei—so that explains the Caucasian population. As for the Koreans, they also have ethnic enclaves—albeit smaller—but they seem to be the most evenly spread out of all the major ethnic groups. They seem to fit in just about everywhere and have numbers averaging around 5 per cent in many of the populated areas on O'ahu.

In my town house complex, the majority of my neighbours are Filipino. My next door neighbours are immigrants from the Philippines who have been here for several years. They are a pair of brother and sister in their 50s and the former works as a security guard at a small discount store. Upstairs is a younger Filipino couple with a daughter. The father works on one of the military bases.

In the building across from me is a friendly Filipino man and his family. He works as a security guard on one of the military bases and he taught me that some Filipino words are substituted with Spanish, like *buenos noches* for good evening.

Above the Filipino family lives a friendly older Samoan couple. They're happy because their son, daughter-in-law and new grandson will soon move in with them. Their place is a small two-bedroom condo, but Samoans—like their Polynesian cousins, the Hawaiians—love to be close to their family.

Contrast that with the second or third generation Japanese grandpa at my daughter's kindergarten. He has to pick up his three grandchildren from the kindergarten and watch over them. He said it was his full-time job. I said he must be very happy he can spend so much time with them. He looked at me like I was crazy.

Another one of my neighbours is a mainland white guy who used to be in the air force doing

My ex-neighbour, a white guy from New York, is married to a local Filipino lady. They were both working at a local bank but he decided that there weren't any decent jobs here so he moved his wife and two young kids to New York. His wife wasn't happy about it, because she liked Hawai'i and had family here. He is a good example of the struggle to get a decent paying job here. If you aren't in the military or have a security clearance, it is a tough to get a job. Additionally, if you are from the mainland, then you probably don't have the connections to get a job either.

computer and technical work. He is now a contractor to the military doing IT administration. He has been here for four years and said he still doesn't have any friends that are local. His wife is a native Japanese from Okinawa and they have a little boy.

One of my other neighbours, a black guy, just got out of the military after ten years. He registered with unemployment and two weeks later, they had a job for him because he already had a security clearance. He was a mechanic in the military and is now a contractor to the military as a mechanic. He fixes big trucks and Humvees. His wife is a white girl from Minnesota and they have a new baby. She will finish her commitment with the military this year and she wants to move back to Minnesota. He has lived here eight years and likes it here. He has lived in Kailua before and thought everyone was real friendly there.

MEETING THE PEOPLE

Having lived in Japan and California, I was used to being a white minority among Asians, but this didn't prepare me for Hawai'i. Some spoke English that was hard for me to understand and many were dark-skinned, stout and Rubenesque. I couldn't tell the difference between Japanese, Filipino, Chinese, Korean, Hawaiian, or even Caucasian.

Everyone wears 'locals' and 'surfah' slippers, shorts and local T-shirts like 'North Shore Surf Hut'. Many local ladies wear Hawaiian jewellery—an array of large gold bracelets with Hawaiian words on it. Some people called them 'cans' because they are as big as tin cans. Even young children wear them.

First Impressions

One Hawai'i long-timer, originally from Colorado, had a first impression that everyone was speeding around in Hawai'i. But then he went to Taiwan and other parts of Asia and found that Hawai'i wasn't as bad. A Caucasian girl from the mainland had the first impression that everyone was very cliquish.

The people also seem to have a lot of aunts and uncles here. In Hawai'i, children call friends of the family 'Auntie' and 'Uncle'. It's kind of like the Japanese way of calling older people *ojisan* or *obasan*—which can be translated as 'uncle' and 'aunt'. Even the kids at my daughter's preschool called the teachers Auntie Spring and Uncle Steve. And the nurse at the paediatrician's office is called Auntie Erin. However, older women are called *tutu* (the Hawaiian word for grandma).

Culture Shock and Rock Fever

My Colorado family's first impression was that the people seemed very sedentary. No one was out riding their bikes or taking walks. Where are all the bike paths and walkways? They wondered what kind of, if any, recreation was popular here.

After driving around the whole island, they wondered how people didn't get rock fever. Rock fever is a common excuse for newcomers to leave Hawai'i. They feel confined and restricted on the island with nowhere to drive to or travel about. Other people say rock fever is just an excuse to cover up the negative effects they have experienced with the culture shock of living here.

ON THE ROAD

There are turtle, dolphin and shark stickers on the back of cars. Some people with Hawaiian blood have a 'Hawaiian' sticker or something written in Hawaiian. Asians put Chinese language characters on the car with various meanings like 'fast guy'. Others put dedications to deceased family members on the back windscreen, 'In loving memory of...'. The military families put yellow or star-and-stripes ribbon stickers on their cars with slogans like 'keep 'em safe' or 'the price of freedom isn't cheap'.

Our second-hand car came sporting a yellow ribbon 'support our troops' sticker on the window. We already felt like a local. The windows on the car looked dirty when we bought it but I figured we could wash it. I was wrong. It was hard-water spots. I had to buy a water spot remover and scrub the windows hard to get the spots out.

It wasn't until I drove the highways everyday that I learned that the problem with Hawaiian drivers is that they just don't know how to merge. They give you a friendly wave of the hand when you let them into traffic, but sometimes they change lanes without looking or signalling. Be a defensive driver. There is a mix of people on the road. Some drive at the island pace while others are reckless speedsters. On

O'ahu island, the driving skill seems to diminish the further towards the Ko'olina on H-1 that you go.

When stopping off somewhere to get directions, do remember that people do not use the terms north, south, east or west. To the east, they may say 'go toward Diamond Head' or 'on your way into town (Honolulu)'. To the west, they may say 'going towards Wai'anae or Ewa' or 'it's on the leeward side'. To the north is 'going up to the North Shore'. This can be confusing to a newcomer, because a lot of the time you don't know these places to which they are directing. The leeward side of the island faces south or west and the windward side faces north or east.

They will also say it is on the mountainside or oceanside of the street. Some people will say it in Hawaiian—*mauka* or *makai* respectively. They also use place names instead of street names to give directions. They will tell you to turn at the Zippy's restaurant and it's across from the fire station. They also don't use the highway numbers but instead the name of the road. For example, highway 99 is Kam or Kamehameha highway.

Getting Around

When you first arrive, you will probably have no idea where the cities are located. The best street and city map is the one that comes in the phonebook. We tore it out and put it in our car. If you get tired of searching for a city name on the map, you can always go online at http://www.mapquest.com to locate the city.

POLYNESIAN TATTOO

It may surprise the newcomer to see so many people with tattoos that scroll across their arms, back, legs and sometimes face. It's not like the military guys' tattoos that are often pictures of girls, a fighter jet or something appropriate on their arm. Polynesian tattoos are elaborate designs that look like prints you would see on fabrics.

In Hawai'i, tattoos mean something. The tattoo is a tradition that dates back to the old Polynesian islands. The different Polynesian islands had their own unique tattoos.

The Hawaiian word for tattoo is *kākau*. Tattoo is originally from the Tahitian word *tatau*. The tattoo was often a mark of a warrior and had family and rank-related meanings. Historically, the missionaries tried to ban it.

> Some Hawaiians get tattoos as memories on trips to places like Tahiti. Bangkok has several tattoo shops in the popular guesthouse area for backpackers. It is also cheaper to get a tattoo in places like these.

Today's tattoos are a blend of different traditional Polynesian styles. These styles are a way for Hawaiians and other islanders to take pride in and identify with their ethnic heritage. Some even use the traditional method of striking the black ink into the skin with a sharp *moli* (tattoo needle), while others use modern needles. It is an example of the renaissance of Polynesian culture in Hawai'i and mainland USA.

In Hawai'i, it is also popular among surfers to get a tattoo. Some get traditional Japanese designs that are reminiscent of the *yakuza* (Japanese mafia) tattoos you see in the movies. Others get traditional Hawaiian symbols like a turtle or a shell for protection and to guard over them.

Like the backs of cars in Hawai'i, some people's backs have tattoos with writing in Hawaiian and others have dedications to lost loved ones 'In loving memory of....'.

TELEVISION

Looking at the immigration statistics, it is easy to understand why there are so many multi-ethnic broadcast television programmes and stations. These are regular broadcast stations so they are available with a regular television antenna; you don't need to pay or subscribe to cable television. KIKU has NHK news, Japanese cartoons, samurai serials like *Abarenbo Shogun* and *Shinsengumi*, murder mysteries and dramas (night-time soap operas). Almost all the Japanese language programmes have English subtitles. KIKU also has some Filipino and Vietnamese programmes. The Univision channel (KHLU) has Filipino and Spanish language programmes.

The Korean channel (KBFD) has news, comedy talk shows and the famous Korean dramas (subtitled in English) which have taken off in popularity in Hawai'i. They used to be broadcast late at night but are now shown during prime time.

KBFD television station that broadcasts them has become very successful.

The Dangers of 'Ice'

In the first few months we lived here, there was a television show called *Ice—Hawai'i's Crystal Meth Epidemic*. The Department of Human Services sponsored this award-winning television documentary on the ice addiction. It's their attempt to educate the public about the effects of ice on families, crimes and cost to society.

COOLERS, LAWNCHAIRS, BOUNCERS AND TENTS

Did someone spit on me? I have heard the mist of rain in the air called rainbow showers and pineapple juice. The first time I looked up and wondered if it had flown off the roof from the large air conditioners because it was another beautiful sunny day in the middle of August. What was this mist of water floating this way and that in the air? How does it rain like that without clouds and raindrops, just a wet mist flying on the wind?

Also, the homeless in the parks and on the beach can be a bit of a shock. According to the government, there are something like two thousand homeless people on the Wai'anae coast of O'ahu. People tell you not to go to the parks and beaches after sundown because that is when the homeless consider it their home and you will be invading. At night, my wife has had some of them walk up to the car when she was at the traffic light. They have also approached her asking for a dollar when she got out of the car to go into the Waipahu Daiei supermarket

No one pays any mind to the mystical showers and they use the parks and beaches regardless. Every weekend in the parks, there are several groups gathered under the shade of trees or portable tents (not the camping kind—just a large tarp on top of poles to keep off the sun). Not far off are large inflated children's 'bouncers', the kind you pay a buck or two for your child to bounce on at festivals. It is usually

Friends and families having a good time at a barbecue at Kaimana
Beach Park.

some child's birthday, and balloons and a cake are around
the picnic table.

This isn't much different from what you see at the
beach—people lounge around in foldable lawnchairs under
tents and at picnic tables. They are in for the duration of the
day, fortified by drinks from the cooler and plentiful food
from the picnic table. Whether it is a barbecue at the beach
or a birthday in the park, as long as there is shade to sit in,
they make an all-day event of it.

CUSTOMER SERVICE

I approached a store clerk at a big-name department store.

"Could I look at the instruction manual for this air
conditioner to see how it is installed?"

"Hawai'i's windows are different from the mainland—we
have jalousie windows. It has to be installed differently."

Did he mean that the instructions were written for
mainland windows? Or was he implying that I was from the
mainland and that I didn't know what the windows were
like in Hawai'i?

"My place has regular sliding windows. Can I see
the manual?"

"You have to buy a different kind of air conditioner."

"No, I can remove the window panes; can I see the manual?"

He reluctantly got it and handed it to me.

"So 10,000 BTU's should be good for about 300 sq ft?"

"It's different from the mainland here…"

Did I say anything about the 'mainland'?

People in Hawai'i call the part of the United States on the North American continent as 'the mainland'. Whether you're from the mainland or not, sometimes you're treated like you are. My parents visited and went to a local restaurant. The local waitress couldn't understand some of the English expressions they were using (they're from Colorado) and asked them if they were from the mainland. On the other hand, make sure you don't call the mainland the United States or America. People are sensitive to when people talk like Hawai'i isn't part of the USA.

SOUNDS

Red cardinals chee-chee and whistle, while pigeons coo incessantly in the back yard. Nearby is the sound of the Kamehameha highway traffic instead of the crashing waves of the ocean. Outside is the noise of landscapers, lawnmowers, weed-eaters and blowers. At 6:00 am, a landscaper wrestles with a dead palm frond on the tree outside my window.

The first week in our new town house, they butchered the long row of beautiful trees lining Kam highway, taking off all the green and shaping them like light bulbs. Two weeks of rumbling chainsaw massacre only drowned out by the military helicopters flying lower than should be allowed!

Civil Defence Siren

Civil defence sirens become louder as they rotate in your direction then fade as they turn in another direction. You are supposed to turn on the TV or radio to get further information on what to do in case of an emergency like a tsunami. If it isn't an emergency, you will see a test message on the TV screen.

I got tired of the stink of the exhaust from mowers and chainsaws, so I drove down a street in Mililani where all the trees were lit up with purple flowers, rolled down the windows and the fragrance filled the car.

CREATURES

Lying in bed, a strange scratching sound came from next to my son's bed. We turned on the light but saw nothing. A few minutes later, there was a rustling in the closet. I thought it was a mouse. I lifted a bag off the dresser and out sped a purple-green, eight-inch-long centipede—the kind you see in horror movies. Centipedes are scary but dumb. They don't move if they are covered up. I threw a pile of clothes on it and tossed it outside on the *lānai* (porch, balcony or deck). It slithered off into the yard.

Centipedes are like cockroaches and can get inside the house alongside the openings that are made for the water and drainage pipes. We taped off all the openings at the bottom of the kitchen cabinets. This cut back considerably on the centipedes and cockroaches.

Bugs can be a problem in Hawai'i and some homeowners associations cut down papaya trees and other fruit trees because they attract bugs. In my yard, curled up under patches of crabgrass were two-inch long, purple centipedes. I got rid of the weeds and I don't see them anymore. Centipedes—both large and small—bite, so be careful. One man was hiking and felt something bite him on the neck. A purple centipede had landed on him as he walked through some low-hanging trees. His neck swelled up for days.

The previous owners let the backyard of our town house go wild. I picked up a large rock in the corner of the yard and there was a family of slugs underneath. I got rid of all the rocks in the yard and I don't see the slugs anymore. Snails climbed all over the side of the house and on the fence leaving faeces trails. I threw away all the snails, cut the grass short and cleaned out the debris under the trees. They stopped coming. One other solution is to buy a snail pesticide and spread it in a line around the yard. I didn't use this because I have small children that dig around and play in the yard.

We put a storage cabinet on our *lānai* and a month afterwards, we had a good rain and a rat decided to make

a home behind it. The property manager had the pest guys set traps and caught it a day later.

The constant geckos in the yard don't bother me, but sometimes they lay eggs in places like the windowsills and when you crush them, a plague of ants come and eat the remains. If ants start parading into the house, we find where they are entering from and spray them with Raid (an insect spray). We leave them alone if they are on the outside of the house, because the Homeowners Association (HOA) has the bug man spread pesticide regularly around the premise.

HISTORY OF THE RAINBOW ISLANDS

CHAPTER 2

'What I have always longed for was the privilege
of living forever away up on one of those mountains
in the Sandwich Islands overlooking the sea.'
—Mark Twain, *Letters From Hawai'i*

GEOGRAPHY

There are 137 islands in the Hawaiian archipelago. The major inhabited islands by population are Oʻahu (876,156), Hawaiʻi (148,677), Maui (117,644), Kauaʻi (58,308), Molokaʻi (7,404), Lānaʻi (3,193) and Niʻihau (155).

The majority of Oʻahu's population is concentrated in several areas: the southern half of the island around Kailua and Kāneʻohe on the windward side; Honolulu west to Pearl City, Waipahu and Waipiʻo on the leeward side; and central Oʻahu around Mililani, Schofield Barracks and Wahiawa. The largest centre of population on the Big Island of Hawaiʻi is Hilo. Maui's largest population is centred at Kahului and Wailuku on the windward side and at Kīhei on the leeward side.

Mark Twain called Hawaiʻi 'the loveliest fleet of islands that lies anchored in any ocean'. This fleet is anchored 3,862.4 km (2,400 miles) from mainland USA and 6,196 km (3,850 miles) from Japan. Alaska lies 4,506.2 km (2,800 miles) straight north of Hawaiʻi. The equator is 2,365.7 km (1,470 miles) due south and Tahiti lies another 1,496.7 km (930 miles) beyond the equator.

The average temperature doesn't vary much over the course of the year. For all of the islands, the warmest months are in the range of 21–26°C (70–80°F) and coolest months in the 16–21°C (60–70°F) range. However, the temperature varies according to elevation. Our friends in Wahiawa (the centre of O'ahu) sometimes use their fireplace in the wintertime, as do people living higher up the mountain on the Big Island of Hawai'i. The trade winds come from the windward (north-east side) of the islands, and as a result cities like Kailua and Kāne'ohe receive the most rain. Mount Wai'ale'ale on Kaua'i is the wettest spot on earth, and Hilo, located on the Big Island, is considered one of the wettest cities in the US.

YOU MUST BE FROM MOUNT WAI'ALE'ALE

On all the islands, the leeward side (south and west side) of the islands (i.e. on O'ahu: Honolulu, Pearl City, Wai'anae) face away from the trade winds, but still receive their cooling effect. These trade winds blow almost 70 per cent of the time. The leeward side of the islands is very dry and has an almost desert-like climate. The height of the ocean waves varies with the seasons. During the winter months, the waves are the highest on the north shore.

The Big Island of Hawaii and Maui have some of the highest mountains. The highest peaks, Mauna Kea and Mauna Loa on the island of Hawai'i, are almost 4,250 m (13,943.6 ft).

If you measured Mauna Kea from its base under the water, it would have a higher elevation than Mount Everest.

Historically, there have been earthquakes, tsunamis, hurricanes and volcanic eruptions. The volcanoes of Kīlauea and Mauna Loa on the Big Island of Hawai'i are still active and erupt frequently. In the last one hundred years, several hurricanes have hit the island of Kaua'i and many large earthquakes have shaken the Big Island. Many earthquakes occurred out in the Pacific Ocean and created tsunamis that hit all of the Hawaiian islands and caused significant damage.

Many people don't realise that the Hawaiian islands stretch another 2,414 km (1,500 miles) north-west to Midway Island and the Kure Atoll. An atoll is an island that was once a volcano worn down over millions of years into a sandy coral reef with lagoons. Plants, wildlife and sea life thrive on these deserted islands.

The active underwater volcano Lō'ihi, about 32.2 km (20 miles) off the south-east coast of the Big Island, is

Diamond Head: the top of a long dormant volcano that towers over Waikīkī, O'ahu.

currently the location of a hot spot that was originally under the Kure Atoll. The hot spot stayed in the same place, but the pacific plate moved south-west and all the islands of the Hawaiian archipelago were created along the way. Lō'ihi will be the spot of the next volcanic Hawaiian island.

Finding Out More

To learn more about Hawai'i's north-western islands, watch the PBS Cousteau special. It is a rare glimpse of the amazing underwater wildlife around the north-western islands that is missing on the populated islands—especially O'ahu.

You will learn that the Kure Atoll is part of the state of Hawai'i and that the other islands are part of the National Wildlife Refuge. Apparently, the Kure Atoll used to have a tennis court. Visiting boats would park in a nearby monk seal habitat which caused the endangered monk seals to decrease.

Midway island is famous for its place in history as a turning point in a World War II battle. Forty people live on the island while doing nature and wildlife preservation. Volunteers live on the island for three months at a time and clean up old fishing nets and old military garbage.

The Big Island is well known for its many tourist attractions, while O'ahu can boast that it has more golf courses than all the other islands, with Maui coming in second. There are multiple daily inter-island flights between Honolulu and Līhu'e, Kaua'i; Moloka'i; Lāna'i City; Kahului, Maui; and Hilo and Keāhole airports on the Big Island. Tourists and residents can easily enjoy the natural beauty and historic sites of all the islands.

The top three income producers in Hawai'i are tourism, federal spending on the military and agricultural exports. Pineapple, sugar, macadamia nuts, coffee and papaya are some of the top agricultural products grown throughout the islands. From 1890, agricultural production (sugar and pineapple) was the biggest income producer in Hawai'i, but during World War II and after 1970, income from military spending was higher. During the mid-1980s, income from tourism topped military spending and is now the major economy in Hawai'i.

HISTORY
Historical Chronology

AD 400–1200	Polynesians came to Hawai'i from Marquesas and Tahiti.
1778	Captain Cook first visited the island of Kaua'i and was killed a year later in 1779 along with four of his marines in the same bay. Other explorers and traders began to visit Hawai'i.
1810	Kamehameha I united the islands into the kingdom of Hawai'i through conquest and diplomacy.
1820	American missionaries from Boston arrived. Missionaries began the process of converting the Hawaiian language to a written alphabet.
1840	Kamehameha III proclaims the First Constitution of Hawai'i on 8 October.
1843	A British commander forced King Kamehameha III to give the islands to Great Britain without approval from London. The British supported Hawaiian independence and gave back rule to the king.
1843	Herman Melville sailed to the South Seas in 1841 on the whaler Acushret, but deserted ship at Marquesas Island after 18 months. He escaped aboard an Australian trader a month later before leaving it at Tahiti where he was briefly imprisoned for deserting the ship. He worked for a time as a field labourer in Tahiti and then shipped to Honolulu, where in 1843 he enlisted in the US Navy.
1848	The Great Māhele. The king of Hawai'i divided the land of Hawai'i among the chiefs and commoners

	and allowed private ownership of the land for the first time.
1852	First Chinese immigrants arrived to work on the sugarcane plantations.
1866	Mark Twain, American author of *The Tales of Huckleberry Finn*, arrived as a roving correspondent for a Californian paper and wrote about Hawai'i.
1868	First Japanese arrived to work on the plantations.
1878	Portuguese plantation immigrants arrived from the Madeira Islands.
1782–1893	The reign of the Hawaiian monarchs, Kamehameha I through Kamehameha V. As there was no successor to Kamehameha V who died in 1872, two successive kings were elected—Lunahilo (ruled from 1873–1874) and Kalākaua (1874–1891). The last monarch was Kalākaua's sister, Queen Lili'uokalani (1891–1893).
1893	Queen Lili'uokalani was overthrown by the annexationists, a conspiracy of American sugar plantation owners. The annexationists feared her proposals for a stronger constitution would empower the monarchy of Hawai'i. The American minister to Hawai'i supported the conspiracy by ordering US military men to leave their boat in the harbour and aid the annexationists.
1894	The Republic of Hawai'i was established. Sanford B Dole was made president.
1895	Queen Lili'uokalani and her supporters tried to retake the

The Hawaiian flag still flies over 'Iolani Palace, the former home of the Hawaiian monarchy. Queen Lili'uokalani was imprisoned in the palace during the overthrow of the Hawaiian monarchy.

government but failed. Fearing for the safety of her supporters, she abdicated the throne and pledged allegiance to the Republic.

1900	The Republic of Hawai'i became the US Territory of Hawai'i with Sanford Dole as the governor. President McKinley signed the Organic Act on 30 April, making Hawai'i a Territory of the US.
1901	Hawai'i's first legislature (as a Territory of the US) was convened in Honolulu.
1900–1906	Okinawans, Koreans and Filipinos started immigration to Hawai'i.
1890s–1940s	The rise of the 'The Big Five'—the nickname for the five business firms (many started by missionaries) that controlled Hawai'i's political and economic power. These firms

	started with the sugar industry and their ownership and power spread to other industries. They owned a large percentage of the land (In 1922, James Dole bought the whole island of Lāna'i for a pineapple plantation.)
1910–1940s	Several strikes on the plantations finally led to the unionisation of the plantation workers.
1941–1943	The Japanese attack on Pearl Harbour instigated the internment of Americans of Japanese Ancestry (AJA). Many of the people of Hawai'i—including AJAs—joined the military and fought in Europe. Military presence and bases in Hawai'i expanded.
1941	Martial law was declared in Hawai'i and revoked only in 1944.
1945	Samoans began to immigrate to Hawai'i.
1948	President Harry S Truman endorsed statehood for Hawai'i in his report to Congress.
1950	In an effort to obtain statehood, a Hawaiian Constitutional Congress was convened. The resulting consitution was later ratified by voters.
1959	President Eisenhower and Congress designated Hawai'i the 50th state (Alaska being the 49th) on 18 March. On 28 July, the first senate election after statehood took place and incumbent Territorial Governor William F Quinn was elected as first state governor.
1959	Daniel K Inouye was elected to the US House of Representatives—the

	first American of Japanese descent to do so.
1960s to the present	AJAs came to power in Hawai'i with the democratic party. AJAs, Senator Inouye and Senator Spark M Matsunaga among others, represented Hawai'i in Congress. George Ariyoshi was the first AJA governor (1974–1986). The democratic party increased social welfare programmes. Employers provided mandatory health insurance for anyone working 20 hours or more.
1970s to the present	Many refugees (Vietnamese, Cambodian, Hmong, Laotian, Burmese) came to Hawai'i from South-east Asia.
1970s to the present	A traditional voyaging canoe, named Hokule'a (Star of Gladness), was built and sailed to Tahiti in 1976. A renaissance of Polynesian culture (music, *hula* dance, dress, canoes, tattoos, etc.) began in Hawai'i and continues today on the island and on mainland USA.

Current Events

1993	President Clinton signed a resolution apologising for the US government's role in the overthrow of the Hawaiian monarchy.
2003	Korean Centennial commemorating the first arrival of Korean immigrants in Hawai'i.
2006	Filipino Centennial commemorating the first arrival of Filipino immigrants in Hawai'i.
2009	Hawai'i's 50th anniversary as the 50th state.

MORE ON HISTORY
Polynesia
The Polynesian islands form a triangle from Easter Island over to New Zealand and up to Hawai'i. They include Hawai'i and the islands of the South Pacific: Samoa, Tonga, Cooks, Marquesas Islands, Society Islands and Easter Islands. The Polynesians came to Hawai'i from the Marquesas Islands and Tahiti (part of the Society Islands) approximately one thousand years ago. Using only canoes in their migration, their long-distance voyage was an amazing feat.

Polynesian life revolved around the voyaging tradition, and all of the Polynesians shared similar food, plants, language, traditions and customs. For example, they

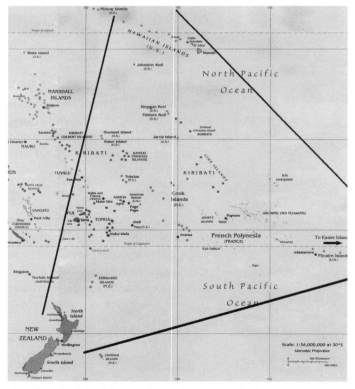

The Polynesian islands form a triangle from Easter Island over to New Zealand and up to Hawai'i.

A taro patch grows in front of the Kamehameha V cottage (built in the 1850s) at Moanalua Gardens. Taro was brought to Hawai'i by the ancient Polynesians and is used to make traditional food such as *poi*.

all farmed an edible root called taro, they practised communal child rearing, and they presented humans as a sacrifice to the gods. They also had practices that were taboo, and therefore forbidden and punishable by death. A woman eating with a man was taboo; in contrast, nudity in public was considered natural and acceptable. Captain Cook, a visitor to the islands, observed their practices and later introduced the original Tongan word *taboo* to the English language.

Mark Twain on his trip to the islands joked about the Hawaiian's altar of human sacrifice in his book *Letters From Hawai'i* as:

'An ancient heathen temple—a place where human sacrifices were offered up in those old bygone days when the simple child of nature, yielding momentarily to sin when sorely tempted, acknowledged his error when calm reflection had shown it to him, and came forward with noble frankness and offered up his grandmother as an atoning sacrifice.'

Western Contact

Two hundred and fifty years ago, naked dark-skinned Polynesians paddled their canoes out to meet the ships of explorers, traders and whaling ships visiting the islands. The Spanish, Dutch, English and French all explored and traded with the islanders. Hawai'i was one of the last of the Polynesian islands to be visited by the ships from European nations.

Captain Cook is credited as the first non-Polynesian discoverer of Hawai'i; however, some evidence points to the Spanish as being the first European contact with Hawai'i. Cook's ships landed on Kaua'i in 1778, and Cook named his discovery the 'Sandwich Islands' after his friend the Earl of Sandwich. The name became obsolete after 1844 and the traditional Polynesian name 'Hawai'i' was used.

Upon discovery, Hawai'i was quickly introduced to the practices of the Western world. The Hawaiians needed iron but didn't know how to make it. Captain Cook's crew traded

nails and other pieces of iron for food and water. Likewise, the Hawaiians introduced their Polynesian customs to the ship's crew. However, after travelling throughout the South Pacific, the sailors were no longer shocked by the Polynesian cultural practices of human sacrifice or their sexual freedom.

The Hawaiians also suffered from Cook's discovery. They innocently submitted to Cook's authority as they thought he was their god 'Lono'. Mark Twain remarked in his book *Letters From Hawai'i* that 'Cook desecrated the holy places of the temple by storing supplies for his ships in them, and by using the level grounds within the enclosure as a general workshop for repairing his sails, etc.—ground which was so sacred that no common native dared set his foot upon it.' This did not increase Cook's favour with the Hawaiians. In 1779, there was a dispute over a boat the Hawaiians had stolen to scavenge its iron nails. A Hawaiian chief was killed in the ruckus. Captain Cook and his crew took hostage of the great chief and as they prepared to take him to their ship, the angry Hawaiians killed Cook. Twain further commented, 'Small blame should attach to the natives for the killing of Cook. They treated him well. In return, he abused them. He and his men inflicted bodily injury upon many of them before they offered any proportionate retaliation.'

The Dream Continues

The death of Captain Cook did not tarnish the lure of Polynesia to the adventurers of the Western world. Since the first discovery, many travellers, authors, artists and movie producers have captured their impressions of these magical islands through every media form.

Australian historian Gavan Daws, in his book *A Dream of Islands*, records the biographies of famous men who were drawn to the Polynesian islands—men

Authors Charles Bernard Nordhoff and James Norman Hall wrote *Mutiny on the Bounty*, a fictional account based on historical events that took place of a tyrannical captain whose cruelty motivated his crew to mutiny in favour of living in the heavenly paradise of the Tahitian islands. The authors also fell in love with Tahiti. Both men married half-Tahitians and Nordhoff settled in Tahiti for many years before leaving for the US where he died. Hall lived the remainder of his days on the islands where he was buried.

like Herman Melville who wrote *Moby Dick*, and Paul Gauguin, the French artist. Gauguin painted Polynesian nudes and he later died on the island of Marquesa. Also, Robert Louis Stevenson, the author of *Dr Jekyll and Mr Hyde* and *Treasure Island*, dined with the Hawaiian king Kalākaua and went 'native' on the island of Samoa. Lastly, Mark Twain was well known for his obsession with Hawai'i and the 'balmy breezes and fragrant flowers'.

Kamehameha I to V

Kamehameha was the chief of the Big Island of Hawai'i. Different chiefs ruled the other islands of Hawai'i. Kamehameha began his campaign to unite the islands in 1782. In 1795, he succeeded in uniting all the islands except Kauai. In 1796, he tried but failed to conquer Kaua'i. In 1810, through forceful diplomacy, he brought the island of Kaua'i into his kingdom. The kingdom of Hawai'i lasted almost a hundred years. There was a succession of five kings of the Kamehameha family. After Kamehameha V, there was no successor, so two elected kings succeeded him—King Lunalilo and King Kālakaua. The last Hawaiian monarch was Kālakaua's sister, Queen Lili'uokalani.

In 1893, Queen Lili'uokalani was overthrown by a group of annexationists. The group consisted largely of the local American sugar plantation owners. They formed the Republic of Hawai'i with Sanford Dole (cousin to pineapple magnate James Dole of Dole Pineapple) as leader.

President Grover Cleveland in a speech to Congress called it a 'lawless occupation of Honolulu under false pretexts by the United States forces. By an act of war, committed with the participation of a diplomatic representative of the United States and without the authority of Congress, the Government of a feeble but friendly and confiding people has been overthrown'. He refused to sign the treaty of annexation.

In 1895, Queen Lili'uokalani tried to regain the throne through a failed coup d'etat. Despite this, a resolution of annexation was approved by Congress and signed by President McKinley. In 1900, Hawai'i became a US territory.

The famous statue of King Kamehameha in downtown Honolulu.

After the annexation of Hawai'i by the US, Hawaiian names for children were banned until the law was later repealed. The Hawaiian language was also pushed to the side, and almost pushed out of existence in favour of the English language for instrumental use.

Even today, some Native Hawaiians still resent this injustice done to the Hawaiian people by the American government and the sugar plantation owners, and wish to become a sovereign nation again.

Finding Out More

The best way to understand the history and culture of Hawai'i is to visit the Bishop Museum in Honolulu. There are very few extant artefacts representing the ancient Hawaiian culture. Some of these artefacts are ivory jewellery made out of whales' teeth (that was worn by the chief class) and the huge, carved-wood totem poles of the ancient Hawaiian gods (these were unearthed in fields and swamps). One exhibit explains the Hawaiian monarchy, each of the members of royalty and their legacies. There are also historical objects from the whaling and missionary eras. On the third floor of the Hawaiian history wing, there are some historical artefacts of the various ethnic groups (Japanese, Chinese, Korean, Filipino, etc.) in Hawai'i.

The Bishop Museum has a planetarium show that explains how the ancient Polynesians navigated by the stars. Their artefacts and island histories are in a special section of the museum.

The museum is a good place to visit before going to the Polynesian Cultural Center (located next to and owned by Brigham Young University). The center organises shows and demonstrations of traditional dance, music, art and games. The recreated historical villages include replicas of original costumes, canoes and traditional architecture such as life-size huts and temples.

Lastly, take the tour of the 'Iolani Palace, the former home of the Hawaiian monarchy during the reign of King Kālakaua and Queen Lili'uokalani (the last two monarchs). The palace is the only royal palace in the United States. The tour guides at both the Bishop Museum and the 'Iolani Palace are very informative.

Missionaries

European explorers colonised Polynesia in the 18th century by claiming various islands for their homelands of Spain, France, Germany, England, etc. Hawai'i had its own kingdom during this period, even though some countries like France and Great Britain tried to claim it as a colony. The colonisation of Hawai'i began with the arrival of the American missionaries in the 1820s. Mark Twain in his *Letters from Hawai'i* shares.

'[Missionaries]... showed him [the Hawaiian] what rapture it is to work all day long for fifty cents to buy food for the next day with, as compared with fishing for a pastime and lolling in the shade through eternal summer, and eating of the bounty that nobody laboured to provide but nature.'

'They [Hawaiians] are amazingly unselfish and hospitable. To the wayfarer who visits them they freely offer their houses, food, beds, and often their wives and daughters... The example of white selfishness does not affect their native unselfishness any more than the example of virtue does their native licentiousness.'

'The missionaries had deprived the natives of their innocent sports and pastimes' (such as the 'lascivious *hula hula*', and the promiscuous bathing in the surf of nude natives of opposite sexes).

The missionaries required the Hawaiian women to wear *muumuus* (a long dress covering the arms and legs) and banned the *hula* dance because it was licentious (lacking moral and sexual restraints). They also convinced the Hawaiian chiefs to ban women from visiting sailors on the whaling ships.

The Hawaiians died from diseases brought by Westerners. Venereal disease, plague, influenza, smallpox, mumps, leprosy and other diseases brought the Hawaiian population down to less than half of what it was before Westerners arrived 50 years before in 1778. Hawaiians infected with leprosy were

> One selfless missionary from Belgium, Father Damien (1840–1889), dedicated his life to helping the Hawaiian leprosy victims on Moloka'i.

banned to a leper colony—the village of Kalawao on the island of Moloka'i.

The Great Māhele (1848–1850)

The Hawaiians did not fully understand the concept of 'private ownership of land'. In their culture, land was treated as common and the king decided the use of the land. The king gave *ahupua'a* to his chiefs to oversee. An *ahupua'a* was a pie-shaped piece of land, a land division that runs from the mountain ridges to the oceans. In ancient Hawai'i, this piece of land was a self-sustaining system ruled by a chief. Farming was practised in the valley with fishing at the sea level. The farmers would come down to exchange food with the fishermen.

In 1841, a law allowed foreigners to lease land from the *ali'i* (chiefs) for up to 55 years. In 1848, American capitalists and missionaries convinced the king of Hawai'i to privatise the land. The missionaries believed a division of the land would benefit the Hawaiian commoners. A *māhele* (division) of the lands was made between the king and the chiefs. In 1849, the king gave simple ownership of land to commoners. This was an amazing act of good will from the king to his people, giving up the lands of his kingdom to the common people of Hawai'i. However, the greed of many men turned this generous act into one that hurt the commoners of Hawai'i. Foreigners and capitalists understood the value of having title ownership to land and secured as much land as they could. Many Hawaiians didn't understand that they had to file with the government for

This is the only building left of the huge, old Waipahu sugar mill. The photograph was taken before it was recently renovated into a YMCA gym.

the lands they occupied, and so they lost it. Others sold their rights to the capitalists and descendants of the missionaries. By 1886, non-Hawaiians owned two-thirds of the land in Hawai'i.

Plantation

Plantation Numbers

An exhibit in the Hawai'i Plantation Village shows the year that each ethnic group started migrating to Hawai'i to work on the plantations:

- Chinese   1823   A total of 46,000
- Japanese   1868   A total of 180,000
- Portuguese   1878   A total of 30,000
- Puerto Rican   1878   A total of 5,200
- Okinawan   1900   (Included in the Japanese total)
- Koreans   1903   A total of 7,000
- Filipinos   1906   A total of 120,000

This does not include all the Native Hawaiians who worked on the plantations.

At the beginning of the 1900s, the plantation owners imported immigrants to work the plantation fields because many of the Native Hawaiians refused to work on the plantations—first Chinese, then Japanese and Filipino, as well as smaller numbers of Puerto Ricans, Portuguese and other nationalities. The workers had labour contracts that couldn't be broken without the penalty of prison. They had to buy living essentials from the company store, and ended up spending more than they made. The plantation owners used control tactics, like separating newcomers by race and making them wear number tags. The owners fought hard to keep the workers from unionising and getting better wages.

By 1933, there were five large companies—know as the Big Five—that owned nearly all the sugar and pineapple production and many other businesses as well. Many of the families of the Big Five were descendants of the missionaries. They had enormous wealth and power.

Picture Brides

Visit the Hawai'i Plantation Village located on Waipahu street in Waipahu to learn about the plantation era and its associated culture. Their small museum exhibits historic photographs and antiques of this period, as well as historical plantation houses and an old steam train engine.

Many plantation workers were single men and there was a shortage of woman so they started the practice of arranged marriages through letters and pictures sent back home. One museum photograph portrays a Japanese picture bride. She received a picture of her husband-to-be in Japan, and when she arrived in Hawai'i, she found out the picture was taken of him 20 years before. Many matchmakers used this trick to entice picture brides to come to Hawai'i. There is an excellent movie depicting this historical era, called *Picture Brides*. It was made in Hawai'i and the star is a Japanese actress.

Pearl Harbour

With the 1941 attack on Pearl Harbour, the property of the Americans of Japanese Ancestry (AJAs) was confiscated and they were put in internment camps. Some Hawai'i resident AJAs were placed in internment camps on the mainland. Fortunately, AJAs were a third of the population in Hawai'i so it was impossible to put them all in camps. Being one-third of the population, their removal would have crippled the state's economy. Only a small percentage—those pinpointed by the FBI—suffered in the camps. A total of 1,875 Hawai'i resident AJAs were detained in War Relocation Authority Camps and Department of Justice Internment Camps. The redemption for the AJAs came when thousands of them volunteered for the army. Many died for their country, and their units received many medals of honour. In January 1943, a Japanese-American combat team was formed. It included the 100th Infantry and the 442nd Combat Unit, which was the most decorated unit for its size and length of service in the US military history. One of those decorated soldiers is Hawai'i's US Senator Daniel Inouye.

Renaissance of Polynesian Culture

In 1975, a traditional style voyaging canoe, named Hokule'a, was built for a scientific experiment to test the possibility of sailing from Tahiti to Hawai'i. The Polynesian Voyaging Society (PVS) succeeded in the sailing voyage and have since sailed over 100,000 miles around Polynesia and beyond. This

The author with his mother and children at the Polynesian Cultural Center.

double-hulled canoe has become a symbol of the renaissance of Hawaiian/Polynesian culture.

A strong interest in Hawaiian/Polynesian culture has developed on the mainland, as well as through art, dance, music and festivals—especially in California. According to John Charlot in his book *Chanting the Universe*, America was influenced by Japanese culture through art, architecture and even values from Zen philosophy. He believes Polynesian culture is the next popular influence on American culture.

Since 1978, the Hawaiian government has taken part in the revival of Hawaiiana by requiring that educational programmes on Hawaiian culture, language and history be made available in schools.

THE LOCAL CULTURE

CHAPTER 3

'One thing I went notice about this place.
All us guys we tease the other race.
It's amazing we can live in the same place.'
—lines from a popular local song
called 'Mr Sun Cho Lee'

DECEPTIVELY DIFFERENT

Turn on the TV in Hawai'i and football games and golf
tournaments are playing. The people in Hawai'i are crazy
about sports, especially football, just like mainland USA. There
are several Christian programmes on TV, and Christianity is
the largest religion on the islands. On the surface, it doesn't
seem that much different from the mainland. It may appear
that there are many mainland values in Hawai'i, but make no
mistake—Hawai'i differs in many ways from the mainland.
It's much deeper than just *sumo* wrestling on TV in Hawai'i.
Confucianism, Buddhism and Hawaiian spirituality, as well
as the concepts of saving face and bring a group-centred
society, all exists in Hawai'i.

Immigrants can change on the surface and look and act
like everyone else, but it is harder to change the deeper
culture inside. AJAs are currently in their fourth generation
in Hawai'i and like everyone, dress in sandals, T-shirts
and eat mixed plate lunches; but their underlying beliefs
and values are similar to their distant cousins in Japan.
For example, the Japanese-Americans in Hawai'i still
hold Confucian and Buddhist
beliefs: respect for parents and
the elderly, the importance of
education, humility, shame,
perseverance, etc. The majority
of Japanese-Americans don't

I used to live in California, and
the Asians of California act much
more like mainland Americans
than the Asians of Hawai'i. The
Asians of Hawai'i have held
onto their cultural heritage and
values better.

speak Japanese yet still use the Japanese high-context style of communication where there is much unspoken content. Content that is communicated through certain behaviours, signs and invisible social cues are inevitably missed by the newcomer.

The native Hawaiians have also held onto their cultural heritage through an oral history that is conveyed through chants, songs and stories. Despite efforts by early missionaries, some Hawaiian philosophy and spirituality have also managed to survive.

COLLECTIVISM IN HAWAI'I

Group-centred behaviours dominate in Hawai'i's culture. The primary group is the family and extends outward from there to work, the community, etc. This is called collectivism—the group takes priority over the individual. This is the opposite of mainland USA where Americans are famed for their highly independent and individualist attitude.

Advertising Hawaiian Values

The majority of countries in the world are collectivist. All of Hawai'i's major ethnic subcultures (Hawaiian, Japanese, Filipino, Chinese and Korean) are collectivist, with the exception of the Caucasians.

The Hawaiian word *'ohana* means family and is used often in Hawai'i. *'Ohana* is central to Hawaiian society and reflects the group value. The Bank of Hawai'i had a commercial using the phrase *'bankohana'* as a play on their Bankoh (Bank of Hawai'i) nickname. Adding the *'ohana* gives it a sense of being local, a feeling of being part of the group or family. Central Pacific Bank used a collie dog (dogs represents the virtue of loyalty in American culture) in its ads and stressed the word 'loyalty'—also a group-centred value.

The Filipinos and Japanese are stereotyped as being clannish. In a collective society, there is more ethnic clustering and therefore ethnic enclaves. The people on the outside of the group are paid little attention, such as people coming in from other cultures. For the people in Hawai'i, loyalty lies with locals before newcomers.

The next group layer are people in the same culture but from different ethnic groups. Their loyalty lies with their ethnic group before the local culture. The result of this may be occurances of racial preference in hiring practices.

Lastly, there are also group divisions within races with different dialects or from different areas. The Chinese divide themselves between the Punti and Hakka; the mainland Japanese from the Okinawans (Okinawa is part of the chain of islands south of mainland Japan); and the Filipinos are divided by their different dialects—Ilicano, Tagalog and Visayan.

Even the Caucasians have their own group. Some Caucasians admit that the longer they stay in Hawai'i, the more collectivist they become. This adds up to a lot of different in-groups.

MOVING FROM AN INDIVIDUALIST COUNTRY

Individualists are culturally programmed to ask just about any question or make any comment with little sensitivity as to the effect of that question or comment. They prefer the efficiency of direct communication over the risk of offending someone. Group societies don't like being direct and prefer to beat around the bush. They also spend more time talking individually to one another in an effort to create consensus before speaking up in a group.

For people in individualist cultures, the primary concern is one's self or ego—they aren't worried about bringing shame to the group but are worried about taking a blow to their self-image/esteem. The fear of bringing shame to the group doesn't control their social behaviour but instead feelings of guilt—like when a societal rule is violated.

Individualists also feel morally obligated to treat all people equal. However, collectivists are expected to treat the people in their group better than those outside it. Ironically, Mary K Pukui, a teacher of Hawaiian ways, in the book *Nānā I Ke Kumu* contrasts that Americans profess equality for all but many act better than others. In ancient Hawai'i, there was an upper class and a commoner class; however, even the chiefs would behave lowly around everyone regardless of class.

Hawaiians and the Asians in Hawai'i all come from collectivist cultures. The local culture of Hawai'i is collectivist.

Mainland Americans have the hardest time adapting because America is one of the most individualistic societies in the world, and they clash with Asians and Hawaiians on their collectivist values. Therefore, mainlanders frequently find themselves in the out-group instead of the in-group until they practise at how to function in a collectivist society. Learning how to interact in a group society can feel like a total reprogramming of your brain. It is like learning another language, an unspoken language.

One local Filipino pastor said the locals have a potential that's buried by fear. That in Hawai'i there is a false humility or inferior complex. A coach asks who can play a certain position, and everyone is afraid to raise his hand, because then others will look at him and say to themselves, "I can play that position better than him. Who does he think he is?"

IN THE REAL WORLD

Collectivism is expressed in the family, work and community. For example, collectivism is seen in the Filipino *bayanihan* system of family and community support organisations. In a collectivist society, people on the street can feel colder, but people inside your groups (family, work and community) warmer than in an individualist society.

The collective family can sometimes be oppressive and intruding, but it is also very supportive and anticipative of your needs. In the individualistic culture, the family can be more distant comparatively. They are willing to help, but you must assert your need and not too often or they may think you are too needy and may avoid you.

In collectivist cultures, there is a loyalty and obligation to the group. You have an obligation to pay back the favours and benefits you have received from the group. In the collectivist workplace, you will feel outside the circle when you do something the group doesn't approve of or which brings shame to the group. When you adjust your behaviour, you will find them welcoming you back like someone who has been away for while. It can sometimes feel like the old high school cliques, with everyone struggling to look a part of the group.

Hawaiian Students

University of Hawai'i professors that come from the mainland complain that students don't ask or answer questions. What they don't understand is that local students have been socialised that way. By sticking out from the group, they risk being seen as placing themselves above the group. By answering a question, they also risk losing face or worse yet—bringing shame to the group. They also need to know what the groups agreed upon answer is before they venture their opinion.

SHAME

It is unacceptable to bring shame to members of the group. This can be as simple as not asking embarrassing questions. People don't ask questions because they risk sticking out from the group, or even bringing shame to the group. They also don't risk answering questions until they know what the agreed upon group response is.

If members of the group aren't modest or bring shame to the group, the group will put them back in their place. If members of the group think a member has done something wrong, with the Japanese it might lead to an internal distancing from the member, whereas with Hawaiians it might mean that sarcasm and scorn will be directed at the member. If these tactics don't work, the group escalates to alienation, in effect kicking the person out of the group.

FACE

Local cultures value privacy and non-confrontation. An article in the *Honolulu Star Bulletin* states that 'the emphasis in cultures such as Japan and China is on the family and community, not on individualism. These cultures develop a sense of saving face, and instinctively their people learn to avoid bringing shame, controversy or negative public exposure to the family.'

For an individualist, it can sometimes seem like they flat out lie to you, but they are doing it to maintain harmony and save face for themselves or their group. They might have even been trying to save your 'face', which is something many Asians understand, but for people from individualist cultures, it can be a brutal experience. They don't realise that the locals' odd behaviour may be a result of trying to avoid confrontation and not bring shame to themselves or their group (which ultimately falls on themselves if they do).

The concept of saving face explained on a local business' billboard.

For example, the Filipinos value *pakikisama* (harmony). This is maintained through saving each other's face and going along with and conforming to the group. *Hiya* is the Filipino word for shame and embodies the fear of losing face. Face is tied with position. The expectation is that you act according to your position. You can lose face if someone implies that you have not fulfilled your duty to your position and ultimately the group.

To avoid creating this situation, some people will use a go-between. For example in Hawai'i, if a landscaper gets a contract through word of mouth and something is wrong with his work, the customer will not complain to the landscaper but instead he will complain to the person who recommended him. This way, the landscaper does not lose face but he is held accountable by making sure he doesn't bring shame to his network of business partners.

The teacher of a class can find ways to limit the pressure of the group and the fear of losing face. According to Geert Hofstede in his book *Cultures and Organizations, Software of the Mind: Intercultural Cooperation and Its Importance for Survival*, it is illogical to speak up without being sanctioned by the group to do so. Instead, he suggests calling on the students individually in the class for their input or breaking them up into small groups. In the latter, a group decision is made and the group selects their own spokesperson to speak for the group.

BREAKING INTO THE GROUP

Locals use connections to get business done. Sometimes, it seems you need to know someone to land a good job, find a good doctor or even get decent service. Part of the group mentality is a strong loyalty to members of your group. If you're not part of the group, you won't be paid much attention. Mention a connection, your position within the group or someone they know and they automatically sit upright and pay attention.

It helps to have a local friend whom you can use as a reference for getting a doctor. The receptionist at the children doctors' office will tell you they are not accepting new patients, but they will check to see if any of the doctors are willing to take someone. In addition to details about your child, they will ask who referred you to their office. Give them a name of someone else who already has a doctor there and the secretary will come back on the line saying one of the doctors is willing to take your child as a new patient.

It is the same in the case of a dentist. Just like doctors, there are lots of dentists available but the good ones aren't accepting new patients. We were having a hard time finding

a good dentist, so my AJA co-worker recommended her dentist. He was very busy but was willing to accept us as new patients on her recommendation. We received excellent service and at a much better rate than the previous dentist we had used in Hawai'i. Interestingly enough, the majority of the dentists in Hawai'i are AJAs.

FEMININE VALUES IN HAWAI'I

In a masculine culture, the man has to be macho, aggressive, ambitious and competitive and the woman has to be talkative and sociable. Money, materialism, success and 'survival of the fittest' are the norm.

In a feminine culture, there is no separation of roles in the home or society. A man or woman can be a homemaker or an executive. It is okay for both men and women to show all the range of emotions and it is not good to flash wealth or status. Quality of life and being friendly are important.

Feminine and Masculine

One can see how feminine and masculine society values are played out in the Korean and Japanese dramas that are popular in Hawai'i. Feminine cultures see life as precious and masculine see it as expendable. In one ancient Korean war drama, the military leader was worried that the lives of his soldiers and even civilians would be lost. In contrast, in the Japanese war dramas, *samurais* (member of a powerful military caste in feudal Japan) frequently commit suicide because their commanders merely request it.

Hawai'i's local culture has a mix of both masculine and feminine, but the overriding local culture is feminine. The local culture has to be feminine to allow all these different ethnic groups to live alongside each other on these small islands without racial violence.

Masculine values are part of the ethnic cultures of the Japanese, Filipinos and Caucasians. Hawai'i's masculine values are integrated with Asian Confucian and Buddhist beliefs—quiet yet in control. A man can be a bodybuilder, macho type but not aggressive, and he can be competitive if it's his group against another. Also, the women are just as tough as the men and work just as hard. The pidgin words for a tough-looking local guy and girl are *moke* and *tita*.

On the other hand, the Native Hawaiians, with their love of the land (environment), *'ohana* (family and community) interest in the welfare of others, especially the love and care of children, openness about sexuality, importance of giving back to the community, and the actions of friendliness and hospitality, represent a society with feminine values. *Aloha* is the love of life, not in the aggressive accumulation of things but in the joy of sharing and giving. Hawaiian values and the *aloha* spirit will turn a tattooed, scary-looking Hawaiian into a big, soft-hearted guy.

MODESTY

'E noho iho i ke opu weuweu, mai ho'oki'eki'e.'
'Remain among the clumps of grass
and do not elevate yourself.'
—Mary Kawena Pukui's *'Olelo No'eau:
Hawaiian Proverbs and Poetical Sayings*

In the Native Hawaiian culture, like other feminine societies, it is important to be humble and self-depreciating, or lower yourself so that you don't stick out from the group. According to Benjamin Young in the book *People and Cultures of Hawai'i: A Psychocultural Profile*, 'An individual seeking public office could not be *maha'oi* (forward, brazen) and advertise personal accomplishments. To do so would be unseemly. So, one has friends go about telling the successes one has had. Then the follow-up is to deny, or state that one's friends exaggerated the statements.'

Another example is of one white man that grew up here and was one of the few whites in his school. He learned about the value of modesty in Hawai'i's culture from his classmates. One day, he was sitting in class and the teacher asked a question. As usual, he did his best to raise his hand and give an answer. After he answered, the kid sitting behind him gave him a slap on the back of the head.

"What was that for?" He asked.
"Don't be a show-off," the kid replied.

LOCAL VALUES—SENSE OF COMMUNITY

'He po'e ho'opiha wa'a.'
'Useless people are like riders in a canoe
who do nothing to help.'
—Mary Kawena Pukui's *'Olelo No'eau:*
Hawaiian Proverbs and Poetical Sayings

Locals often judge you by your actions and not by your word, race or credentials. People often tell you that you need to get involved with the community to be successful here. Caring for others is a feminine culture value. *Malama* is the Hawaiian word for taking care of (each other).

The Hawaiian philosophy of *aloha* is sharing without expecting something in return. However, if everyone is only receiving, then the *aloha* will run out. To keep the *aloha* spirit alive, you have to be a part of it, not just receiving but also giving.

One of the vice chancellors at the community college had come to Hawai'i about the same time as me. A few months later, he was on a television telethon to raise funds for some community organisation. Also, the chancellor's picture was in the weekly paper attending a local business organisation event.

Not everyone is going to be on TV or in the newspaper. Another way to be involved is through your children. My child had a potluck, craft fair and bake sale at her pre-school every semester. They were very appreciative when my wife had made some fabric crafts for the craft sale and a watermelon salad for the summer potluck. We didn't do the bake sale but could have made more points with the group if we had, but for us it was a matter of the lack of time and energy with a couple of young kids at home.

According to one native Japanese immigrant, they also expect you to be involved at the elementary school level too. At Momilani, one of the top scoring public elementary schools, she said they have a high expectation of parent volunteering and involvement but that they also temper that with what your situation is. If you have both parents working or the mother is pregnant, they lower their expectations.

That Local Attitude

Some people may complain of the local attitude. It may frustrate them enough to make them want to move back to where they came from. A special supplement on local culture in the *Honolulu Advertiser* stated: 'There can be a smugness dividing 'us' from 'them,' a small-town-like arrogance of those in-the-know vs those essentially clueless about Hawai'i's ways.' That arrogance can make you feel like a tourist even if you've been living here for years.

Locals like to have the appearance of being in control and the people of Hawai'i admit to being provincial. In addition to provincialism, there is old history like the quasi-slavery on the plantations that still resonates. And today, land and housing prices are going up and jobs are hard to get. It's difficult to compete with people coming from the mainland and other countries so there is bound to be some tension felt by newcomers.

Breaking the Ice

Some locals will test you by being unfriendly at first. They want to see if you will respect local ways and watch how you react. The best strategy is to be humble and try to win their respect and friendship by going the extra mile and showing them you don't think you are better or smarter than them. This isn't just limited to immigrants (foreign or from the mainland); sometimes they test each other too, if they think that person is coming off as better or smarter. Some people will always keep you in the deep freeze, where others, once you melt down this ice barrier, will show their heart and will go overboard to help you and make you feel welcome.

With locals, it will take time for Caucasians to break through the barrier. Whether you're in a business setting or in the neighbourhood, take the time to show your sincerity by getting to know the people first. Take it easy and don't be in a rush to get all their personal details. Keep it low-key and relax and be yourself.

Many people can be reserved or shy and may not look you in the eyes. Nevertheless, smile and greet people even if they don't smile or greet you back. Many men, and sometimes women, greet with an upward nod. If you are a newcomer, you may need to do it first; it is important to acknowledge peoples' presence or you will seem weird or arrogant. The upward nod is done without saying anything and this is all that is needed—just an acknowledgment of others. A newcomer can do it to a room of locals and will get nods back.

Sometimes it can seem like a sales job, you put in the face time and allow your contacts to warm up over time. You are selling them on the concept that you aren't like the stereotype they know of a newcomer (Caucasian, Asian etc). There are some who will never thaw and will always be prejudiced or condescending. Others will open their heart if yours is true.

The Polynesian and Asian custom is to glance down and not stare in people's eyes, but you need to greet people here by looking them in the eye—just don't stare. A lot of local guys here do the bent upward handshake sliding into a regular one or a fist shake or fist bump. A lot of people also greet with a handshake and 'howzit' and say goodbye with a hug and a nose or peck on the cheek.

And of course there is the all-purpose *shaka* for hello, goodbye and thank you. The *shaka* is a thumb-and-pinkie salute that can also mean 'right on' or 'hang loose'. According to the Oʻahu Railway tour guide, the *shaka* originated from a train engineer that had lost his middle three fingers and would wave to people from the train. It is a greeting that symbolises local pride and identity.

Lastly, break the ice by sharing your time more than your opinions. When getting involved, whether at work, outside work, at your kid's school, volunteer organisations, homeowner or community associations, resist the urge to speak up. Find a balance between sharing what you know and holding back. Make your suggestions in a way that considers others' points of view and doesn't cause them to lose face.

Unspoken Rules

In any culture, there are innumerable unspoken social cues and norms. People in Hawai'i won't tell you that you've violated a cultural norm, but you can feel it through their 'stink eye' (nasty look) or by them being uncooperative. As in any culture, the expectation is that you understand the cultural norms.

In Hawai'i, it is important to be polite, friendly and appreciative, as opposed to being assertive. Being assertive is easily interpreted as pushy. When in a retail store, supermarket or library, there is always at least one person working there that is willing to react to an assertive, pushy person. It can be in the form of misinformation from a store clerk; or making you wait a long time at the reference desk at the library; or the cashier at the supermarket triple-checking your ID against your credit card. It may be that you haven't been assertive but you have violated some other cultural norm and that's their way of telling you—by not telling you but instead making things hard for you.

It may be a reaction to the mainland too. If a local from Hawai'i goes to the mainland, they will be expected to act according to mainland culture and may also accept the pecking order (whites on top). Also, they get strange looks if they are behaving in a foreign way like speaking pidgin English. Hawai'i is similar in its expectation that you understand and follow the social rules of Hawai'i.

Finding Your Way Around

One long-time resident had a hard time until her husband and her understood the places they should and shouldn't go. Some people say you shouldn't go to Wai'anae, Kalihi or Waimānalo without a local friend and that the locals there can be territorial and act like you're intruding. When you first move here, it takes making many mistakes and going to the wrong places until you find out how to live here. She went with her husband to the beach in Wai'anae and sat near a camping tent. They were too new to realise that the tent was someone's home. Some of the tent dwellers blocked in their car with other cars so they couldn't leave and one woman started throwing coconuts at her. They managed to get away and have been living here successfully for many years.

First you learn what not to do and where not to go, and then later you begin to make friends. You find there are some really good people here too. Being a newcomer, you tend to step on all the landmines but eventually you find the safe places and friendly faces.

Ethnic Jokes and Talking Stink

One local born AJA thinks 80 per cent of locals can identify the race of another local. Criminal profiles on TV used to mention a specific race like Japanese or Filipino, which was funny because that meant the person being robbed or whatever was able to tell that person's race in a matter of a few seconds. Now, they will just use the term 'Asian' instead. On the other hand, a Caucasian professor who moved here from California and has been living here 30 years says he still can't tell someone's race.

Everyone here, like other multi-ethnic communities, has grown up talking about racial differences with each other, although not always with the newcomer. One local Chinese-American graduate student said you have to become 'thick-skinned' to all the racial/ethnic/local jokes when growing up here. Another local Japanese-American said he knows a Portuguese banker who always sends the latest Portuguese joke to everyone he knows. He said ethnic jokes reflects the diversity here; it depends on the context but they are often used as a source of levity of cultural differences.

It is the newcomers, especially from the mainland, that are thin-skinned because they didn't have to grow up with racial issues, jokes and differences. To adjust to the culture of Hawai'i, you have to be able to laugh at yourself, make mistakes, learn the culture and not be sensitive to racial jokes—especially about your own race. Locals know

Ethnic Humour

Local-born comedian Frank Delima is an icon of ethnic humour in Hawai'i, with funny stereotype characters like the Chinese *mahjong* player, Japanese *sumo* wrestler, Samoan football player and others. There is an old favourite song in Hawai'i called 'Mr Sun Cho Lee'. This song makes fun of many of the ethnic groups in Hawai'i through stereotypes, such as a cockfighting Filipino (Filipinos brought cockfighting to the islands; it's illegal but still practised) and a tightwad Chinese.

An example of ethnic humour in Hawai'i.

newcomers are sensitive to these kinds of jokes and may avoid opening up to them until they know they can be trusted to not take it the wrong way.

The newcomer has to understand that it is a part of the multi-ethnic culture way of taking the power and the sting out of ethnic differences through jokes, and easing the racial tensions and insecurities of people by allowing everyone to laugh at each other and themselves. One *hapa* (part Hawaiian) Filipino grad student from the mainland felt she and the locals actually bonded by talking stink together about other races. Some say that if a newcomer becomes the target of an ethnic joke, that means they have been accepted as part of the group. Even using ethnic labels like *haole* (Caucasian) or *pākē* (Chinese) can be a sign of trust between friends. Lastly, ethnic stereotypes (the kind seen in jokes) are shortcut ways for locals to identify with each other.

THE PEOPLE
The local atmosphere pervades in the areas that have mixed ethnic communities, while the racial enclaves tend to reflect the atmosphere and culture of the dominant ethnic group.

This is why it is important to understand both the overriding local culture and the individual ethnic cultures.

America has been characterised as a melting pot. Hawai'i with its largely Asian population is more like a melting wok. Some people say Hawai'i is more like the Canada analogy— more like a salad bowl. I would have to add my own analogy and say it is more like a bowl of curry with the curry being the overwhelming taste of local culture on top of the individual ethnic meat and vegetables.

While ethnic rituals and traditions seem to fade with the generations, values and beliefs seem to persist longer.

It is easier to understand Hawai'i through looking at the various ethnic groups' contributions to the customs, etiquette, holidays, foods, religion, traditions and rituals in Hawai'i. Many ethnic groups celebrate at temples the Japanese Buddhist holidays of Buddha Day (Buddha's birthday) and Bohdi Day (the day Buddha's became enlightened under the Bohdi tree). The Chinese, Japanese and Filipino all have beauty contests at festivals. Many celebrate the Chinese Lunar New Year and the Narcissus Festival. Everyone in Hawai'i spends lots of money on firecrackers to celebrate the New Year. Firecrackers, illegal in many states, are not in Hawai'i, because it is part of the Asian tradition and the noise is believed to scare away bad spirits.

It is also important to understand where each ethnic group resides on the islands. On O'ahu, the Japanese outnumber all the other races. On the islands of Kaua'i and Maui, Caucasians are the largest number (with the Hawaiians a very close second). While on the Big Island, Moloka'i and Ni'ihau, Hawaiians are the most populous. On Lāna'i Island, the Filipinos are the largest population. There are also racial enclaves within each island.

Just over 70 per cent of the population of Hawai'i is on O'ahu. Caucasians, Japanese, Filipinos and Hawaiians are

> A local born Asian-Indian and his native Japanese wife had a birthday celebration for their only child. There were no other Asian-Indians present, but he still practised various customs like not taking a picture of only the three of them, because in Indian culture to take a picture of three is unlucky.

spread out on all the islands. However, other ethnic groups have the majority of their population on O'ahu. For example, 95 per cent of Chinese, 87.9 per cent of Koreans, 95 per cent of blacks, and 94 per cent of Samoan/Tongan live on O'ahu, which is nicknamed the 'gathering place'. It is truly the multi-racial gathering place of the islands.

STEREOTYPES

There are lots of stereotypes: the Chinese have the money because they are shrewd businessmen (a stereotype about Chinese held in many countries); the whites own Hawai'i's land (the historical legacy of the capitalists and missionaries); and the Japanese have the government (politics, politicians and government jobs).

But how much do these stereotypes hold true? For example, do the Japanese really have the politics? Look at the racial mix in the government: Senator Daniel Inouye is Japanese but Senator Daniel K Akaka is Hawaiian-Chinese (the only American-Chinese in the US senate and the first senator of native Hawaiian ancestry) and Mayor Mufi Hannemann is Samoan. Hawai'i had its first Filipino governor, Benjamin J Cayetano (the highest ranking Filipino-American in elected office in the US), from 1994–2002, and current Governor Lingle is a Caucasian originally from Saint Louis, Missouri.

Stereotypes have a kernel of truth and also say as much about the person making them as it does about the people being stereotyped. Therefore, people avoid stereotypes. However, it is important to understand the stereotypes that people hold in order to better understand the basis of information that ethnic groups in Hawai'i use to interact.

Whether stereotypes are true or not, they provide an understanding of how different ethnic groups make sense of each other and what their moral, values and expectations are. Stereotypes can be used as ethnic slurs but can cut both ways. In one case, it's serious and in another, it's a friendly jab at a friend. Ethnic jokes are part of Hawai'i's local culture, so don't be extra sensitive to the overt racist quality in a joke. One joke every ethnic group says about other ethnic groups is that they all look alike. Which has some truth to it, because it is difficult to tell people of a same race apart until you begin to see their subtle differences. Locals stereotype each other as the clannish Filipino, uppity Japanese, lazy *kanaka* (Hawaiian), arrogant *haole* (white), tight *pākē* (Chinese), etc.

In the next section, we look at the different ethnic groups of Hawai'i, their values, traditions and even stereotypes. First we will look at the Hawaiians, then the Asians, and lastly the Caucasians.

HAWAIIANS

Robert Louis Stevenson in the book *Travels in Hawai'i* explained Hawai'i and Hawaiians: 'The thought that haunts the stranger is that of Italy. The ruggedness of feature which marks out the race among Polynesians is the Italian ruggedness. Countenances of the same eloquent harshness, manners of the same vivacious cordiality, found in Hawai'i and among Italian fisherfolk. I know no race that carries years more handsomely, whose people, in the middle way of life, retain more charm. I recall faces, both of men and women, with a certain leonine stamp, trusty, sagacious, brave, beautiful in plainness; faces that take the heart captive. The tougher the struggle of the race in these hard isles has written history there; energy enlivens the Hawaiian strength. Or did so once, and the faces are still eloquent of the lost possession. The stock that has produced a Caesar, a Kamehameha, a Ka'ahumanu, retains their signature.'

This rugged and cordial race were the first to discover the Hawaiian Islands somewhere around 400–500 AD. They brought with them food, crafts, religion and customs. Their ancient occupations were canoe-making, taro farming and fishing. It is fair to say that things were going pretty well before the arrival of explorers from the West a thousand years later.

The colonial history of the Native Hawaiians resembles the Australian Aboriginals. They both numbered about 300,000 at the time the Europeans arrived around 1780. Then around 1860, their numbers dropped to about 70,000 for the native

Hawaiians and 22,000 for the Aboriginals. One of the big factors in the decline was the diseases that the Westerners brought with them.

Today, the Native Hawaiians (*kanaka māoli* in Hawaiian)—including ones of mixed race—are about 20 per cent of the population. They are represented in all classes and aspects of society, but regrettably, they have one of the highest rates of unemployment and welfare cases.

The Home of Native Hawaiians

According to the US Census, there are various areas on the islands where individual ethnic groups are more than 50 per cent of the population. Hawaiians are present on all the islands but are concentrated with over 50 per cent of the population in these areas:

- On O'ahu—the majority of the west coast from Nānākuli all the way up to the far side of Mākaha valley. Also, on the windward coast (east coast) in the area surrounding Waimānalo.
- On Maui—the coastal area on the south-east side stretching from Kaupō around the tip to Ke'anae.
- On the Big Island of Hawai'i—the area around Hilo International Airport.
- On the island of Kaua'i on the windward side from Keālia up to Anahola.
- The whole island of Moloka'i.
- On Ni'ihau—they make up 80 per cent of the population.

Stereotypes

Benjamin Young in the *People and Cultures of Hawai'i* says: '(Native) Hawaiians have suffered from negative and positive stereotypes. It is not uncommon to hear disparaging comments made toward Hawaiians: lazy, shiftless, unmotivated. Likewise, it is also frequently heard that Hawaiians are easy-going, expressive, loving and generous.' I have even heard part-Hawaiians say these things about Hawaiians, so these stereotypes aren't only held by non-Hawaiians.

Stereotypes of Hawaiians living in poverty, breaking the law and failing school can drown out the positive contributions of upstanding people in the Hawaiian community, such as Native Hawaiian Senator Akaka. Some say strong Hawaiian leadership and social pay-off in their work (i.e. social standing and impact being more important than wealth) is the solution to the Hawaiians' socio-economic problems today. They also say that the Hawaiian values of generosity and sharing clash with the Western Protestant ethic of ambitious, individualistic enterprise. For example, the first motive of the Hawaiian entrepreneur is often said to be hospitality while the Western capitalist is profit.

Though Hawaiians have suffered from negative stereotypes, with the Hawaiian Renaissance, they have found a new pride in themselves and their culture. More Hawaiians are learning the language and participating in cultural practices and spiritual rituals. In 1978, the Hawaiian government enacted programmes in the schools for the study of Hawaiiana-- Hawaiian culture, language and history. The administration of former Governor Cayetano (1994–2002) created Hawaiian immersion schools. At these schools, classes are taught using the Hawaiian language and subjects related to Hawaiian culture are included in the curriculum.

Hawaiian Values

Hawaiian cultural contributions are the performances of *mele* (songs) and chants, *hula* dance, even the modern-day slack-key guitar and the ancient craft of *kapa* (bark cloth and twine baskets). These, along with the Hawaiian language and the Hawaiian spirituality, are being revived. The Hawaiian cultural contributions through the values of *aloha*, *'ohana* and hospitality play a big part in the local culture of Hawai'i. Here are some of the values of the Hawaiians:

Aloha

Peter Adler wrote an article on 'Aloha Spirit' in the book *The Price of Paradise II*: '*Aloha* spirit is not an abstract intellectual idea. It is a life form which must be nurtured and practised if it is to survive. Given the pace of demographic, economic, and

The Hawaiians have contributed richly to the cultural environment of Hawai'i, such as with this graceful dance by a young group of dancers.

political change in Hawai'i, this may become progressively more difficult. It is easier to reduce the notion of *aloha* spirit to a bundle of interpersonal codes than it is to infuse the 'spirit' half of the equation into everyday affairs. But for some people, *aloha* spirit ultimately means just that. It is the divine breath that gives all of us a sense, of humility, balance and grace.'

Some Native Hawaiians from whom the wellspring of *aloha* spirit originated may have the least amount to give. There is the plight of the Hawaiians with high rates of poverty and homeless. An extreme example is the Department of Human Services (DHS) overload of children in danger cases and a high number of children that are taken away from families. Many of these families are of Hawaiian descent. Many families have one or more parents addicted to the drug 'ice'. There are so many addicts and addicted families that the DHS sponsored a special one-time television programme about the ice drug epidemic in Hawai'i. It is a painful programme to watch, and the children of these ice addicts are put into shelters and eventually foster care by DHS.

Generosity and Hospitality

Generosity and hospitality is seen in many Polynesians cultures like Hawai'i. The Hawaiians didn't believe they owned the land but felt they were responsible for taking care of it. Land was the source of life as well as food. They readily shared this land with each new ethnic group that arrived throughout history. For Hawaiians, generosity is a way of life. In earlier times, according to Pukui in *Nānā I Ke Kumu*, 'Hawaiian women were generous with their sexual bounty'; in the same way, the Hawaiians have been generous with their food, family, homes and land.

Reciprocity

Pāna'i in Hawaiian means reciprocity. Hawaiian, Japanese, Filipino and local culture hold the belief in giving back something of greater value in return for something received. *Laulima* means to cooperate and work together. There is an expectation and an obligation to give and take freely, to help and be helped among the extended family. Hawaiians have a sense of fair play where everyone is expected to make a contribution.

'Ohana

'Ohana means family or those you choose to call family. There is a collectivist loyalty and dedication to the welfare of the *'ohana* group. Work must be something that benefits the *'ohana* and not just the individual.

Harmony and Helpfulness

Lōkāhi means unity, harmony, balance or coming together. *Lōkāhi* is maintained by humility in the members of the *'ohana*. The Hawaiian process of *ho'oponopono* is for talking out problems to reach a solution. *Kōkua* or helpfulness is seen in the many fundraisers that are announced at your child's school or in the emails you receive from your co-workers at work.

Hawaiian Time

Hawaiians live in the present and enjoy the moment.
'Ukupau means 'job done'. It is the practice of people helping
one another with their work tasks so that they can finish
early and commence with fun and relaxation. In ancient
times, Hawaiians worked when they needed something
like food or a sleeping mat. This was the beginning of
the piecework system where you finish your work and
you're done for the day, not when the clock strikes five.
This pay-by-the-job system was also seen on the sugar
plantations and some jobs today still use it, such as the
garbage collectors.

Native Hawaiian Animism and Spirituality

According to Hawaiian mythology, the Hawaiian Islands
were born from the woman Papa of the earth and the man
Wakea of the sky. They had several children, the first being
the Big Island of Hawai'i. Later, they gave birth to the rest
of the islands and the people of Hawai'i. The *kumulipo*
(means genesis or source of life) is an evolutionary
mythology chant that explains the origins of Hawaiians
and the universe. It also tells the story of how the chiefs
and royal family are genealogically linked to the creators
of the islands.

Hawaiian/Polynesian Animism is a mythology of gods
and *mana* is the divine power that is in everything. The
ancient system of *kapu* (prohibition) is used to protect *mana*
in things like people, places, animals, objects, etc. *Heiau*
are ancient temples where rituals, including the sacrifice
of violators of the *kapu*, had taken place. A *kahuna* (priest)
performed the rituals and chants. Not only Hawaiians were
sacrificed; in 1792, three English sailors were supposed to
have been sacrificed at the largest *heiau* on O'ahu—Puu O
Mahulea Heiau.

Ancient Aloha is also the spiritual value of a common life of
sharing with others. Traditional Hawaiian culture is based on
the heart and not the head like Western Christian culture (they
did not believe in a devil or a hell and afterlife). Hawaiian
spirituality goes beyond the Confucius/Buddhist/Zen rules

of behaviour. It is based on a philosophy that is grown out of the heart and spirit. It starts with the loving and caring of the family from children to dead ancestors and *kōkua*, the helping of others.

In Hawaiian mysticism, there is a belief that dreams inform and advise one. Dreams can foretell events of good and bad fortune, personal failures, and failures in relationships or duty to their family. Their dead ancestors speak to them through their dreams. Physical illness is the result of some imbalance in their lives, either in their relationships or something they have done wrong, and their *'aumakua* (spiritual ancestors) are punishing them.

Seventy-three years before the overthrow of the Hawaiian monarchy, the Christian missionaries arrived and overthrew the existing Hawaiian religion and gods. They did this so completely that little remains today of Hawaiian spirituality. Whether Christian or not, many Hawaiians still believe in the *'aumakua*—their spiritual ancestors that guide, advise, warn, protect, reprimand and punish them through dreams and life occurrences. *'Aumakua* can protect them from bringing shame to their family or group. The Hawaiians, like the Japanese, feel an obligation to their dead ancestors. Whereas the Japanese are repaying a debt to their ancestors and performing filial piety, the Hawaiians believe they must love their family and dead ancestors or be lonely and unhappy after death. They also still believe in personal gods and that the *'aumakua* reside in animals such as lizards, sharks, birds, and even in plants, rocks and clouds. Today, some Christian churches play a role in continuing the culture through practices such as *ho'oponopono* (see page 63).

Tradition

Traditional Hawaiian customs such as the *lei* and the *lū'au* are world renowned. The *lei* is a custom of welcome or congratulations by presenting a Polynesian garland of flowers. to wear around the neck. There are many varieties of *leis* that can be used. Never hand a *lei* to a person. When placing the *lei* on the person, a hug and a *honihoni* (kiss) will be given on the cheek if the relationship is close; other times its just a brush of the nose on the cheek. *Leis* welcome a new co-worker/employee, congratulate a new graduate, etc. If you receive a *lei*, the custom is to wear it all day, or at least not take it off in front of the person who gave it to you. Even the bride and groom at a wedding wear *leis*. A groom wears a *maile* (shiny shrub leaves of twine) with *pīkake* and *'ilima* flowers and the bride wears a flower headband called a *haku*.

The *lū'au* is a Hawaiian feast with a gathering of people celebrating a special event. The *lū'au* was named after a popular dish of taro tops, chicken and coconut milk. In Hawaiian culture, the first birthday is a very important event and it is customary to have a *lū'au* to celebrate a baby's first year. The baby *lū'au* is celebrated by all the ethnic groups in Hawai'i. If you are invited to a baby *lū'au*, make sure you attend or have a very good excuse not to.

At the baby *lū'au*, there is Hawaiian food, music and games for the kids. As with most events in Hawai'i, the dress code is relaxed and casual unless otherwise stated. People typically wear *aloha* shirts, shorts and sneakers, and the women wear a *muumuu* or a dress. If it's on the beach, slippers can be worn. If it's held at a hotel or hall, the dress code might include slacks and loafers for the man and an *aloha* dress for the woman. In addition to a birthday present, many people include cash in the birthday card to help with the cost of the baby *lū'au*. A cash gift can be anywhere from US$ 10–25 per person, depending on how well you know the family. As with other events, if you are close to the family, you may also help out by setting up the place before the event and cleaning up after it.

> To hold a baby *lū'au* at the Ala Moana Hotel can cost up to US$ 5,000 or more. The parents figure they can get the money back and more in gifts from the guests. They use this money to pay for a college fund for the baby.

Traditional celebrations of Hawaiian heritage are the Makahiki annual Aloha Festivals celebrations, Hula Festivals like the Prince Lot Hula Festival at Moanalua Park and Kamehameha Day parade (the founder and first king of

The author's wife wearing a *lei* and enjoying a meal of traditional Hawaiian food of *poi, kalua* pig, *poke* and others.

Hawai'i). Other holidays include 1 May, Lei Day and Prince Kūhiō Day—birthday of the nephew of Queen Lili'uokalani and republican delegate to congress.

CHINESE

Today, the Chinese (including ones of mixed race) make up about 15 per cent of the population. Of the total Chinese population, only about a thousand are of Taiwanese origin. The Chinese were the first immigrants to come and work on the sugar plantations. They had specialised knowledge in the sugar refining process and signed work contracts that, if broken, could have landed them in jail. After serving out their contracts, they quickly moved out of the plantations and into Honolulu. Many went into businesses.

According to US Census data, the Chinese population is concentrated in downtown Honolulu and Diamond Head and spread out from there in decreasing numbers. Their populations on the other islands are in the single percentages. Ninety-five per cent of the total Chinese population live on O'ahu.

Chinese horoscope, fortune-telling, acupuncture, *feng shui* (Chinese practice of placement and arrangement of space to attempt to achieve harmony with the environment) and Chinese medicine are some of the Chinese cultural contributions in Hawai'i, as well as on the mainland. Chinese medicine intertwines Taoist concepts with that of ancient treatments. This is achieved through specific food and herbs. For example, the Chinese fruit lychee—a popular fruit in Hawai'i—is recommended for tumours. Chinese medicine also considers ginseng a cure-all for many illnesses.

Lysee ('lucky money' in Chinese) is a Chinese custom practised in Hawai'i. *Lysee*—not to be confused with lychee—are red envelopes with money given to others on special occasions like birthdays or weddings. Red is considered lucky and conveys good wishes and good luck. For example, after a wedding, the family gives the bride *lysee* filled with money at a special bridal tea ceremony.

Ching Ming Festival is a time for Chinese to express their Confucianist virtues of filial piety by visiting the graves of their ancestors. During this festival of Pure Brightness, the Chinese place offerings such as roast pig, incense, flowers, fake paper money and paper replicas of gold and silver bars on ancestors' grave sites. *Lysee* and items such as fake money, silver and gold bar replicas used for the Ching Ming Festival can be purchased at some supermarkets like 99 Ranch Market in Honolulu.

The Chinese Chamber of Commerce in Hawai'i began to promote the celebrations of three festivals to stimulate business in Chinatown and preserve Chinese customs and traditions:

- Narcissus Festival
  (http://www.ccchi.org/narcissus/index.html)
  Held in conjunction with the Chinese New Year. This festival was started in Hawai'i and is claimed to be the oldest ethnic festival in Hawai'i. They sponsor a beauty contest with a Narcissus Queen.
- Dragon Boat Festival
  (http://www.dragonboathawaii.org)
  A traditional boat race from China held between May and June.

GREAT NEWS WE'RE IN THE DRAGON
BOAT. NOT SO GOOD HERE'S OUR DRUMMER

- Harvest Moon, Full Moon or Mid-Autumn Festival
  The various names for a traditional harvest festival celebrated in China and by Chinese around the world. In Hawai'i, this celebration encompasses traditional songs and dances, fireworks and dragon and lion dances

The Chinese Lunar New Year starts with the first day of the lunar calendar (depending on the cycle of the moon) which falls some time between the end of January and February. The Lunar New Year is celebrated with big festivities in Chinatown, with special foods and a lion dance where several people cover their heads with a long lion costume and dance down the street. The lion is a symbol of wealth and longevity and is supposed to scare the evil spirits.

Chinese use fireworks in many festivals and rituals to drive away evil spirits, so Chinatown is blasting with fireworks during the celebration of the Lunar New Year. '*Gung hee fat choy*' (prosperous new year) is said to others after the turning of the Chinese New Year. One part of the Lunar New Year tradition is the stacks of oranges (a symbol of gold) displayed inside homes for the occasion.

Visiting Chinatown

Today's Chinatown isn't all Chinese, but a mix of Vietnamese, Laotian, Japanese, Thai, Filipino, Hawaiian, Korean and Caucasian merchants. To find out more, visit their website:

http://www.chinatownhi.com/

You can also find out more at the Chinese Chamber of Commerce in Hawai'i at:

http://www.ccchi.org/.

The Chinese in Hawai'i are still obsessed with luck and this can be seen in the colours and numbers they pick. They believe red is lucky and many Chinese in Hawai'i believe in lucky and unlucky numbers. Even numbers and the number eight are generally considered lucky (although this is also dependent on other factors like how the word sounds, etc.). When we made an offer on our condo, the owner was Chinese. He liked our offer but said it was an

A Chinese lady burns incense and prays at an altar in the Chinatown Cultural Plaza.

unlucky number for him (it contained the number 5—an uneven number), so we raised the offer by a thousand dollars (which changed it to a 6) so that it was lucky for him and that sealed the deal.

Confucius Influence of the East Asians

The basics of Confucius' teachings can help one understand the underlying motivations and core moral values of the Eastern Asians (Chinese, Japanese, Korean) in Hawai'i. Confucius was a philosopher born in China in 551 BC. His teaching spread through Korea and eventually into Japan.

Confucius believed in a hierarchy of five types of social relationships: between ruler and subject; father and son; husband and wife; elder and younger; and friends. It is your mutual obligation and duty to respect and obey those more senior than you, and protect and be considerate to those who are more junior. This is the way to maintain harmony within groups and in society.

'Over his embroidered robe, he wears a simple cloak'—*from The Odes of Horace*. Sometimes, locals may look like they are trying to hide what they know, but it is really a core moral value of humility and self-deprecation.

The principles of Confucius' teachings revolve around developing virtue, as opposed to Western religion that seeks divine truth. Developing virtue starts with oneself and extends out to the family, and ultimately society. Virtue is the development of self as opposed to Western religious ideas of holding particular beliefs of good or evil. The only belief is that developing virtue is the first step to a peaceful and happy world.

The virtue of harmony is important because it shows how 'face' is maintained and how people function in this group-centered (collectivist) society. It is virtuous to maintain harmony—at least on the surface—and respect, and not bring shame to those of one's in-group. Taking care of one's parents financially or physically is also a virtue that is practised in Hawai'i.

Confucius taught that everyone, regardless of background, should continue to improve themselves through education, practice and self-discipline. Although public education is poor in Hawai'i, that does not mean it is not valued, especially among Eastern Asians. The fact that Hawai'i has the highest percentage of private schools of any state in the USA could be viewed as an indication of the value of education on the islands.

According to Confucius, other values that should be cultivated are frugality, patience, reciprocation and perseverance. Also, one should not treat others as one would not like to be treated oneself.

In Hawai'i, all of these virtues—in particular hierarchy, obligation, harmony, modesty and reciprocity—are obvious. In addition, there are the Buddhist values of proper behaviour, filial piety and self-sacrifice.

Many of the Chinese values reflect the Confucianist philosophy. Like other Eastern Asians, the Chinese value hard work and education. They have Confucianist values of being polite and having respect for the elderly (filial piety) and family. Also, like many collectivist societies, they place

A statue of the father of the Republic of China, Dr Sun Yat-Sen, in Chinatown, decorated with *leis*. He was educated in Hawai'i and later returned to China to become the first president of the Republic of China.

the welfare of the family above themselves. Locals stereotype Chinese as being shrewd business people, stingy, aloof, tight-fisted, and having all the money and owning all of downtown Honolulu. This may be because of their famous business sense and the emphasis they place on owning property and entrepreneurship.

> **Learning the Language**
>
> The Chinese and Japanese share a similar writing system and can read each other's newspapers to some extent. There are both Chinese and Japanese language schools in Hawai'i for children to learn their heritage language. (There is a Mandarin language class on the 2nd floor of the Cultural Plaza in Chinatown.)

The Chinese and Japanese have brought similar cultural aspects to Hawai'i, such as the the martial arts of Chinese *kung fu* and *tai chi* and Japanese *karate* and *kendo*. Also, the Japanese and Chinese have similar eye exercises that involve massaging pressure points around the eyes called *tsubo* in Japanese. Both the Japanese and Chinese have the practice of flower arrangement and a tea ceremony. The Chinese Ching Ming Festival is the same as the Japanese Bon Odori—a day for the spirits of dead ancestors. Lastly, both are stereotyped as polite and inscrutable.

JAPANESE

At the end of the 1800s, over 200,000 Japanese were brought in to work on the plantations. It is said that the Japanese are an example of the American dream: having started on the plantations a few generations ago, they are now a force in politics and education and are a major influence on the local culture in Hawai'i.

Okinawans are typically grouped with the Japanese when counting the numbers that migrated. Okinawa is part of Japan, but used to be the largest and most important of the Ryukyu Islands. This island chain was previously known as the Ryukyu Kingdom. They have different customs and values from the Japanese. They speak Japanese but also have a native Okinawan language.

The Chinese and Japanese have been in America for several generations, whereas other Asians such as the Cambodians and the Hmong are relatively new immigrants. Asians constitute about 4 per cent of the total US population but 58 per cent of the total Hawai'i population. Out of this 58 per cent, 42 per cent is reported to be purely

Asian, while the additional 16 per cent have mixed racial parentage.

Out of the former 42 per cent, 40 per cent are Japanese (pure parentage), whereas the Japanese are only 8 per cent of the total Asian population of the US. There is a concentration of five times more Japanese in Hawai'i than on the mainland. This may be one reason why people from the mainland clash more with the Japanese here, as they have had less exposure to them than other Asian groups and cultures (i.e. Chinese or Filipino). In Hawai'i, Asian Indians and Vietnamese numbers are under 2 per cent of the Asian population (about 9,000), whereas on the mainland they far outnumber the Japanese with 26 per cent of the total Asian population.

According to the US Census, there are various areas on the islands where individual ethnic groups are more than 50 per cent of the population. Japanese (including Okinawans) are present on all the islands but are concentrated with over 50 per cent of the population in these areas: on O'ahu, Japanese enclaves spread out like fingers running north off of highway H-1; Upper Mānoa in Honolulu, Moanalua, Pearl City; then up highway H-2 to Mililani Mauka in central O'ahu. The city of Hilo on the Big Island of Hawai'i is the only area outside O'ahu that has a Japanese population of 50 per cent or more.

> One Asian Indian said that the Indians don't go anywhere that doesn't already have a community of other Indians living there, and that is why there are not many Asian Indians in Hawai'i. The same may be true of Japanese, because they have had a community in Hawai'i for almost 150 years.

Japanese History in Hawai'i

The Japanese Cultural Center of Hawai'i (JCCH) has a historical gallery if you wish to learn more about the history of the Japanese in Hawai'i. Visit their website at:

http://www.jcch.com

Traditions

Ethnic groups are slowly taking on the values of Hawai'i's local culture and American culture, and some faster than others.

The Filipinos are said to assimilate faster while the Japanese are characterised as a group that has held onto traditional values and beliefs with successive generations better than any other ethnic group. However, with the exception of the Chinese, the Japanese have been here longer so there has been more time for Japanese ways to erode and be replaced by local and American ways.

Many Japanese traditions have survived over the generations and some have even been transformed. The Japanese and other ethnic groups in Hawai'i still celebrate traditions like Hatsumode, Oshogatsu, Yakudoshi, Girl's and Boy's Day and Obon Odori.

All of Hawai'i celebrates the turning of the calendar new year. Hatsumode, a practice from Japan, is the first visit of the year to a Buddhist temple or a Shinto shrine on or after midnight. During Hatsumode, people receive blessings from a Shinto priest and pray for protection and guidance. At Buddhist temples, bells ring 108 times, the last ring at the stroke of midnight.

Before Oshogatsu (New Year), the Japanese display *kagami-mochi* (a symbol of happiness and luck) in their home. *Mochi* (Japanese rice cake) is rounded into flat balls and stacked with an orange on top (sometimes real food or a plastic imitation). They also display New Year's *kadomatsu*—a pine and bamboo and plum blossom decoration that symbolises vitality. *Kadomatsu* is placed at both sides of the entrance of the home and discarded the first week of the New Year.

Visit Daiei supermarket before New Year and you will find plenty of *osechi ryori* (tradition Japanese New Year's food). *Mochi* is the most popular and is also found at Japanese festivals. Traditionally, *mochi* is pounded in a huge mortar with a wood mallet, but today's families have electronic *mochi* makers in their homes. *Osechi ryori* are symbols of health, happiness and prosperity, like *mochi*, *ozoni* (*mochi* soup), *renkon* (lotus root), *konbu* (seaweed) and *kazunoko* (red herring eggs). Also, red sushi and tuna sashimi are preferred on New Year because red is the colour of luck and happiness. Japanese also celebrate the New Year by eating *toshikoshi soba*. *Soba* is brown buckwheat noodles dipped in a soy sauce soup base. *Toshikoshi* means 'crossing over to the New Year'. I usually get the name confused with *hikkoshi soba*, which is the tradition of eating *soba* after moving house.

Lucky and unlucky days are a belief stemming from Shintoism. There are good luck birthdays and bad luck birthday traditions for the Japanese. *Shichi-go-san* (literally '7-5-3') is a coming-of-age celebration of children turning these ages. Children wear *kimonos* (traditional Japanese attire, a long loose robe tied with a sash) and receive blessings and prayers of protection from a Shinto priest. In Hawai'i, young girls can rent a traditional Japanese *kimono* at the Japanese Cultural Center and have their picture taken. Also, *kanreki* (second childhood) is a man's 61st birthday, and it is celebrated with him wearing a red hat and red vest symbolising him starting life over.

Bad Luck Party

Yakudoshi (literally 'misfortune year') is a bad luck party for a man's 41st birthday or a woman's 32nd birthday. These are considered unlucky years so changes are avoided. My Japanese mother-in-law did experience bad luck during her *yakudoshi* because her father died. A party is held before the birthday to ward off bad luck. Many ethnic groups celebrate this event, especially for the man.

Traditional Events

- Spring Cherry Blossom Festival with a beauty contest for a Cherry Blossom Queen.
- The Shinto Thanksgiving Festival in October at Daijingu Temple, similar to the Buddhist Obon. It is a festival for dead ancestors.
- On Girl's Day (*hinamatsuri*), 3 March, *mochi* is served. In February, an expensive glass case filled with doll replicas of the emperor and empress is displayed in the home. The display must be taken down on 3 March or the girl's chances for marriage will diminish.
- Boy's Day (*kodomo no hi*) is on 5 May and is celebrated with the flying of a *koi nobori* (carp streamer/banner) kite outside the home. Inside the home, an arrangement with a *samurai* helmet or armour and male dolls are displayed.

In addition to a *koi* flag outside, Boy's Day, like Girl's Day, is also celebrated with an ornamental display. The display in the picture includes a miniature traditional helmet and armour with a sword plus a bow and arrow.

- 15 November is Shichi-go-san.
- Bon Odori festival lasts all summer long. (*Read more about the Bon Odori under the Festivals section in* Chapter Seven: Enjoying Hawai'i *on page 196.*)

Customs

Kotobuki is a Japanese custom of giving congratulations (at a wedding or other celebratory events) with a decoration of 1,001 metallic-paper *origami* (Japanese art of folding paper into decorative shapes and figures) cranes woven into a picture. The original Japanese tradition is a thousand cranes but the people in Hawai'i added one for good luck. The crane symbolises longevity and fidelity.

For the Japanese, it is customary to give a *banzai* toast at weddings, banquets and other celebrations. *Banzai* means '10,000 years and long life'. For the *banzai* toast, the arms are raised and '*Banzai*' is shouted. The *banzai* toast is repeated three times from the guests to the couple then as a thank you from the family to the guests. The guests shout '*Shinro*, *shinpu, banzai!*' (literally 'groom, bride, long life'). The family shouts '*Raihin shoku, banzai!*' (literally 'guests, long life'). This custom is practised even by non-Japanese.

Stereotypes

The stereotype of the Japanese being uppity or even power-hungry may be due to their desire to provide for their family and their children's future. They will *gaman*, persist and endure (like good Confucianists), and go to great lengths to achieve their goal. They have achieved some success doing this too. The Japanese, alongside the Asian-Indians, are the top-earning Asian-American groups. According to the US Census, both groups had a median family income in the US of about US$ 70,000. They value education and have almost double the number of Bachelor degrees compared to the average in the US.

The Japanese are also often stereotyped as secretive, clannish and have the reputation of sticking together. They, like other collectivists (and maybe stronger than other groups in Hawai'i), show a preference for their racial in-group. Japan was a closed society for a long time and it may be the reason why they are so in-group oriented. As collectivists, it is perceived as wrong to treat those outside your group better than those inside your group, whether it is sharing information, selecting candidates for jobs, or deciding on a job contract.

Additionally, in traditional Japanese society, it is not appropriate to show emotion, especially anger. Facial expressions are minimised almost to a point where it seems their faces are frozen. Even spoken Japanese minimises the amount the mouth moves compared to English. They are true minimalists, not only in their architecture and interior design.

Another stereotype is that the Japanese tend to avoid risk more

The Japanese are stereotyped as lacking emotions and being impossible to understand or interpret. My Japanese wife had an interesting answer to this question. It is common knowledge that the pupil expands when viewing something pleasurable or when having fun, and contracts during negative encounters. Compared to Caucasians, Japanese eyes are smaller and the eye colour is dark brown, so it's harder to see the emotional response in their eyes.

than other ethnic groups. My wife explains the reason for this. There is a strong ethic against greed and being selfish that is taught in children's folk tales and legends. There are many stories where two men have a choice between a present of little perceived value and one of greater perceived value. The greedy man chooses the greater value present but ends up with nothing and the other man that had chosen the smaller gift ended up with a greater reward inside (gold, money, food, etc.). Concepts like high-risk high-return are considered bad.

Japanese Values

The Japanese of Hawai'i may have lost their heritage language but their heritage values and behaviours persist. One local Filipino woman who works for the University of Hawai'i and helps international students from Japan was surprised to find they are more open than the local Japanese. They will open themselves up to her counselling while the local Japanese remain closed. Today, Japan is a much more individualistic and open country than the one made up of rural farms the Japanese of Hawai'i immigrated from 140 years ago. Like many transplanted ethnic groups, the culture and values of years ago seem to exist in a time warp in the new country. My Japanese wife goes to the local Daiei grocery store and sees the products that were popular in her grandmother's day in Japan but are still popular today in Hawai'i.

Religions from Japan that the AJAs practise are Shinto, Buddhism and Zen. Shinto shrines, *hongwanji* (Buddhist temples) and Zen centres are scattered throughout Hawai'i. Japanese values are written on 12 rock pillars at the Japanese Cultural Center of Hawai'i. They are: *gisei* (sacrifice), *giri* (sense of duty), *meiyo* (honour), *haji* (shame), *sekinin* (responsibility), *chūgi* (loyalty), *kansha* (gratitude), *shikata ga nai* (acceptance with resignation), *ganbari* (perseverance), *gaman* (quiet endurance), *on* (debt of gratitude) and *oyakōkō* (filial piety).

Many Asian Americans in Hawai'i do not realise that some of the values they practise originated from Confucianism. For example, the Chinese, Japanese and Koreans all

Inside the Waipahu Hongwanji. This Buddhist temple, like many on the islands, is over 100 years old and has services in Japanese and English.

practise filial piety (taking care of one's elders)—this is originally a Confucianist virtue. Japanese have a double dose of maintaining harmony: the virtue comes both from Confucianism and the Japanese religion of Shintoism. They also have a value of *enryo* (holding back, self-restraint) that also comes from the Shinto religion. Because of *enryo*, the Japanese may appear inscrutable, lacking emotion and even dense, but they are actually smart and just holding back—being careful not to stick out or show off. Also, their group identity and value of self-sacrifice come from the Buddhist religion.

In the Japanese and other Eastern Asians, the Confucian virtue of persistence and working hard in combination with the Buddhist virtue of self-sacrifice may create an extreme work ethic; one that is different from the local island pace and Hawaiian sense of time. Like the Filipinos, the Japanese survived through the hardship of the plantation days with their values of perseverance and quiet endurance.

They, like their brothers in Japan, believe in sacrificing themselves for the benefit of their children, yet also expecting their children to later repay *on* (a debt of gratitude) by taking care of them in their old age. *Oyakōkō* or filial piety is once again an Eastern Asian Confucianist value of fulfilling obligations to family, elders and society.

Although the Japanese of Hawai'i share many values with their cousins in Japan, they still feel separate from Japan. Unlike other ethnic groups that have strong ties to their motherlands, the Japanese in Hawai'i have relatively little connection or affiliation with Japan.

Indirect Communication

The Japanese like indirect and non-confrontational communication. The concept of harmony and maintaining it by not outrightly objecting or refusing can make communication difficult and confusing. If you propose agreement on something and get no objections, then find out later they are not following your proposed agreement, it can seem like passive-aggressive behaviour. Talking to others one-on-one will get more realistic responses and opinions than in a group.

Lastly, they also employ high context, non-verbal communication and depend a lot on unspoken cues and understandings. You have to learn the subtle ways and signals they use to show disagreement. It is safer to take silence as a 'no' than a 'yes'. And a 'yes' as an 'I understand you' and not 'I agree with you'.

Mainland Americans get their information through direct questioning, whereas Asians often get it through the grapevine. This can also be the reason why Asian cultures may seem to gossip more than mainland American culture. My Japanese mother-in-law says she likes the fact that mainland Americans (Caucasians) spend a lot less time gossiping about co-workers and family members than the Japanese do.

Contributions

Hawai'i comes alive when you understand the unique contributions made by each ethnic group—customs that are practised by everyone in Hawai'i and not just the Japanese. Simple things like the porcelain *manekineko* cats in the front

of stores beckoning with a paw for customers to come in. It is believed these cats bring prosperity and happiness. If the right paw is raised, it is for money; if the left paw is raised, it is for welcoming customers. The higher the paw, the more welcoming it is. There many different types of *manekineko*, but the one most popular is a white, gold and black cat. This is considered lucky because real cats with three colours are rare.

Like the Chinese culture, the Japanese culture is seen everywhere in the US and especially in Hawai'i: calligraphy, *haiku* (a poem of 17 syllables, in three lines of five, seven and five), *bonsai* (the art of growing ornamental, artificially dwarfed varieties of trees or shrubs), *ikebana* (flower arrangement) with Hawaiian flowers, *karate* (unarmed combat using the hands and feet to deliver and block blows), *sumo* (heavyweight wrestling), *kendo* (fencing with two-handed bamboo words), etc. Musical instruments and music have been brought over from Japan. *Taiko* is a Japanese barrel-shaped drum. Japanese *taiko* playing groups are popular in Hawai'i and they even have after-school *taiko* lessons at some elementary schools. *Shamisen*—also called *sanshin* in Okinawa—is a three-stringed lute traditionally made with the skin from a cat, dog or snake. The *sanshin* is played in the bandstand at Obon dances. The Japanese TV station KIKU also broadcasts a weekly local karaoke contest in Japanese.

Many wedding displays of 1,001 *origami* cranes are in the shape of the *kamon*—a round, black and white family crest from Japan. My wife's family crest is the *sagari fuji* (weeping willow) and my father-in-law claims it has been passed down from the *samurais*. You will see a *kamon* on the front of some businesses or buildings in Hawai'i.

The art of Japanese *origami* has spread all over America, and Hawai'i has added its own twist with Hawaiian-print, *origami* paper. It is folded into traditional Hawaiian symbols such as turtles, slippers and *aloha* shirts.

FILIPINOS

Starting from 1906, Filipinos from the Visayan Islands (central region) and the Ilocos (northern region) of the Philippines were recruited to work on the sugar plantations. Filipinos labourers, called *sakadas*, were the last group of immigrants brought over to work on the plantations. The sugar planters had an office in Manila that gave fares to Hawai'i for those who signed three-year contracts. Approximately 120,000 were brought in during the first half of the 1900s.

Filipinos come from different areas of the Philippines, each group having their own socio-economic differences. The Philippines has over 7,000 islands with different dialects and cultures spread throughout. There are many regional languages such as Visaya, Ilocano, Tagalog and others. Most Filipinos speak more than one regional language. For more than 300 years, the Philippines was a colony of Spain, therefore some Filipinos may speak Spanish and its influence can be found in the terminology in everyday conversation, as well as in the names of people and places. The Spanish also brought the Roman Catholic religion to the Philippines and many Filipinos are Christian.

The Philippines, like Hawai'i, was at one time a territory of the US. In 1898, when the US won the Spanish-American war, the Philippines (then a Spanish colony) became a territory of the US. In 1946, the Philippines became an independent nation. However, to this day, there are still US military advisors in the Philippines.

There were several waves of Filipino immigration to the US and many Filipinos became American citizens by joining the US military. However, a major issue with this group is that Filipino war veterans are still struggling to receive the same benefits as other US veterans, despite the key role they played in freeing the Philippines from Japanese control in World War II. Additionally, the Filipinos in Hawai'i, like the Japanese in Hawai'i, proved their allegiance to the US by fighting in World War II.

The US Census figures show the Filipinos are the second largest immigrant (who are not born in the US) group in the US, after the Mexicans. It is predicted that the Filipinos will soon be the largest Asian-American group in the United States, outnumbering the Chinese.

Factoring in their rate of immigration, Filipinos will soon surpass the Japanese as the largest Asian-American group in Hawai'i. Unlike the Japanese who are the strongest voter bloc in Hawai'i, the Filipino vote is relatively low in numbers and is more fractured. Some speculate it is because of the divisions within the Filipino community among the different regional groups. Others speculate that the community is divided by socio-economic factors and the contrasting interests in the range of classes. Several Filipinos have had positions in the Hawaiian government, the most notable being local-born-Filipino former Governor Benjamin Cayetano (1994–2002), and the present Senator Ron Menor, who are well-known figures within the Filipino community. There are also some Filipinos represented in government administration and business. They have doctorates and are in leadership positions.

However, the Filipinos are still largely under-represented in professional jobs. The Chinese, Japanese, Koreans and Caucasians hold many more professional and managerial positions, while the Hawaiians and Filipinos mostly hold the labour (such as farming, fishing and forestry work) and service jobs, though some are in key positions in the academic and corporate domains.

The Filipinos per capita income is lower than the average for Hawai'i because they occupy so many of the low-income jobs. They form half of the farm/plantation/mill workers and hold a quarter of both labour and service jobs in Hawai'i. They are very under-represented in the higher paying jobs, professional and government positions.

Filipinos are the largest percentage of students in public, private and Catholic schools in Hawai'i. Leeward Community College has a huge percentage of Filipino students yet many of the teachers are Japanese and Caucasian. In schools like Waikele elementary, the student population is half Filipino.

Since 1906, Filipinos have been immigrating to Hawai'i and are still immigrating today. Yearly, approximately 6,000 people immigrate to Hawai'i from other countries and more than half are Filipinos. Little more than half the Filipino population has been born in Hawai'i. Filipinos are the third largest ethnic group in Hawai'i. On the 2000 census, about 170,000 reported being full Filipino, and 275,000 reported being part Filipino.

According to the US Census, there are various areas on the islands where individual ethnic groups are more than 50 per cent of the population. Filipinos are present on all the islands but are concentrated with over 50 per cent of the population in these areas: on the island of O'ahu, Waipahu (near the old sugar mill) out to Barbers Point, Wahiawa (near the Dole pineapple plantation) and the area around Kalihi in Downtown Honolulu. On the island of Lāna'i, known as the 'Pineapple Island', Filipinos are more than half the population.

Social Values

In comparing the Filipinos with the Japanese, the latter have been in Hawai'i longer and have a smaller group of immigrants still coming from Japan. The values of the Japanese in Hawai'i are from a Japan of years ago transformed through decades in Hawai'i. They have seen a slow assimilation to American values. On the other hand, the Filipinos were the last major group to immigrate to the plantations and are one or two less generations in Hawai'i than the Japanese. In addition, there are many new Filipino immigrants still coming to Hawai'i. The values of Filipinos in Hawai'i today are closer to their relatives in the Philippines than the local Japanese are to their counterparts in Japan.

However, the culture of the Philippines is different from a hundred years ago. New Filipino immigrants bring a different culture from the one the Filipino old-timers brought to Hawai'i.

The Filipinos brought with them the *bayanihan*, a spirit of supporting each other through family, extended family, neighbours, organisations and labour unions. These collective Filipinos feel an obligation to pay back these groups with loyalty and support. Filipinos are the largest group of Roman Catholics in Hawai'i and the church is one place they find support and community.

They value the extended family and feel ties to the greater Filipino community. They created organisations such as labour unions to fight for better conditions during the plantation days. In difficult times, they pulled together, like when they created the labour unions and other social connections. These alliances were collective and demanded loyalty. They had the obligation to help each other out and pay back favours or face losing support of the group. Those who fell outside their groups were paid little attention.

The Filipino Community Center

Today, many groups and institutions support Filipino business, community and other interests. One such institution is the Filipino Community Center (FILCOM Center) in Waipahu. Organisations like these are helpful for the Filipino newcomer immigrant and are a source of physical and emotional support. The FILCOM offers free classes in citizenship for new immigrants. They also have a *hanapbuhay* (means 'livelihood' in Filipino) workshop with help and information on how to start a small business in Hawai'i. Visit them at:

http://www.filcom.org/.

The *bayanihan* spirit is extended to new immigrants from the Philippines. The Filipino community is the opposite of the Japanese community and opens its arms to newcomers from the home country. '*Mabuhay*' is a Tagalog greeting similar to '*aloha*'. Filipinos immigrating to Hawai'i will find help (similar to the *aloha* spirit) from other Filipinos finding a job or even a place to live while they get their feet on the ground.

Historically, plantation workers created groups and alliances as a way to create an extended family of *bayanihan* mutual support that single men were not able to bring with them when migrating to work on the plantations. Extended family such as the aunts, uncles and grandparents will live with the family. It is through *bayanihan* of the extended family households that they can pool together to buy a home. These can be the bigger stone veranda houses you can see in Waipahu with the iron rod gates and 'beware of dog' signs; houses that fit more than just the immediate family.

Utang na loob is a debt of honour or gratitude, a form of reciprocity and exchange of mutual benefit. Similar to the Chinese and Japanese, they feel a debt to their parents and elderly for raising them and repay this debt through caring for them financially and physically. When they receive a favour or a service, they feel debt of gratitude and an obligation to repay this debt either in the future or when the other is in need of help or through gifts. This can also happen even when they perceive they have received a favour. The obligation to their family takes precedence over their work and even community activities.

Hiya is the Filipino word for shame. It is important to save face by not bringing shame to themselves, their group and others. They feel shame if they perceive themselves to be socially unaccepted by a group. Sometimes, a Filipino will go to any length to save their face, even if it means going into debt.

Pakikisama seems to have a wide meaning. It is the Filipino word for harmony through smooth interpersonal relations and the value of friendship. It is the value of 'going with' the crowd and the leadership, avoiding confrontation and conforming to the desires of the group—the collectivist value of placing the group before yourself.

Amor propio means self-esteem. Filipinos will strive to protect their reputation. This is also part of not losing face; if they don't live up to the expectations of others, then their reputation will suffer. And conversely, this may be where they get the stereotype of being susceptible to flattery.

This is also where the Filipino stereotype of oversensitivity or of being shy and unable to express emotions comes into play. Because of *pakikisama*, they need to be considerate and aware of others' feelings and desires and go to great lengths to avoid giving offence. Yet, some Filipinos are also easily offended and especially sensitive to attacks on their *amor propio*.

Filipinos value the extended family, close family ties and loyalty that reaches out to grandparents and even to distant cousins. They respect a hierarchy in relationships and defer to the authority and the decision of elders. Filipinos also value work and education as a way to elevate their status and their family. Patience, perseverance and a strong work ethic have enabled the Filipinos to work on the plantations in the past and survive in Hawai'i today. Lastly, similar to the Hawaiians, they value hospitality. The guest is treated like a king even to the detriment of the host.

Several values of the Filipinos are shared with other ethnic groups in Hawai'i. The Filipinos have the value of hospitality in common with the Hawaiians. In Filipino, harmony is *pakikisama*, in Hawaiian it is *lōkāhi*. Even Eastern Asians must cultivate the Confucianist virtue of maintaining harmony. Hawaiians and Eastern Asians share the Filipino value of *utang na loob* (obligation of reciprocity).

Customs and Traditions

Music and dance are an integral part of Filipino culture. The Spanish influence can be felt in the sound of the Filipino music at fiestas. The *pandango* (money dance) is a tradition brought from the Philippines that is often performed at weddings. *Tinikling* (bamboo dance) is a dance you can see at gatherings and festivals. Two people hold long bamboo sticks and a third person dances in the middle. The sticks are held near the floor and clapped against each other while the dancer steps in between and over them.

A large majority of Filipinos are Catholic and there are many churches in the Filipino enclave of Waipahu. Catholicism is seen in the traditional holidays they celebrate, and in their customs and values. As Catholics, they practise regular weekly church attendance, have traditional Catholic mass weddings and other Christian traditions such as baptism of children. Also, many immigrant Filipinos use the services of the Catholic Charities and the Catholic Immigration Center.

Traditional Events

The biggest Filipino cultural event is the Filipino Fiesta and Parade sponsored by FILCOM. There is a parade in front of Waikīkī Beach that ends at Queen Kapi'olani Park. At the park bandstand, Filipino entertainers perform next to fiesta booths with cultural crafts and vendors sell foods such as *lumpia* (egg spring roll made with pork and vegetables or banana) and the popular Filipino desert *halo-halo* (a variation of shaved ice in different flavours, sometimes with beans).

There is also the Barrio Fiesta on Maui and the Fiesta Filipina that crowns a beauty queen. Beauty pageants also function as community fundraisers in Hawai'i. The Fil-Am Festival at Kapi'olani Park is a cultural festival created to bridge the gap between Filipino and American culture.

The Filipinos continue to celebrate Flores de Mayo and Philippine Independence Day (12 June).

Latecomers

It has been said by some that the Japanese, Chinese and Korean consider themselves all part of the same local group but do not consider the Filipinos as part of the Asian in-group. The Japanese and Chinese have been in Hawai'i much longer and are economically on the high end. The Japanese and Chinese share the same writing character system. Some Korean writing is also similar to the Japanese/Chinese character system. Geographically, the three countries are close. These three countries also share the Buddhist and Confucianist philosophies.

Filipinos have a Spanish and American historical colonial influence in their language and religion. Many are Catholics. The Filipinos were the last group to migrate here for plantation work. Also, as the relative newcomer to Hawai'i, they are economically on the low end.

Stereotypes

The Chinese are stereotyped as Oriental Jews and the Filipinos as the Oriental Latinos. They are seen as dark-skinned Asians with a hot Latin temper. Along the lines of the Latin stereotype, they are perceived as frequently singing and dancing, especially at weddings. There is also a stereotype of them being extra sensitive to criticism and status. This may come from their *amor propio*; they are careful to protect their pride and reputation.

A local stereotype of Filipinos is that they are not college educated, and that their test scores are lower than average. This may be a result of their lack of access to good education and low-income restrictions. Some speculate that this could also be the reason for the high percentage of Filipinos in gangs.

Another stereotype is that they are employed in low-wage jobs, such as landscaping and picking of weeds. However, according to the US Census, the median family income in the US was US$ 50,000. The Filipinos were far above average (US$ 65,000) and the Chinese were less than the Filipinos (US $60,000). The Koreans had the same median family income as the Vietnamese (US$ 47,000).

Filipinos do value education. According to the US Census, 43.8 per cent of Filipinos in the US have a Bachelors degree or higher. That is about 2 per cent higher than the Japanese (41.9 per cent). The average for the total population of the US was only 24.4 per cent. The Korean rate was 43.8 per cent and the Chinese was 48.1 per cent.

Lastly, the Filipinos, like other Asian groups, often avoid prolonged eye contact and are seen as clannish. Avoiding eye contact is a custom that is still practised in the Philippines. Even the old Filipino guy that lives next door still greets me with a nod upwards and points to things with lips in the Filipino way. As for clannish behaviour, it's about alliances and collectivism. The Filipinos are disinterested in those outside their alliances or groups.

Filipinos, like the Hawaiians, are also starting to rediscover their culture. Young Filipinos are reconnecting through Filipino food and dance. According to one University of Hawai'i Filipino student, there is a revival of learning the languages of the Philippines. The university is one of the only (if not the only) university that offers Filipino and Ilocano language classes for university credit, and you can get an entire bachelor's degree in Philippine Language and Literature. There are also classes on Filipino dance, film and literature, as well as a Center for Philippine Studies that is quite active.

Going Back to Your Roots

One local-born Filipino woman said that she would have loved to have been involved in all the Filipino culture related groups that are available to youth today, but that there weren't any of these groups when she was younger. There was a time in Hawai'i when minority ethnic cultures were looked down on, and in the case of Hawaiians, even suppressed. Just like how people in post-colonial countries are reclaiming their ethnic heritages today, the Filipinos, Hawaiians and many ethnic groups in Hawai'i are reviving interest in their ethnic heritage.

CAUCASIANS

The Caucasians are the largest immigrant group, but have difficulty considering themselves immigrants. Approximately 30,000–40,000 people immigrate to Hawai'i from the mainland each year. Caucasians make up the majority of this group. There are even some Caucasians that emigrate from Canada to Hawai'i each year. I met a Caucasian Canadian woman who moved here because she landed a nursing job at Pali Momi Hospital. The military also constitute a large percentage of the Caucasian population on O'ahu.

To determine the Caucasian enclaves, it might be helpful to look at a map of federal lands. The US government- or military-owned lands on O'ahu are the Pearl Harbour Navy Base and the Hickam Air Force Base (both on Pearl Harbour); Schofield Barracks Army in Wahiawa in central O'ahu; on the windward side are Kāne'ohe Marine Base and Bellows Air Force Base; and the National Guard in Kapolei on the leeward side.

If you overlay Oahu's census data map, Caucasians number 50 per cent or more in all these military areas. The other non-military-related lands of Kailua (in between

ONE OF THOSE CAUCASIANS SPREAD OUT ON THE ISLAND

the Kāneʻohe Marine Base and Bellows Air Force Base) and Waikīkī have over 50 per cent Caucasian population.

On Maui, the majority of the island has a percentage of 50 per cent Caucasian with the exception of downtown Kahului; the area around the coast on the south-east side stretching from Kaupō around the tip to Keʻanae; and the Waiheʻe and Lahaina coasts. On the Big Island of Hawaiʻi, Caucasians comprise the majority of the island with the exception of Hilo and the surrounding valley. On the island of Kauaʻi, Caucasians inhabit the northern quarter of the island from Hāʻena to Kīlauea.

Because of the immigration, Caucasians are becoming a larger cultural and economic force on the islands. This raises the question of whether they may once again replace the Japanese as the political power or if it will be the sleeping giant of the Filipino community. California is the top state that US immigrants come from. Californian culture has had and will continue to have an effect on the culture of Hawaiʻi.

Historically, Caucasians avoided the back-breaking labour of the plantations and took on supervisory roles instead. Thus, the emotional baggage of the locals comes from the plantation history and present-day struggles. The Native Hawaiians lost their religion, land and sovereignty to

American missionaries and capitalists. The Asians on the plantations were little more than imported slaves. This past resonates with locals today when new Caucasian immigrants come from the mainland or foreign countries and buy up homes and take jobs.

Caucasians in Hawai'i represent all walks of life: surfers, retirees, military, veterans, artists, federal government workers, long-time residents, corporate expats, university professors, university employees and students, regular working class and professionals. Military personnel and their dependants are around 10 per cent of the population of O'ahu, so they have a significant effect on the economy and can be considered as another subculture here. The military keep the mainland culture strong in Hawai'i.

Values

The majority of Caucasians are Christian. Christian values are fairness, decency and kindness. The Protestants are known to have strong work ethics and value education, which generally fit with the local culture and especially the Asians. Additionally, they can be entrepreneurial and value building wealth.

They differ on other values. For example, Asians value filial piety while Caucasians are not expected to take care of their elders and rely more on community services like adult day care and nursing homes. Caucasian retirees like to come here because the Asian-influenced culture respects the elderly.

Many ethnic groups in Hawai'i value harmony. For Eastern-Asians (Chinese, Japanese and Korean), it is a Confucianist virtue. It is also the Hawaiian value of *lōkāhi* and the Filipino value of *pakikisama*. This is notable because it is a value shared by all these ethnic groups except the Caucasians. Most Caucasians believe that when it means getting the job done, it is OK to step on some toes or have someone lose a little face. And in social relations, they would much rather tell it as it is and speak what's on their mind than tiptoe around in fear of offending or annoying someone.

Signs of cronyism and racial jokes in Hawai'i may offend the Caucasians' liberal idea of equality and political correctness.

Their rational-objective mode of thought may be affronted by the subjective nature of the local culture; for example, that family takes priority over work and business matters.

Some Caucasians may observe local ways but may not necessarily prefer provincialism. Compared to other ethnic groups in Hawai'i, the Caucasians in Hawai'i lack loyalty to each other. However, the military has its own support and social structure and they tend to stick together.

Caucasians also value success, wealth and achievement. However, it is not OK to show off or flash wealth in Hawai'i; this conflicts with the Asian Confucian virtues of humility and self-deprecation and the Hawaiian value of modesty.

Stereotypes

Caucasians are often stereotyped as being superficial and unneighbourly. One Persian friend of mine used the metaphor that Caucasians will let you in the garden but not into the house. It's all business and we don't open our hearts or our homes to new acquaintances like how many people in other countries or the Native Hawaiians do.

The majority of Caucasians come from North America (mainland USA and Canada), which are individualist, masculine societies. Many of the things Caucasians are stereotyped for are traits of this type of society. So the stereotypes are a result of a culture clash with the collective and feminine local culture of Hawai'i.

The individualist says 'I' and 'me' and the collectivist says 'we' and 'us'. Caucasians get their identity from being an individual and have a need for autonomy. They are often stereotyped as insensitive because they are frank and to the point. Caucasians sometimes ask personal questions that may appear nosy, whereas locals tend to gossip, so they both end up hearing the same personal information—just that one is more direct and the other more indirect. The indirect method may appear more conniving, but it's really just a matter of avoiding a loss of face or giving offence. Caucasians do not worry about the collectivist behaviours of saving others face or shaming the group.

American sociologist Frederick Samuels, in his book *The Japanese and Haoles of Honolulu*, interviewed one person who said, 'The Japanese seem to think that the interaction between themselves and the Haoles leaves something to be desired.' Another person claimed, 'They (Japanese) stick together because they have faith in each other. They cannot depend on the Haole.' One Caucasian he interviewed said, 'Haoles are show-offs. About money, job, talent, socially. We are pushy, aggressive…'

The Caucasian stereotypes of being ambitious, aggressive, assertive and materialistic are part of their masculine culture. However, the Asian ethnic groups in Hawai'i may be as materialistic with their houses, cars and consumer goods. In regard to the Caucasians being stereotyped as acting superior and arrogant, this may be because ego-building is valued in masculine societies, whereas modesty is valued by feminine cultures such as Hawai'i's local culture.

While the Japanese may be stereotyped as humourless, the Caucasians are stereotyped as bad at local humour and overly sensitive to ethnic humour. Local humour might be considered a play on human relationships, perhaps revealing people's minor weaknesses or mistakes. This is different from Caucasian humour, which may be considered shocking or crude. Caucasians living in Hawai'i, if they don't already have it, develop the ability to laugh at themselves and their mistakes.

Keeping the Noise Down

Caucasians are often perceived as loud. A Caucasian rented a town house a few doors down from us. He had a noisy souped-up old truck with a huge Los Angles Raiders sticker on the window. Before work every morning, he revved up his truck and cranked the music. Despite the fact that the locals have obnoxious car alarms, they tend to be more considerate of neighbours in regards to noise.

The stereotype of the Caucasians as being colourless may have some truth in various aspects, because some Caucasians traditions and customs pale in comparison to the rich traditions and customs of the other ethnic cultures that reside in Hawai'i. For example, Caucasian funerals are drab compared to other ethnic communities. The Chinese have a tradition of burning fake miniature replicas of houses, cars, paper money and other items at funerals, as the dead are supposed to be able to use these things in the next life. Many ethnic groups have feasts with funerals.

There are also good stereotypes of Caucasians as ambitious, hard-working, friendly and generous. Caucasian Americans have an individualist way of giving and are some of the

Gold bars and hell money for the Chinese Ching Ming. The paper is folded into gold and silver bars and later burned at a Taoist funeral for dead ancestors to enjoy in the afterlife.

highest singular individual donors to humanitarian causes in the international community. Even military personnel stationed in Iraq give their own money to help the local schools of the Iraqis.

KOREANS

The first wave of Koreans arrived between 1903–1905 to work the plantations. They, like the Japanese, were short of women and used the picture bride process to bring over the first wave of about 600–1,000 Korean women to marry. With the end of the Korean War in 1953, many more Korean brides of US military men came to America.

Koreans continue to immigrate to Hawai'i and now number about 41,300 (including mixed races). Koreans are about 3.4 per cent of Hawai'i's Asians but around 10.3 per cent of the Asian population in the US.

According to the US Census data, Koreans are concentrated in Honolulu, Hawai'i Kai, Salt Lake, Pearl Ridge and spread out from there in decreasing numbers, with single percentages on the other islands. Looking at the census maps, they seem to be the most evenly spread out of all the major ethnic groups, and seem to fit in just about everywhere. Yet like many other ethnic groups, they are concentrated on O'ahu with 87.9 per cent of Koreans living there.

Korean, Japanese and Chinese languages and writing have some similarities. Many older people speak Japanese as a result of the Japanese colonisation of Korea (1910–1945). Shamanism is the oldest Korean religion, with Buddhism, Confucianism and Christianity arriving later.

Koreans have an honour system based on family and friends. They also follow a social hierarchy and have a Confucian respect for parents. This is reflected in the Korean dramas where the daughter and son strain under the debt they feel they must repay their parents for raising them.

Koreans are sensitive to status and appearance and will go to great lengths to save face. They are like the Japanese and rely on many non-verbal clues when communicating. *Kibun* is the Korean word for sensitivity in interpersonal relationships and preserving harmony. This goes back to the concept of high-context communication and being sensitive enough to interpret subtle non-verbal signals.

Keeping the Traditions

One first-generation Korean-American mother that was born in Hawai'i didn't really think about the customs that she practised. She had her picture taken in a *hanbok* (the traditional Korean dress) when she was 100 days old. She also practised the New Year's tradition of bowing to the spirit of her ancestors by placing her hands outward on her forehead and touching her palms to the floor. Her husband is Filipino and she said that the Japanese have kept their heritage culture better than the Koreans, but the Filipinos kept theirs even less than both the Japanese and Koreans.

The Korean Festival is as popular as Korean dramas and *kimchi* (spicy pickled cabbage, the national dish of Korea). This huge festival held in Kapi'olani Park has music, entertainers, food and craft booths. The number of people attending the festival is testament to Korean culture in Hawai'i. It is of the same magnitude as the Japanese Okinawan festival, and contrasts with the Thai festival that is more like a get-together of a small community of friends and family.

Koreans have found their way into both professional and political positions. Mayor of the Big Island, Harry Kim, is an

A traditional Korean performance at the Kapi'olani Park Bandstand, which is actually a huge gazebo.

Kimchi is the biggest contribution to food in Hawai'i from the Korean culture. There are several varieties of this spicy pickled cabbage available at the supermarket. People in Hawai'i enjoy eating *kimchi* with all kinds of foods. It's also used as an ingredient for dishes like *kimchi* fried rice.

example of the Koreans' success in Hawai'i. He is the first Korean-American to be elected mayor in the US. In 2003, Koreans celebrated their 100th year anniversary of the first immigration to Hawai'i.

PACIFIC ISLANDERS

The Pacific Islanders are a much smaller immigrant group compared to the Asian immigrants, but share a similar Polynesian culture with the Hawaiians. Hawai'i is part of the Pacific Islands, which comprise the triangle of islands within Polynesia as well as the islands of Melanesia and Micronesia (the two groups of islands west of the triangle of Polynesia). There are too many islands to list, but the ones of importance to Hawai'i are Samoa and Tonga. The highest number of Polynesian immigrants come from Samoa and Tonga. The Polynesian Samoans and Tongans have populations of about 16,000 and 4,000 in Hawai'i respectively. Other groups such as Micronesian (including a large number from the island of Guam) number about 8,000 in Hawai'i.

According to the US Census data for O'ahu, in a couple of areas in Kalihi, 30–50 per cent of the population is Samoan. Samoans constitute almost 25 per cent of the population of lower Waipahu (the area below Farrington Highway where many of the street names start with 'Pupu') and around Lā'ie (this is the city where the the Polynesian Cultural Center is located) on the windward coast. Ninety-three per cent of Samoans/Tongans lives on O'ahu and there tends to be higher populations where there is also a high Native Hawaiian population, probably because they share similar Polynesian culture.

Pacific Islanders have 13.8 per cent of people completing college degrees compared to the US national average of 24.4 per cent. They are over-represented in service and labour jobs and under-represented in managerial and professional occupations. However, they have found their way into both professional and political positions. O'ahu Mayor Hannemann is an example of Samoan success in Hawai'i.

Hawaiians (3.21 per household) have larger families than the national average (2.59) and Samoans (4.43) have even larger families than the Hawaiians. Samoans, like Hawaiians, love to be close to their family and children. My Samoan neighbour and her husband couldn't wait for their son, daughter-in-law and grandson to move in with them into their small two-bedroom apartment. She beams everyday when she takes her grandson out for a walk in the stroller. Like many Samoans and Hawaiians, they are strong Christians and their grandson

The Samoans brought the *lava-lava* (a sarong) to Hawai'i. Samoans are stereotyped as the big guys, the ones you see on the football and rugby teams. One local Japanese girl said, "Don't get in a fight with Samoan because he will show back up with all his big Samoan brothers."

was given the good Christian name of Judah, which means 'Lion of Christ'.

Some Samoan Words
- *Talofa*   Greetings or Hello
- *Fa'afetal*   Thank you
- *Loe*   Yes
- *Leai*   No
- *Tofa*   Goodbye

PORTUGUESE

A total of 17,500 Portuguese immigrant workers and their families were brought in after 1878. Many Portuguese, like the Filipinos, are Roman Catholic. They comprise 4 per cent of the population of Hawai'i and have made many contributions to the local culture. The *ukulele* (a small four-stringed guitar) was a creation inspired by the guitars brought by Portuguese immigrants. Several pidgin words are from Portuguese, and local favourites such as sweetbread and the popular *malasadas* sugar doughnut are from Portugal. The Portuguese are stereotyped as talkative and have been credited with bringing 'talk story' to Hawai'i. Portuguese are included with the Caucasians in the US Census data.

BLACKS

Blacks are concentrated in the government military-owned lands on O'ahu: Pearl Harbour and Navy Base, Hickam Air Force Base, Schofield Barracks Army Base and around Wahiawa in central O'ahu, on the windward side around Kāne'ohe Marine Base down to Kailua and Bellows Air Force Base. 94 per cent of blacks live on O'ahu and have single percentages on the other islands.

VIETNAMESE

Vietnamese are concentrated in Honolulu, especially in Pālolo (east of Chaminade University) and the areas surrounding Chinatown. In the areas outside of Honolulu and on the other islands, they number less than one per cent.

RELIGIONS IN HAWAI'I

- Hawaiian/Polynesian Animism—an ancient mythology of gods and *mana* as a divine power that is in everything. The revival of Hawaiian religion is taking place with the ritual practice of guidance from the *'aumakua* (spiritual ancestors).
- Buddhism (from Japan, China and Korea)—the path to enlightenment and nirvana is through the elimination of desires.
- Taoism (from China)—based on the text the 'Tao-te-Ching', focuses on living in harmony with life through non-action and letting things take their natural course. Many practices are similar to Buddhism.
- Confucianism (from Japan, China and Korea)—based on the ideas of social and moral behaviour conceived by the Chinese philosopher Confucius. It is a philosophy turned religion that now includes the worship of ancestors and various other gods.
- Shinto (from Japan)—worship of a divine power, ancestors and nature gods like the sun god Amaterasu.
- Zen Buddhism (from Japan)—derived from Buddhism. The belief to achieve enlightenment through meditation.
- Christian—the belief in the Christian doctrine, practices (church attendance, baptism, wedding, etc.) and of Jesus. Includes Catholics, Protestants and Mormons.

The Japanese religions of Shinto, Buddhism and Zen all have their own separate temples. These temples are everywhere on the islands. The Confucianist, Buddhist and Taoist religions of the Chinese are all practised inside the same temple. For example, there is a Chinese temple Kuan Yin on Vineyard and the Hsu Yun temple at Kawānanakoa Place, both in Honolulu.

Christianity is the largest religion in Hawai'i and therefore has churches around every corner. Catholicism is the main religion of the Filipinos and Portuguese in Hawai'i. Chaminade University of Honolulu is a private Catholic university. Also, Brigham Young University and the Polynesian Cultural Center are Mormon institutions on O'ahu. The Makiki Christian Church in Honolulu was built in the traditional

A Japanese shrine in Chinatown prepared for an October festival.

Japanese Edo period style architecture so that it looks like an ancient Japanese castle—a true symbol of the mixing of culture and religion.

HAPA AND THE MIXING OF RACES

When looking at the ranking of the racial charts below, the middle column shows the results for groups that are of a single race, while the right column records those of one race or more (including the statistics from the middle column).

Races in Hawai'i (2000, US Census Bureau)		
Race	One Race	Combination
White	294,102	476,162
Japanese	201,764	296,674
Filipino	170,635	275,728
Native Hawaiian	80,137	239,655
Chinese	56,600	170,803
Korean	23,537	41,352
Black or African American	22,003	33,343

Races in Hawai'i (2000, US Census Bureau)		
Samoan	16,166	28,184
Vietnamese	7,867	10,040
Other Micronesian (excl Guamanian or Chamorro)	6,492	8,401
American Indian and Alaska Native	3,535	24,882
Tongan	3,993	5,988
Other Asian	3,418	10,020
Laotian	1,842	2,437
Guamanian or Chamorro	1,663	4,221
Asian Indian	1,441	3,145
Thai	1,259	2,284
Other Pacific Islander	872	5,059
Other Polynesian (excl Native Haw, Samoan, Tongan)	588	3,019
Indonesian	292	709
Cambodian	235	330
Fijian	214	459
Malaysian	115	354
Sri Lankan	114	176
Pakistani	35	97
Other Melanesian (excl Fijian)	26	44
Hmong	20	22
Bangladeshi	6	10

For the Hawaiians, there are about 80,000 by race alone but in combination, there are about around 240,000—that's triple the number of the race alone. The Hawaiians and the Chinese (also triple) have had the most marriages with other races and mixing of races. That is double the amount of mixing the Japanese have done. Out of the major ethnic groups, the Japanese have done the least mixing and the Chinese and Hawaiians the most.

Hawaiian restaurants have an appetiser plate called a *pūpū* platter. The *pūpū* platter is popular and has several ethnic foods all on one plate, separate but creating a delicious variety. Some people believe this is the state of ethnic relations in Hawai'i. Separate but co-existing on the plate, creating a delicious variety.

Many think that mixing is and will be the solution to racial harmony in Hawai'i. This is suggested through the huge rate of mixed marriages, releasing people from ties and dividing lines of race. Others mention the fact that even people with mixed ethnicity sometimes talk bad about one of their own races, so mixing isn't going to solve racial tensions.

A KALEIDOSCOPE OF ETHNICITY

We have tried to understand Hawai'i's people through generalisations of each ethnic group, but we must also recognise that there are a thousand possible combinations of people and culture here. There are many races: Japanese, Chinese, Korean, Caucasian, Portuguese, Hawaiian, Puerto Rican and Filipino, to name just a few. Mix them over a few generations and you have a thousand combinations.

I was confused when I signed up my child for kindergarten. Which box do I select: Caucasian or Japanese? She is half of both. How do the people of Hawai'i approach this? Do they select the race they feel the strongest ties to? This was a new experience for me since I had only had to check off one box my whole life. I had no clue how the hundreds of thousands of multiracial people in Hawai'i approached this problem.

This was symbolic of my journey to Hawai'i—coming from a one race existence to a

Beautiful Keiki

Keiki is Hawaiian for children. Hawai'i is basically east meets west and is filled with racial mixes. Ask anyone in Japan and they will tell you that Asian and Caucasian mixed babies are beautiful. In Hawai'i, the weekly newspapers frequently have ads for beauty pageants and contests like the Tropicana sun lotion contest looking for beautiful *keiki* of Hawai'i.

A Waikele elementary kindergarten class is a kaleidoscope of ethnicity.

multiracial reality. An awakening to a new paradigm. Like the one I had when I saw a history book rewritten from a non-colonialist point-of-view in a graduate Asian Studies class. It wasn't a matter of adding women, black and Native American voices and narratives to American history. It was a complete rejection of colonial history and a replacement with the voices, culture and historical truth according to the local people. About putting back together the pieces of a lost culture and rediscovering the past and present.

Two paradigm shifts in myself I never foresaw happening. As for the checkboxes, I suppose they do like the US Census and check all boxes that apply. I selected both the Japanese and Caucasian boxes. We want our children to grow up identifying with both races and cultures.

CULTURE CONFUSION

I asked one girl who was Chinese-Thai-Caucasian what she was eating. She said it was something her mother made but wasn't sure if it was Thai or Chinese food, or maybe it was a mix that had developed only in Hawai'i or even just in her family. I enjoy knowing what food, tradition, custom, and behaviour comes from what country, but not all people have this interest. Some people say they ignore race as a way to maintain harmony, but its seems that culture is also ignored as a result.

My neighbour, a Caucasian girl that grew up here in Hawai'i, married a Caucasian military guy from the mainland. That is a cross-cultural marriage, despite the fact they are of the same nationality and race. Caucasians growing up here have a different culture than the mainland.

Those with mixed backgrounds have different allegiances. A Waipi'o lady in her 70s who was Hawaiian-Chinese-Portuguese complained that the Kamehameha schools benefits the rich and that the rich part-Hawaiian people put their kids in the school and pay the same low subsidised tuition as the poorer Hawaiians. She also said that the poorer kids cannot pass the entrance test. The schools were set up to help the disadvantaged Hawaiian children but may have lost their vision.

Despite the kaleidoscope of ethnicity, the ethnic mixing and culture confusion, we cannot ignore that individual subcultures do exist. For example, the Hawaiian/Polynesian concept of spirituality is vastly different from Asian Buddhism and Confucianism. The Confucius philosophy of acquiring virtue is very different from the Caucasian and Filipino Christian concept of living religious truths. However, when we socialise with the people of Hawai'i, it is best to understand local ways that have evolved from the contributions of all the ethnic groups.

FITTING IN

CHAPTER 4

TRIGG

'I feel lucky to have been accepted into this crazy, weird, lovable, mixed up, special place called the Hawaiian Islands. And I've finally come to grips with my inner outsider. I am home. Now, when someone sees me and calls out, "Hey, *haole*!" I take it as a term of endearment, and rarely flinch.'
—Charles Memminger,
Hey Waiter, There's an Umbrella in My Drink!

LABELS

Certain things have not changed in the last 140 years. You will find that locals still use the word *haole* and according to census data, even today, the majority of newcomers are from California.

Every culture has its word for foreigners. The Japanese call them *gaijin*, the Thais call them *farang*, and the Hawaiians call them *haole*. However, nowadays *haole* is attributed to Caucasians only. Many contend that it is not a racial slur while others agree that it is tainted.

Mark Twain wrote in *Letters From Hawai'i*, 'To the natives all whites are *haoles*—how-ries—that is, strangers, or, more properly, foreigners; and to the white residents all white newcomers are 'Californians'—the term used more for convenience than anything else.'

Kanaka is the Hawaiian word for man. Historically, Westerners in Hawai'i used to called the Native Hawaiians *kanakas*. The term *kanaka* has faded in favour of Hawaiian. However, *kanaka* is still used by Hawaiians and others, like *kanaka māoli* for Native Hawaiian.

In California, many Asians do not like the word 'oriental' and would prefer to be called Asian. The *Oxford English Dictionary* states that the term 'oriental' is dated and often considered offensive. However, AJAs in Hawai'i often use oriental to refer to themselves, and aren't aware that some Asians do not like the word. There are also Caucasians in

Hawai'i that use *haole* to refer to themselves, while others want to be called white or Caucasian.

People disagree if these words are politically, historically or linguistically correct. Nevertheless, people do use these labels.

HOW LOCALS SEE THE NEWCOMERS FROM MAINLAND USA

A foreign immigrant has his fellow immigrants to rely on. The new arrival gets advice from the long-timers. They tell him all the tricks to getting physically oriented, like how to use the bus and telephone. They explain the social expectations, such as taking off your shoes before entering anyone's home, and also social etiquette like waving when you cut someone off in traffic.

A newcomer from the mainland USA may be seen as an FOB—an immigrant 'Fresh Off the Boat' who does not understand local customs and culture. The mainland FOB does not have the advantage of an expatriate community and housing. As a matter of fact, some former mainlanders who are accustomed to local ways are embarrassed to see the FOB acting like a cultural misfit and may avoid them, while some locals will watch and wait for the newcomer to make mistakes.

A way to lose one's FOB status is through frequenting a place over a period of a few months, and after a while, people will start recognising you. Locals can tell if you are local by what you wear, whether you are in control and seem to know what you're doing, if they have seen you around a few times and whether you are knowledgeable of local ways, food, music, etc. However, trying to speak the local English accent will turn heads and trying to speak pidgin English may annoy some people.

NATIVE JAPANESE IN HAWAI'I

The native Japanese have left several impressions with the local people of Hawai'i. The Japanese tried to take Hawai'i on 7 December 1941 with an attack on Pearl Harbour. In the 1980s, the Japanese bought many hotels, businesses and properties in Hawai'i. Some people put signs on their houses saying it was not for sale so that they would not be bothered by Japanese asking to buy their property.

Japanese tourists frequently take pictures of this huge banyan tree in Moanalua Gardens because it was featured in a popular Hitachi television commercial.

Today, the Japanese are storming the beaches of Hawai'i, not as military invaders or foreign investors but as tourists. A few million Japanese visitors arrive in Hawai'i every year, spending a couple of billion dollars during their time here. On O'ahu, there is a non-stop flow of Japanese tourists from Waikīkī to Ala Moana Shopping Center and the Waikele Outlet Stores.

The Japanese love shopping in Hawai'i and getting discount prices on big name brands. Shopping in Hawai'i is expensive compared to mainland USA, but it is still relatively cheap compared to Japan, especially comparing prices of branded items like Louis Vuitton and Christian Dior. However, the trend is changing and many Japanese tourists are no longer single women with money to burn on branded items but instead new families with kids. These families are filling shopping carts at the Kmarts and Wal-Marts.

According to a Japanese saleslady who works at a famous hotel chain that sells timeshares, the Japanese retirees are buying up timeshares like candy, which isn't surprising. A chart of Japan's population based on age is shaped like the letter 'V'—a huge population of old people at the top and a small birth rate at the bottom. Hawai'i is popular with Japanese retirees, and Japanese retirees in general receive a huge lump sum of money at retirement. Many are spending part of this lump sum on timeshares in Hawai'i.

Recently, Japanese companies have sold the last of the large hotels—bought during the Japanese bubble economy of the 1980s—to companies from mainland USA. Yet, 85 per cent of foreign investment in Hawai'i is still from Japan. Hawai'i is one of the highest states for foreign ownership of land—almost 10 per cent. The people of Hawai'i are sensitive about this issue because of the long history of Americans and foreigners buying the land out from under the people of Hawai'i.

Local Japanese and the Japanese Newcomer

In addition to the buying up of land, locals have a stereotype of immigrants from Asia as clumsy and awkward. Immigrants from Japan will find that many AJAs are less than kissing cousins. They also have different values. For example, immigrants want to send their children to art and music classes while the AJAs, like typical Americans, want to send their children to learn sports.

Because the Japanese culture that has persisted in America is old and outdated, the Japanese immigrants consider their American cousins amusing country bumpkins and dismay at their inability to speak Japanese. In Hawai'i, starting in junior high school, the Japanese language can be studied, but very few AJAs speak Japanese or have any affinity for Japan or her people. Japanese immigrants see AJAs as bananas (yellow on the outside but white on the inside).

Locals may have interesting perceptions of their racial group and other racial groups. A local Japanese recounted that on her trip to Japan, she was shocked to see Japanese working in menial positions at places such as McDonalds. This made her realise the racial bias she had growing up in Hawai'i, seeing the local Japanese in better positions while the non-Japanese did the lower-paying and non-prestigious work.

There are even stereotypes of Japanese Americans coming from mainland USA. Canadian anthropologist Elvi Whittaker wrote in her book *Mainland*

One of my wife's native Japanese girlfriends is married to a local Japanese. Her mother-in-law told her son to marry a local Japanese instead of one from Japan. He got married to a native Japanese. Because of this, there is tension in the family and the mother-in-law isn't as helpful in taking care of her grandchildren. It's ironic because this is the kind of discrimination native Japanese show to foreigners in Japan.

Haole, 'The Japanese are surprised to find that a common ethnic origin does not necessarily ensure a smooth passage into island Japanese culture, but rather exposes them to new ethnic differentiation, namely *katonk*, the designation for mainland (USA) Japanese.'

ETHNICITY AND RACE RELATIONS
Racism, ethnic tension and prejudice in Hawai'i are things the newcomer has heard little or nothing about. In some ways, this is because even the people in Hawai'i are in denial over it. The *aloha* spirit and multi-ethnic pluralism are what people think about Hawai'i. The people of Hawai'i insulate visitors from the reality of race relations in Hawai'i.

Hawai'i has not completely been without racial violence. The 'Kill Haole Day' was the last day of school where school children verbally and sometimes physically abused Caucasian school children. This was banned, but much like the confederate flag with its racist connotations, may still linger. However, we have not personally seen or heard of any racial violence. Racism, it seems, takes subtle and passive-aggressive forms in Hawai'i.

In Hawai'i, some locals hold stereotypes and prejudice learned in the home or learned through personal experience of colliding with mainlanders and foreign immigrants. One of my neighbours, a local Japanese, works at her family's petrol station. There have been times when a military personnel customer would ask her if she speaks English. That really pissed her off, to be born and raised in Hawai'i and be treated in her home like a foreign immigrant.

On the other hand, Canadian anthropologist Whittaker found there were several cases of and reactions to prejudice. Many of the people she interviewed complained of rude store clerks, librarians, etc, where the locals would attend to others before the Caucasians, or have a condescending attitude or make the Caucasians wait an inordinate amount of time.

Whittaker found that some Caucasians, in trying to cope, cast themselves as the hero in a battle of good versus evil. Some will choose to ignore and avoid these people, while others try to take on a self-effacing manner. It seems the best route is being patient, smiling and appreciative.

Prejudice isn't only against whites. One of my wife's native Japanese girlfriends is married to a black guy. He isn't in the military but is frustrated because everyone stereotypes him as one. He also feels that the local Japanese discriminate against him and prefers that his children do not go to dominantly Japanese schools.

My wife and her other native Japanese girlfriends have experienced prejudice in Hawai'i. One heard racial slurs from her Caucasian neighbours. At Kmart, a Caucasian woman called my wife *baka* (Japanese for 'crazy' or 'stupid') as she passed her in an aisle at the store.

Some say they experience no prejudice. However, they may also live in an insulated racial enclave community, much like an expatriate community or military base in a foreign country. Others say it's just certain groups that experience it, such as Caucasians, blacks or Japanese immigrants, etc.

HOW NEWCOMERS SEE LOCALS

If you are a newcomer, make sure you are not mistaking culture clash or culture differences for racism. It is easy to see difficulties with locals as falling along racial lines. Take extra care and go the extra mile to understand. It may just be a personality or culture clash.

As immigrants, we must also be aware of our own prejudice. According to Frederick Samuels, 'The phenomenon of attributing negative actions of the dark-skinned locals to the Japanese, and positive actions to the Hawaiians is not uncommon among the newly arrived.'

When we adjust to a new culture, we have to understand and overcome our own prejudice and stereotypes of it as well. If we are to be happy in our host culture, we need to make changes within ourselves. Sometimes, this means relearning or reprogramming our own thoughts and responses. This is part of the awakening of the cross-cultural experience. Not only do we learn the social language of Hawai'i, but some things we take with us for life.

HIERARCHY AND TERRITORY

Hawai'i has a pecking order based on being local—which means having been born here, growing up here, graduating from a high school here, understanding local ways, food, music, values and looking and acting local. Some contend that looking local is more than simply wearing *aloha* shirts and slippers; it is also the colour of your skin. Acting local is also more than speaking pidgin or a *shaka* wave; it is a complex set of social rules.

There is also a pecking order among locals. Native Hawaiians and the Asians in Hawai'i come from hierarchical societies. Some say theirs is a hierarchy that resembles skin colour—from lighter to darker (Caucasian, East Asian, Filipino and Hawaiian). Others say the hierarchy in Hawai'i is based on the order that plantation immigrants came to Hawai'i: Chinese (1823), Japanese (1878), Korean (1903) and Filipino (1906).

The Eastern Asians (Japanese, Chinese and Korean) tend to have a solidarity that excludes the Filipinos because the Filipinos were the last group to immigrate to Hawai'i, and it also excludes the Native Hawaiians. One of the results of

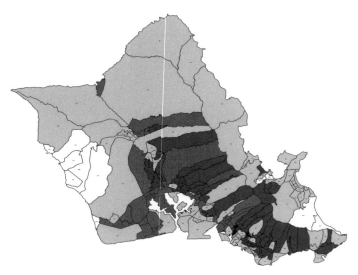

The US Census reports that these racial groups have the highest population percentage in the shaded areas: Hawaiian (white coloured areas); Caucasian (light grey coloured areas); Filipino (grey coloured areas); Japanese (dark grey coloured areas); Samoan (black coloured areas).

this may be that the Filipinos and Hawaiians hold the lower paying jobs.

The pecking order can also depend on which part of the island you are on. There are ethnic enclaves all over the islands—areas where more than 50 per cent of one race are present. This doesn't seem like a lot until you consider how many races there are in Hawai'i: Hawaiian, Chinese, Caucasian, Japanese, Korean, Samoan, Blacks, South-east Asians, Pacific Islanders, Filipinos and others.

None of these races have higher than about 25 per cent of the total population. Everyone is a minority in Hawai'i, but in some areas, they are the racial majorities. In these areas, it may be more important to pay attention to the dominant ethnic culture as opposed to the local culture that is throughout Hawai'i.

Ethnic Territories
It is important to recognise whose territory it is and where yours fits in. One Caucasian from the mainland who is a student in Honolulu felt that racial tolerance was area specific. When he went to the leeward coast or north shore, he had occasionally experienced the stink eye from the locals and one Samoan told him he didn't belong here. Recognising where the various ethnic enclaves on the islands may you help understand this.

RECIPROCITY AND OBLIGATION
Reciprocity is important to the local culture and is part of the ethnic cultures of the Hawaiians, Japanese, Chinese, Korean and Filipino. It is a core virtue in Confucianism and Buddhism. Local values can be seen through the potluck party.

University of Hawai'i anthropologist Jocelyn Linnekin was quoted in the *Honolulu Star Bulletin*: 'there is a sense of obligation, shame and reciprocity'. In terms of food, this translates to 'bringing a dish to a party whether asked to or not (obligation), having an abundance of food on the table (shame), and ensuring that there is enough food so that guests can take home a meal (reciprocity).'

Having enough food to take home is also an old Native Hawaiian custom. There would be a sense of shame if there wasn't enough food and the host would lose face. There is a story of one Hawaiian chief who ran out of food for his party and left town in shame.

These values are part of the Asian heritage too. In Japanese, *on* and *giri* mean obligation and *ongaeshi* means an obligation to repay someone's kindness. Reciprocity means to 'return in kind', which is a core Confucianist value. This is also different from the Western way of showing gratitude.

The Filipinos have a value of *utang na loob*, that is a debt of honour or gratitude. They also have a sense of reciprocity and an obligation to return favours in the future when the other is in need or through gifts.

GIFTS

Gift-giving is a custom that is practised in a similar way as the mainland. Gifts are given at birthdays, Christmas, weddings, graduation, etc. There is also the Japanese custom of *omiyage* that is common in Hawai'i. When you go on a trip, you purchase small gifts for your family and friends. For your co-workers, it is usually something like some famous candy or treat unique to the area that you visited.

Most people in Hawai'i practise the Japanese tradition of *omiyage* and bring some casual gift (like food) from their vacation like food to family, friends and people at the office. Gift-giving here is more casual compared to Japan, and in Hawai'i, everyone opens the gift when presented to them. If given a gift of food, they may return the plate with something they have made. Similar to the Asian tradition, gifts of money are always given in envelopes.

You may also need to bring a gift when visiting someone's house. It doesn't have to be packaged or expensive, it can be something small, usually food. Anything will do, even mangoes, avocados or papayas off your tree or your neighbour's. Flowers or wine is also acceptable. It is the feeling of *aloha* and sharing that is remembered when you give a gift.

One exception to bringing food would be birthdays. You can bring a present but don't bring food unless asked to. Usually the host provides everything needed for the birthday party, including food, tents, chairs, etc. We've seen a lot of birthday cakes from Costco.

When giving little gifts of snacks or candy to classmates or teammates, these are usually put in ziplock bags and marked with 'to' and 'from' on the bag.

Soccer Treats
On the last soccer game of the season, we had goody bags that were put together with contributions by the parents to give to the kids. When treats are brought to a game, they always include some for the younger siblings that are present.

At the end of the school year and at Christmas, many children give presents to their teachers. At Halloween and Christmas, everyone brings treats for everyone else, such as cards with candy canes or Christmas cookies and the like.

There is a general custom in Hawai'i that gifts of money are given at funerals to help pay for the funeral. At funerals, a gift of money is usually given inside a regular sympathy card. Many people cremate their dead instead of burying them in the ground.

WEDDINGS
In Hawai'i, there are many religions and many types of weddings: Shinto, Buddhist, Christian, etc. My wife and I had a Shinto wedding in Japan. The Shinto wedding in Hawai'i is the same and involves a Shinto priest chanting in front of an altar and a ceremony called the *san-san-kudo* (three-three-nine). During this ceremony, we had three servings of *sake* that we had to sip three times. I was nervous and screwed it up and sipped only one time. I saved face by giving my vows in English and Japanese without screwing up and then I laid the ceremonial twig on the altar. We didn't get to kiss because you don't kiss in a Shinto wedding and it would have messed up my wife's traditional white make-up anyway. Buddhist and Shinto wedding traditions are similar. Our friend's Buddhist wedding had the same rituals of chanting of sutras and the *san-san-kudo*.

For guests of weddings in Hawai'i, money is the appropriate gift. At our wedding, one of the Japanese customs was for the wedding guests to give money in an envelope to the wedding couple. The other tradition was one of reciprocation where we gave presents to guests after the wedding. This custom of a reciprocal gift is still practised in Hawai'i. We gave our guests gifts of a set of traditional Japanese wood bowls.

In most Christian weddings, the bride wears a traditional (usually white) gown and the man a tuxedo (usually black). The *pandango* (money dance) is a tradition brought from the Philippines but followed by everyone in Hawai'i. Money is given to the couple during their first dance. The money is thrown on the floor, put in the bride's mouth, pinned to their clothes or taped in a string around the couple. The dance continues until the guests are finished with their gifts of money. Filipino weddings usually consist of a Catholic Mass with an extravagant reception afterwards. Chinese serve a seven-course meal at the reception and have a lion dance with fireworks to scare away evil spirits and bad luck. Japanese will have the *kotobuki*, a picture of 1,001 cranes.

Wedding feasts resemble other Hawaiian celebrations with all the same mix of ethnic foods that the locals love. A *banzai* toast is a part of the wedding where someone from the family gives a speech then repeats *banzai* three times while raising their arms high. And the crowd reciprocates.

Native Japanese also love to come to Hawai'i to have weddings at a chapel on the beach. It's a big business in Hawai'i, and local wedding companies such as Watabe Wedding and Best Bridal have packages starting at US$ 5,000. They also have a minister who is bilingual in Japanese and English. It's highly profitable, considering they buy their *haupia* wedding cakes from the local Zippy's restaurant for US$ 10!

SETTLING IN

CHAPTER 5

'A man who knows that there have been
many cultures, and that each culture claims to be the
best and truest of all, will find it hard to take too seriously
the boastings and dogmatisings of his own tradition.'
—Aldous Huxley, *Playboy* magazine

ACCORDING TO A STUDY BY Mercer Human Resource Consulting of the quality of life among major cities in the world, Honolulu ranked number 25, together with San Francisco. Many European cities headed the top of the list. The study was based on criteria such as safety, economy, medical, health, climate, housing, schools, recreation, etc. In the same study, Honolulu ranked number 61 for cost of living, whereas Tokyo was number one and Manila was second to last at number 143.

RESIDENT PERMIT, WORK AND STUDY VISAS

The US Citizenship and Immigration Services (USCIS is formerly known as the dreaded INS) is a mess. Getting a visa is a slow, demeaning process and shows little regard for our future citizens. Many people get up early in the morning and stand in line for hours waiting to apply for a visa or resolve the many complex issues and problems that arise when getting a visa. The local office and website is located at:

US Citizenship and Immigration Services (USCIS)
Honolulu District Office
595 Ala Moana Boulevard
Honolulu, HI 96813
Website: http://uscis.gov/graphics/fieldoffices/honolulu/aboutus.htm

There is also a National Customer Service Center. Call USCIS toll free at (800) 375-5283 for information and help on matters concerning immigration services and benefits.

Resident Permits

The USCIS has a Diversity Lottery (DV) Programme that makes 55,000 immigrant visas available through a lottery to people who come from countries with low rates of immigration to the United States. For information on this programme and the many other ways to obtain a Green Card (lawful permanent residence), go to the USCIS website:

http://uscis.gov/graphics/services/residency/index.htm

Getting Your Green Card

To apply for a Green Card for an immediate relative (spouse, parent or unmarried child under 21 years old), you will need to file the following forms and fees:

- I-130: This must be filed by a family member (spouse etc.) who is a citizen or permanent resident. It costs US$ 190 for the initial immigrant visa.
- I-485: Application to Register Permanent Residence. Fee: US$ 325 for 14 years old and above, US$ 225 for under 14 years old.
- G-325A: Biographic Information. No fee.
- I-864: Affidavit of Support. No fee.
- I-693: Medical Examination of Aliens Seeking Adjustment of Status. No fee. This has to be performed by a civil surgeon who has been designated by USCIS and you must pay for the exam.

Until you get your Green Card you will need to apply for a work visa:

- I-765: Application for Employment Authorisation. Fee: US$ 180.

If you wish to leave the country while your application is being processed, you will need to apply for a travel visa:

- I-131: Application for Travel Document. Fee: US$ 170.

Until you receive your Green Card, you will have to apply for work and travel visas each year.

It took three years to get my wife's ten-year Green Card. My wife and I spent many long days at the INS (now called the USCIS) going through the application and interview processes. Including work and travel visas, it cost us more than US$ 1,000 to get her Green Card. Still, this was cheaper than using a lawyer but took a lot of work on our part.

THREE YEAR WAIT FROM THIS POINT INS.

I would highly recommend using the US embassy or consulate in the country you are coming from. It can take a matter of weeks to process instead of years if you apply at the US embassy or consulate before moving here. This is because the State Department, instead of the Justice Department, runs the embassies. The State Department isn't flooded with applications like the Justice Department. They are also friendlier at the embassies, because they are staffed by foreign service officers instead of low-paid, overworked immigration officers.

For further information on a visa for an immediate relative and to download forms, visit website:

http://uscis.gov/graphics/formsfee/forms/index.htm.

Work Visas

If you have an employer wishing to sponsor you, your employer must file Form I-140, Petition for Alien Worker.

The filing fee of US$ 195 will not be refunded. The form is available at website:

http://uscis.gov/graphics/formsfee/forms/i-140.htm.

Certain aliens who are in the United States temporarily may file Form I-765 to request an Employment Authorisation Document (EAD). The form is available with a list of addresses to apply to at website: http://uscis.gov/graphics/formsfee/forms/i-765.htm. Submit your application with two passport-style colour photos and a copy of Form I-94 Departure Record (front and back), if available. The filing fee of US$ 180 will not be refunded.

Student Visas

For student visas, contact the international student services of the university or college you are attending.

Hawai'i Pacific University (HPU) claims to be 'one of the most culturally diverse universities in the world'. Out of 8,200 students, HPU has approximately 1,600 international students who come from over 100 different countries.

Origin of students from the HPU website:

- US mainland and Canada: 29 per cent
- Hawai'i: 38 per cent
- Asia and the Pacific: 16 per cent
- Europe: 13 per cent
- Latin America, South America, Caribbean: 2 per cent
- Africa and the Middle East: 2 per cent

University of Hawai'i at Mānoa (UHM) has 20,000 students in total and 1,600 international students who come from about 93 countries. At UHM, the huge majority of students come from Asia but there are also quite a few from Europe and Canada.

For students who need help with visas (F-1, J-1 etc.), please contact:

- Hawai'i Pacific University (HPU)
  International Center
  1164 Bishop Street, Suite 1100
  Honolulu, Hawai'i 96813
  Tel: (808) 543-8088
  Email: international@hpu.edu
  Website: http://www.hpu.edu/international

- University of Hawai'i at Mānoa (UHM)
  International Student Services
  2600 Campus Road, QLCSS 206
  Honolulu, Hawai'i 96822-5076
  Tel: (808) 956-8613
  Email: issmanoa@hawaii.edu
  Website: http://www.Hawaii.edu/issmanoa/

Help for Foreign Immigrants

The Pacific Gateway Center (PGC) offers services to immigrants and refugees. The programme helps immigrants get jobs and refugees secure visas. They have volunteers teach English, review information necessary to pass the US immigration citizenship test, and help immigrants with their taxes. PGC has a programme that funds small business ventures of immigrants. In one project, they helped an immigrant with a background in farming start his own farm. PGC also hires immigrants to work at the centre helping other immigrants.

The Department of Child and Family Services also offers help to immigrants and refugees through English classes, job placement and housing. Goodwill is another organisation that helps immigrants find jobs. Many universities and community colleges offer ESL classes for regular students and non-students in the daytime and evenings.

Below is a list of organisations that either specialise in assisting foreign immigrants or have several programmes that help immigrants.

- The Pacific Gateway Center
  720 North King Street, Honolulu, HI 96817
  Tel: (808) 845-3918
  Website: http://www.pacificgateway.org/index-files/Page438.htm
  Offers general immigrant services, citizenship classes, small business loans and services for immigrants, interpreter services, ESL classes and employment services (job counselling, placement and follow-up).
- Catholic Charities Hawai'i Community and Immigrant Services

250 Vineyard Street
Honolulu, HI 96813-2495
Tel: (808) 537-6321, (808) 521-4357
Fax: (808) 523-8773
Website: http://www.catholiccharitieshawaii.org/
Offers housing counselling programmes, general immigrant services (citizenship/naturalisation), an Innovative Employment and Training for Asians and Pacific Islanders programme, pre-employment and job placement services for immigrants and a job preparation language programme.

- Child and Family Services
91-1841 Ft. Weaver Road
Ewa Beach, Hawai'i 96706
Tel: (808) 681-3500
Email: cfs@cfs-Hawaii.org
Website: http://www.childandfamilyservice.org/

FINDING A HOME

Some mortgage companies will not give you a good faith estimate without an actual property address. So you may have to start your home search alongside your search for a mortgage company. You can start by looking for a good realtor at the Honolulu Board of Realtors website (http://www.hicentral.com). It has listings of realtors as well as the complete MLS of all the houses currently on the market. Your realtor has special access to this website and can get more detailed information, such as giving you a comparison analysis of all the properties that are in the range and area you are looking and with a detailed history of what has been sold and for how much.

Finding a good realtor can be a difficult task when you are a newcomer without any contacts. A realtor should know the area you want to live in and be able to tell you about the advantages and disadvantages of the different areas on different islands. It is important to know things like local school reputations and neighbourhood reputations. Surprisingly, many realtors don't know these things or don't wish to be honest about them. If you are still at a loss for who to trust as your realtor, you are welcome to email me (BrentMassey@BrentMassey.com) with the area you are looking and I may have a few realtors to recommend.

When buying a property, there is a choice of leasehold or fee-simple. Leasehold means the land under the home is being leased on a long-term basis. Fee-simple is the same as buying property on the mainland and you own the land the home is on. In the case of town houses, you own a percentage of the land that the whole complex is located on—ours is as little as 0.36 per cent of the total land.

A home inspection may be required by your lender, but if it isn't, get one anyway. The quality of the construction isn't as good as the mainland USA, so don't make the mistake of assuming that it is. My realtor was a nice guy and paid for my home inspection himself. These inspections usually run a few hundred dollars, but an inspection may save you more than that. My inspector found faulty electrical outlets in the kitchen, which we had the seller fix. It is all a matter of negotiation and the state of the market. If it is a sellers' market, you probably don't want to nitpick every little thing that is wrong, but if it's a buyers' market, you have a lot of leverage because the deal hasn't been closed yet and you can walk away if the seller refuses to fix anything you requested.

Tax Exemptions on Homes

When selling your home in the US, there are tax exemptions. Tax exemption is on gains up to US$ 250,000 if you are single, and US$ 500,000 if married. Previously, when selling a home in the US, you had to reside in it for two years or pay a capital gains tax of up to 25 per cent. Recently, a new law allows sellers who have lived in their home for less than two years to get a partial exemption. For example, if you are married and sold your house after living in it for only one year and made a US$ 150,000 gain, you wouldn't owe any taxes. This is the reason why: you lived in your house for one year so you get half the exemption of US$ 500,000—a total of US$ 250,000. You only made US$150,000, and that is less than US$250,000, so you don't owe any taxes.

The beautiful Mākaha Valley, on the leeward coast of Oʻahu, has the Kāneʻaki *heiau*.

Go past Waiʻanae on the west coast and you will reach Mākaha Valley. According to a local realtor, Mākaha Valley is beginning to boom. It is a nice valley but a pretty far drive from anything, especially downtown Honolulu. It does has splendid views that rival the other valleys such as Mānoa. There are also no high-rise hotels (like in Waikīkī) smack in the middle of the view. The people in the valley are friendly. A 1,500 sq ft, three-bedroom house built in the 1970s goes for almost a million in Mānoa Valley (above Waikīkī). A similar house in Mākaha Valley goes for about US$ 250,000.

Mortgage

Whether you're renting or buying your home, you're going to need a credit check and to put some money as down payment. Hawaiʻi is like everywhere else in the world and real estate prices rise and fall and the rents follow suit. At this time, the rental and real estate market is tight and expensive. The housing market took a dip after 11 September, but since 2001, real estate has doubled and even tripled in price.

If you have really good credit, there are some no-down-payment loans. These loans usually consist of a first loan for 80 per cent of the mortgage at the going market interest rate and a second loan for the remaining 20 per cent at a much higher interest rate. Some loans allow you to roll all the costs of getting the loan into the loan, so you may not have to pay anything.

Some people go with a very low interest one-year adjustable loan. They are gambling that their income will go up as interest rates go up. For the military, this isn't a bad deal because they have a housing allowance that rises with the cost of living and they may only be in their home a few years before being transferred. Choosing this loan is a matter of your tolerance for risk.

There are also high risk interest-only loans that give you a low payment while the mortgage amount continues to grow. This is based on the gamble that the housing market will increase faster than your mortgage will. I would advise avoiding this type of loan, unless you don't mind losing sleep at night wondering if the housing market bubble will pop.

Qualifying for loans like these require a good credit rating from the credit agencies. The credit agencies give you a score that the mortgage companies use to determine which loans you qualify for. A score of over 700 usually qualifies you for loans with the best rates. It seems that there are a lot of people here with bad credit, so when you are bidding on a home or making an application for a rental unit, your good credit could be the advantage you need to land the deal or get the rental in a tight market.

A mortgage company doesn't charge a commission like a real estate agent but has a list of various fees required for the financing of the mortgage. It is best to request a good faith estimate from the mortgage company. This is their best estimate on the total cost of getting the loan from them. Review all the fees and compare them with other mortgage companies to make sure you are getting the best deal. There are several websites that you get advice on fees and interests rates, one of the larger ones is http://www.bankrate.com.

When there is a hot real estate market, there is a backlog of closings at the title companies so it may take longer (a couple months) to get the deal closed.

Checking Your Credit

When companies query credit rating agencies like TransUnion for your credit history, they are bringing down your credit rating score every time they do this. So be careful with how many credit checks you get before you want to qualify for that big home loan. There can be credit checks for setting up your phone, for getting a rental apartment, for a car loan, etc.

One way to get the credit card companies to stop checking your credit and sending you pre-approved credit card offers is to sign up at the Opt-Out Prescreen.com website (http://www. optoutprescreen.com). This website is by the official Consumer Credit Reporting Industry and it sends an opt-out notice to all the major credit rating agencies. This bars credit card companies, insurance and others from checking your credit file and filling your mailbox with pre-approved credit and insurance offers. But this still allows you to get a credit check if you request a company (like a mortgage broker) to conduct one.

Association Fees

Homeowners Association (HOA) fees for town houses in Hawai'i are expensive. These fees can range anywhere from US$ 200–400, or even more in downtown Honolulu. This should be taken into consideration when buying a condo or a home. If you buy a home without HOA fees, you can afford a higher loan payment. However, you do not get the services offered by the HOA, such as building maintenance, landscaping and a pool, paid utilities such as water, sewerage and refuse as well as basic home insurance. Mākaha Plantation in Mākaha Valley has a HOA fee of US$ 400, but that also includes electricity, security guards, security gates and a front office.

In many places, you have to pay for the community association fees. Waikele has a US$ 30 community association fee. This pays for landscaping, water, electricity and improvements. The association also puts together community-building events. This year we went with 600 other people from Waikele for an all-day event at Hawaiian Waters Adventure Park. The tickets and lunch are normally about US$ 50, but it was US$ 10 for adults and US$ 5 for kids. And at Christmas time, we had an evening of free ice-skating and food at the Ice Palace.

Rental

As a renter, you won't have to pay any HOA or community association fees. To rent an apartment, you will need at least one month's deposit and the first month's rent. Most rental leases are for six months to a year. It is near impossible to find a month-to-month lease. The newspapers and the Internet have rental listings. You can view rentals advertised in the *Honolulu Star Bulletin* (http://www.starbulletin.com) and the *Honolulu Advertiser* (http://www.honoluluadvertiser.com). Both websites are completely user-unfriendly and the search engine is almost worthless so it may be easier to buy the newspaper. The Honolulu Board of Realtors at http://www.hicentral.com also has a few rental listings.

Breaking a Lease

There is a law in Hawai'i that allows you to break a lease by giving 28 days notice. However, you will be held accountable for the rent until they find a new renter. Since the apartment complex wouldn't let me sign a month-to-month lease and it was near impossible to find a monthly apartment, I signed a six-month lease. After a month of searching, we found a town house to buy so we gave our 28 days notice to the apartment manager. Before we moved out, they already had someone who wanted our apartment. We ended up paying about two weeks extra rent because of the timing that the new renter moved in and the one week of cleaning required. We were charged for the cleaning but got almost all of our deposit back.

House Tint and Air Conditioning

People tint the windows on their homes to keep out harmful UV rays and keep down the high costs of cooling the house. Electricity is expensive in Hawai'i. The bill for my family runs US$ 100–120 a month and I'm quite frugal. One 'Aiea family put in a window air conditioner and after a month, the father saw the electric bill and decide that was enough of that and took out the air conditioner. Now they use one or more fans running at night in the bedrooms.

The people of Hawai'i talk a lot about tradewinds; the weatherman calls them the 'trades'. Technically, it is supposed to be a continuous wind from the north-east. However, when buying a home, this can't be relied on and it's really just a matter of opening up all the windows and doors to see if air breezes through the place. Even if there is a breeze, that isn't a guarantee that it will be year round, but it's better to buy a house with a breeze than one without, because you will be in air conditioning all the time otherwise—no matter how tinted the windows on the house are.

There is no central air system in Hawaiian homes. So that means there are no air ducts running through the walls or a heating system to attach a whole house air conditioner to. It costs about US$ 1,500 for a separated unit—the cooling fan is on a block outside and a line runs to the cooler fan mounted on the upper part of the wall inside the house. This unit only cools the room that it is in and is a luxury at that price. The majority of people settle for the bulky one-piece air conditioner installed in the window. This costs a few hundred dollars including installation, or if you're a little handy, you can save yourself a hundred bucks and install it yourself.

If you want to save money, then think like a local and adjust your way of life. Long-timers here adjust to the heat and rely on fans and the tradewinds instead of air conditioners. One trick we use is to put the fan in the window or use a standing fan in front of the screen door. In the evening, this will bring the cool air into the house even if there are no tradewinds. Another popular option is to put blinds on the *lānai* (Hawaiian for porch or veranda). These roller window shades can even be purchased with zippers on the sides so the whole *lānai* is sealed off and protected from mosquitoes and other insects but still lets in light and tradewinds.

Hawai'i averages some of the highest daily hours of sunlight in the US, so to save money, install solar panels for electricity and hot water. If you can't afford solar, one other option is a heat pump for your water heater which costs a little over US$ 1,000. This attachment uses the heat from the outside air to warm the water going into the water heater. This will cut down on your utility bill, especially if it's an electric water heater because they are twice as expensive as gas.

TELECOMMUNICATIONS

In your new home, just plug in a phone into the phone-jack (the one that doesn't have phone service yet) and the recording will tell you the number to dial to be connected to Hawaiian Telecom customer service (http://www.HawaiianTel.com). They will take your order to set up the phone line under your name and if it's not the weekend, they should be able to get it set up the same day. There will be a US$ 45 set-up fee. The monthly service charge is US$ 26. They will do a check to see if you have any outstanding phone bills before setting up.

You will also have to decide on a long distance carrier. You can use Hawaiian Telecom for your long distance service or any other provider that has the best discount calling plans. The long distance provider AT&T is expensive but we use it because it has a country plan. You can choose a country and get unlimited calling to that country for US$ 50 a month.

Our neighbours found that it was better for them to get a family plan with free cellphones and free calls between the family's cellphones than it was to pay the US$ 45 set-up fee, but they had to pay a US$ 39 monthly fee and for regular non-family calls during business hours.

If you do get a mobile phone, please be respectful of others and don't shout into your phone while other people are standing around. Turn off your phone or make it silent at the library, class, concerts or other public places and events. And don't drive and talk on the phone—this causes more traffic accidents and is just plain rude as you aren't paying attention to your speed or the other drivers around you.

Hawaiian Telecom and others offer DSL over your phone line for Internet and email services. The cost is US$ 30 a month. If you want higher speed, you can get a cable modem for around US$ 50 a month from the local cable company.

They will install the cable jacks in the room of your choice for free and usually waive the installation fee or give you a discount over the first few months.

INTERNET ACCESS

Hawai'i public libraries have computers with Internet access. If you have a library card, you can use them for up to one hour a day. There is no charge for this service, but you can only use the computer once a day. There are also computers with Internet access available in the University of Hawai'i system of libraries. For example, UH Mānoa Hamilton library and Leeward Community College library both have many computers with Internet access and no login account is required. If the computers are all busy on the first floor, try the second floor of both these libraries. There are computers tucked away in various locations in these libraries. Places like Kinko's also have computers you pay by the minute to use (20–40 cents a minute and 50 cents for laser printouts).

Borders bookstores, Kinko's, The UPS Stores, UH library and several Waikīkī hotels have Wi-Fi Hotspots. This is wireless access for your computer through subscription wireless services like AT&T, etc. If you subscribe to a wireless service, you can freely access the Internet at any store or location with a Wi-Fi Hotspot.

BANKING

To open a savings or current account at a bank in Hawai'i, you will need a photo ID and a minimum deposit of US$ 100 (varies from bank to bank). Most banks offer online account access. After you set up a user name and password, you can make transfers and view statements over the Internet.

One way to save money on fees and get more favourable interest rates is to bank at a credit union. There are many federal credit unions (FCU): University of Hawai'i, Hawai'i Schools, Hawai'i State Federal, Honolulu Federal Employees, Hawaiian Telephone, etc. The downside of credit unions is that they don't have many ATMs. The Bank of Hawai'i has ATMs everywhere, but there is a service charge to use them if you don't have an account with Bankoh. However, many credit unions have shared banking agreements with the majority of other credit unions so you can use their ATMs and bank tellers without a service charge.

Some banks in Hawai'i seem to be a little more cautious. I go by my middle name but they required that my first name be on the bank account. So now whenever I try to deposit cheques that have my middle name on them, some branches will refuse the deposit or they have to get managerial approval.

Both credit unions and commercial banks offer free notary services. Some require that you make an appointment beforehand, but this can save you a fee of US$ 12 or more when you need to get a legal document notarised.

TAXES

The General Excise Tax (GET) is a 4.166 per cent tax on all business purchases. This tax seems like a good deal when compared to other states, but the general excise tax is different than a sales tax because it isn't just at the restaurant or retail store. Businesses have to pay it too, so this compounds what we end up paying at the retail store, and thus results in much higher prices. My realtor asked for his 3 per cent commission plus the GET when we made a contract on our town home. That way, the seller paid the taxes on his commission. See http://www.hawaii.gov/tax/tax.html for further information on taxes.

Property taxes are actually quite reasonable, especially considering the US$ 40,000 exemption given yearly. This exemption is for property that is occupied by the owner. So if your personal home is determined by the state assessors office to be worth US$ 300,000 that year, you only have to pay taxes on US$ 260,000. From age 55 up to 70, the exemption stair-steps up to US$ 120,000 a year. This is one advantage of retiring in Hawai'i.

In contrast to some states with a fixed rate of income tax (in 2004, Colorado was fixed at 4.63 per cent), Hawai'i has a tax rate that increases gradually with income. For example in 2004, the tax on an income of US$ 100,000 after deductions was US$ 7,000 for a married couple filing jointly, or US$ 7,600 if single or filing separately. In the lower tax bracket, an income of US$ 25,000 after deductions was US$ 1,200 if married and filing jointly or US$ 1,500 if single or filing separately.

Paying Your Taxes

Federal income taxes are also stair-stepped according to income bracket. These are the tax rates for 2006 based on income after deductions and married filing jointly:

- US$0–15,100   10 per cent
- US$ 15,100–61,300   15 per cent
- US$ 61,300–123,700   25 per cent
- US$ 123,700–188,450   28 per cent
- US$ 188,450–336,550   33 per cent
- US$ 336,550 and up   35 per cent

Taxes in the US are lower than some European countries, but you get what you pay for, as can be seen in the health insurance explanation below.

HEALTH INSURANCE

In the 1970s, the AJAs came to power with the democratic party and increased social programmes. One product of this decade was the passing of a mandate in 1974 that required all employers to provide individual insurance policy for those working more than 20 hours. With so many Americans without health insurance, Hawai'i is actually one of the states with the highest percentage of covered individuals.

In a regular full-time position, an employer will help you pay part or all of the insurance premium for your family. For example, through the universities group policy, my monthly insurance cost for my family of four was US$ 250. Whereas, through my wife's part-time job, it was US$ 600 for the monthly cost for a family of four (also a company group policy). Because she was part-time, they only paid the cost to insure her, therefore the cost was much higher.

Hawai'i Medical Service Association (HMSA), a member of the Blue Cross and Blue Shield Society (http://www.hmsa.com), insures the largest number of people in Hawai'i, and Kaiser Permanente (http://www.kp.org) is the second largest. If you don't have insurance through your employer, HMSA has

a catastrophic plan for about US$ 100 a month. You have to pass a health and medical history exam. These exams can be hard to pass. I had applied to Blue Cross on the mainland and just because I didn't record every single medical insurance claim I had ever made, they rejected my application.

The HMSA Catastrophic Plan only covers something major and has a huge deductible and doesn't include vision, dental or drugs. Families that would normally be rejected for an individual policy directly from HMSA—because they are high risk or for other reasons—can still get HMSA insurance through their employer's group policy health insurance. Group plans usually have vision, dental and drug coverage, but sometimes for an additional fee.

The American health insurance system shocks many foreign immigrants. People from countries like Canada or Japan feel the system is barbaric, stone-aged and uncivilised, and no better than a third-world country. You may not be able to afford insurance or the insurance companies refuse to insure you. If you don't have insurance and have a catastrophic accident, you can go bankrupt very easily with the medical bills. According to Congressman McDermott, this is the number one cause of bankruptcy in America today.

The Cost of Medical Services

My daughter dropped a weight on her toe and knocked off a toenail. We phoned the paediatrician and they told us to take her to the emergency room (ER) at the hospital to check to see if it was broken. We waited around in the ER for a few hours while they took X-rays. It wasn't broken and she didn't need any stitches so they just cleaned it and bandaged it. This all cost US$ 1,000, so you can imagine what something catastrophic would cost.

Fortunately, Physicians for a National Healthcare Plan (http://www.pnhp.org) are working on changing it. PNHP is a growing group of doctors that are trying to convert the US to government-funded health insurance. However, one local doctor said that a national health care plan would put an end to cutting-edge medicine. People from other countries come to the US for its advanced medical procedures. The Japanese

Mānoa Falls, Moanalua Gardens and other areas have signs around the streams warning against the leptospirosis bacteria in the water and mud. Leptospirosis is not related to the disease leprosy, but is a bacteria transmitted from infected animals to humans through the water. Hawai'i Department of Health reports that this is a problem throughout Hawai'i. You can get infected through open cuts and may get sick. Don't put your head under the water and don't go hiking barefoot in the mud. Swim at your own risk!

come for heart transplants because their health care system doesn't allow it. He thinks that without the profit motive and competition (as well as prestige) in medicine, no one and no university would try to research new cures or invent new medical technologies. However, many believe the benefits of national health care far outweigh these possible yet unproven disadvantages.

DEPARTMENT OF HUMAN SERVICES

The DHS offer free or low cost health insurance. One programme called Med-QUEST has free health insurance for families that meet income and asset guidelines (refer to http://www.med-quest.us for more information). Children qualify for free health insurance if the overall family income is less than 200 per cent of the Federal Poverty Level. For a family of four, this is an income limit of US$ 3,710 a month (this increases every year). For the parents to get insurance, an income below US$ 900 would be required. There are also other programmes from DHS if you are denied the Med-QUEST programme because of too much income or assets. Quest-Spenddown and Quest-Net programmes give partial assistance to pay for health insurance. The asset limits go as high as US$ 8,000 for a family of four.

The DHS also has the national Women Infants and Children (WIC) assistance programme known as the Special Supplemental Nutrition Program for Women, Infants and Children that provides food for children under the age of five and pregnant or lactating or post-partum women. This programme has income limits of about US$ 3,432 a month for a family of four. They provide vouchers worth about US$ 80 a month per child, to pay for milk, juice, cereal, etc. A lot of military families qualify for the WIC programmes because housing assistance and other allowances are not counted as income.

Both of these programmes are available to all newcomers immediately, and for foreign immigrants that are residing in the USA legally.

EDUCATION
Childcare
In Hawai'i, it is hard to get your toddler into childcare. One of the chain childcare providers, Kama'āina Kids, quotes up to a year waiting list for some locations. Others only take three-year-olds and above.

Some providers have scholarships for the financial needy. There are also government assistance programmes to help lower income families pay for childcare and preschool. The government-funded PACT Head Start programme helps three- to five-year-olds attend preschool. If your income is low enough, preschool is free. Early Head Start is another programme for children from birth to three years old that is funded by PACT.

The Department of Human Services has the Preschool Open Doors programme that has higher maximum income requirements. Applications for the Open Doors programme must be received in March and April. The

Department also has a Child Care Connection programme for childcare subsidy assistance. Some programmes require both parents to be working to qualify for financial support. Many programmes take a couple months to process an application—so plan ahead.

The University of Hawai'i system also has childcare centres at Honolulu Community College and Leeward Community College. These programmes are for students, faculty and staff, but if they have room, they will accommodate others. They follow the fall and spring semesters class schedule. Therefore, on summer and winter vacations, as well as many holidays, the childcare centres are closed. These centres cost a little less than commercial programmes like Kama'āina Kids, but have a smaller range of hours.

Kindergarten

Moving up to kindergarten can be a challenge in Hawai'i. The first place to start is the Department of Education website (http://www.doe.k12.hi.us/). At this website, you can select the location you are interested in and see a list of schools. Each school has a School Status and Improvement Report available in PDF form. The reports include math and reading test scores for the school. These scores are compared on a chart with the state average scores. Keep in mind that state average scores are very poor.

Failing Schools

A failing school is one that fails to make yearly progress for three consecutive years according to the Department of Education. This can be based on test scores, teacher-student ratio, teacher credentials and licences, the number of students suspended and adequacy of the school facility space in administration, library, cafeteria and classrooms. If enough kids ditched school, that school could fail each year. The SSIR reports are available at:
http://arch.k12.hi.us/school/ssir/default.html

One person who works for the special education department at Hawai'i Department of Education claims that some schools try to push out or to encourage the special education kids and lower scoring students to change schools before the end of the year when statewide tests are taken. By doing this, the schools test results are higher and the school

Hawai'i is the only state with a single, unified school system—all the taxes go to all the schools, not just one area. Also, just like there is Americana, there is also Hawaiiana, which is taught as a regular class in the schools. Children are taught about Polynesian and Hawaiian culture and history.

doesn't fall into the Adequate Yearly Progress (AYP) failing school category.

Private Schools

Some people say that the better students end up going to private schools. Private schools do not have to follow the state curriculum, so they may have a better curriculum. One preschool administrator said that in the high-scoring public schools, the focus is so much on passing the exams that other programmes like art and social studies suffer. So going to a high-scoring public school may not provide a well-rounded education. Parents look at ways to supplement this or go to a private school, which is always an alternative to the public school system if you can afford to make payments of US$ 500–1,000 a month (based on 12 months). In the US, Hawai'i has the highest percentage of students attending private schools.

The largest private school system in Hawai'i is the Kamehameha Schools. Princess Bernice Pauahi Bishop, a descendant of Kamehameha I, founded the Kamehameha Schools. Her wish was that the Kamehameha schools benefit Native Hawaiian children. The school is for preschool and K-12 students of Hawaiian ancestry. In the past, this policy has been challenged as discriminatory. I called the school office and they said that my child could attend if there were any openings after the Hawaiian children were placed. One person of Hawaiian ancestry complained that the school benefits rich Hawaiians who pay the same low monthly fees as a poor family would.

Private schools do not have to be eliminated as an option just because they are expensive. Many schools have need- and

merit-based scholarships. For more information on private schools, visit the Hawai'i Association of Independent Schools (HAIS) at http://www.hais.org/.

A + For Kids

There is an after-school programme called A + (plus) for children from kindergarten through sixth grade (see website: http://doe.k12.hi.us/programs/aplus.htm). This programme takes care of children after school until their parents can pick them up —as late as 5:30 pm. The programme is subsidised by the government at only US$ 59 a month. There are no income requirements for this programme so nearly everyone is eligible. There are also free and discounted breakfasts and lunches for those who meet income requirements.

Geographic Exception

After reviewing the report available on the Department of Education website, you may decide that you do not want your child attending their home school because it's a failing or poor school, or for other issues such as racial mix, number of suspensions, or you just see a school you like better. Then the option for you is to request a Geographical Exception. This application form is available at any public school. If your child is entering kindergarten, your chances of getting a GE are a little better because other grades require a student to have left and opened a spot, which is pretty rare in the good public schools.

Selection of students for the GE is based first on a programme by the US Department of Education called No Child Left Behind. This program gives first priority for a GE to children of failing schools and low-income families. So even if you aren't low income, if your home school is a failing AYP, you get higher priority. The next priority for selection of GE candidates is children of teachers of the school. After that, selection is based on children who already have siblings that attend the school. The remaining spots go to anyone, based on a lottery system.

Choosing the Right School

High test scores don't necessarily mean that it is a better school or a good fit for your child. We got my daughter into one of the top public schools using a GE. We were lucky because our home school was failing so that put us at the top of the list. My daughter spent a month and a half at the school and never liked going to school. The teacher was too strict and yelled at the kids. My daughter was also having a hard time making friends. We thought she would fit in because she is half Japanese and this school was in a Japanese enclave with all AJA teachers and more than half the students were AJAs. She didn't like going to kindergarten and didn't have any friends after a month and a half so we transferred her back to our home district school.

At the home school, more than half the students were Filipino because we lived in the Filipino enclave. The school had an interesting programme of mixed-age education where they looped two grades together. Parents had a choice of regular classes or looped ones. We put our daughter in a kindergarten class that was looped with a first grade class. They gave us some research on looping that explained that these classes didn't get lower test scores than non-looped classes, but the children enjoyed school more and had better concepts of self. There seemed to be more of a sense of community and the children socialised better and helped each other out.

Some schools have open houses for GE applicants. The parents and children meet the principal and teachers and get a tour of the classrooms. If you are lucky, within the next month you will receive a phone call or letter telling you whether your child got in or not. Usually you will get your notification around April, but it can take longer at popular schools.

Middle School and Beyond

Some feel the junior high and high schools are so bad (poor education, gang or drug problems, etc.) that after finishing a public elementary, they will send their kids to a private junior high and high school. Some even move back to the mainland so there kids can get a better education after elementary. However, one local woman who grew up here and attended public schools said you just have to have faith in the public school system. She has two Bachelor degrees from Colorado State University.

As for the University of Hawai'i, UH professor Richard Rapson wrote in his book *Fairly Lucky You Live in Hawai'i*, 'The University of Hawai'i is definitely mediocre. It excels in special areas such as studies related to Asia and the Pacific, and in scientific study related to the seas, the stars, or to tropical agriculture... Yet it does not have the feel of a university; it generates little excitement; many of its administrators and Regents know little about education and seem to care less; the faculty forms no intellectual community; the University has become increasingly ingrown and provincial.'

The former University of Hawai'i president Evans Dobelle, proclaimed the dream of making UH the 'Berkeley of the Pacific', but he was ousted for political reasons and the dream was never realised. UH students take several years longer to graduate than mainland students. For this reason, many parents will send their kids to mainland universities so that they finish in four years. However, the dream of many of these students is that they can find a job in Hawai'i after they graduate because they want to live in Hawai'i.

The prominent Aloha Tower beckons visitors to Honolulu, and in its vicinity is a popular marketplace consisting of shops and restaurants.

Searching the tidepools for fish, crabs, eels and other creatures is a fun activity for children and adults alike. A net and a bucket comes in handy.

During the Aloha Festival, parades take to the streets, celebrating the unique culture and traditions of Hawai'i.

The Ho'omaluhia Botanical Gardens in Kaneohe boasts of stunning scenery and a well-stocked catch and release fishing pond, where no fishing license is required.

A well-kept secret on the North Shore past the Dillingham Airstrip is YMCA Camp Erdman. Among other things, the camp has cabins on a beautiful stretch of secluded beach and this new ropes course.

The Korean Studies Building at the University of Hawai'i. The university is a leader in Asian and Pacific studies.

LIBRARY

If you are a Hawai'i resident, you can get a library card for free. All the state libraries are interconnected so you can borrow a book at one and return it at another. The Hawai'i state library system has 51 locations throughout the state and more than three million books. The University of Hawai'i library system is separate from the public library system and encompasses all the state universities and community colleges. It has four million books with the main branch at UH Mānoa holding three million of them.

You can request for books from other Hawai'i state public libraries online or through your local public library. If you are affiliated with the university, you can request interlibrary loans (borrowing books from other UH libraries) from any UH system library. They have UH libraries on Maui, Kaua'i, Hawai'i and O'ahu.

The UH library system has tons of books the public library system doesn't have—and vice versa. For example, if you search the public library system website (http://www. librarieshawaii.org) you will find several *CultureShock!* books but the UH library system (http://www.uhmanoa.lib.hawaii.edu) has many more.

The public library system has a collection of foreign language books at each branch. There are books and magazines in Japanese, Korean, Filipino, Chinese, etc. However, it is difficult to search for foreign language books using the website so it is best to visit the library. Each library has a different collection so it is worth checking out a few different libraries. The Hawai'i state public library (the main branch) has the largest collection.

The public libraries website (http://www.librarieshawaii.org) also has some online resources. One handy resource is the Hawai'i newspaper index. This index is maintained by the major newspapers and is a searchable database. Articles are available online through the newspapers individual websites:

- *Honolulu Star Bulletin*
  Website: http://www.starbulletin.com
- *The Honolulu Advertiser*
  Website: http://www.honoluluadvertiser.com

The Honolulu Advertiser charges a fee of US$ 3 for any articles older than two months. The *Honolulu Star Bulletin* has back issues available online for free. Articles are also available for free on microfilm through the main Hawai'i State Public Library on King Street in downtown Honolulu or through the University of Hawai'i at Mānoa in the Hamilton library.

You can get access to the UH library system if you are a student or employee, or if you know someone who is. They can designate you as a proxy and let you use their library privilege.

SHOPPING

If you don't have friends with fruit trees who can give you a free share of the crop, probably the best deal is the farmers who set up tables on the road and other places. For example, off Waipahu road near H-1 in Waipahu, local farmers set up a stand one or twice a week for selling fruits and vegetables. Also, local farmers come to the Leeward Community College once a week with a table of produce to sell.

The next best deal is the scheduled open markets and farmers' markets in parking lots. Every Sunday from 8:00 am to noon, a farmers' market is set up in the Mililani High school parking lot. Waikele has one in the parking lot at Waikele Community Park. Kapiʻolani Community College has one from 7:30 am–11:00 am every Saturday. You can find deals on locally grown fruits, vegetables and other products that are better priced than the supermarkets—like a two pound avocado for a buck.

Then there are the swap meets/flea markets selling anything and everything. The mother of all swap meets is at the Aloha Stadium. You have to pay a few bucks just to get in. You can find crafts, clothing and second-hand items such as electronics. It is more for entertainment sake, as you do not need most of the stuff you find there, like the pink gecko keychain my daughter bought. There is also another large weekly swap meet held in the parking lot of the old drive-in movie theatre at Pearlridge mall. Both swap meets

A market in Chinatown provides a variety of vegetables and food stuff at affordable prices.

are held on Wednesdays and on the weekends. Whether it is a street stand, farmers' or flea market, they are open to bargaining with you.

You cannot bargain with the clerks at the malls and outlets but if you go during their regular sales, you may find a bargain. Tourists take the trolley all the way from Honolulu to visit the Waikele Outlet Stores, one of the most profitable outlets in the US.

The more well-known several shopping malls include:

- Ala Moana Center
  1450 Ala Moana Boulevard
  Honolulu, HI 96814
  Tel: (808) 955-9517
  Website: http://www.alamoanacenter.com
- Aloha Tower Marketplace
  1 Aloha Tower Drive
  Honolulu, HI 96814
  Tel: (808) 528-5700
  Website: http://www.alohatower.com
- Kāhala Mall
  4211 Waialae Avenue
  Honolulu, HI 96816
  Tel: (808) 732-7736
  Website: http://www.kahalamallcenter.com
- Hawai'i Kai Towne Center
  6700 Kalanianaole Highway at Keahole Street
  Honolulu, HI 96825
  Tel: (808) 396-0766
  Website: http://www.hawaiikaitownecenter.com
- Pearlridge Center
  231 Pearlridge Center
  Aiea, HI 96701
  Tel: (808) 488-0981
  Website: http://www.pearlridgeonline.com
- Victoria Ward Centers
  1210 Akuahi Street, Ste.115
  Honolulu, HI 96814
  Tel: (808) 593-2376
  Website: http://www.wardcentre.com

- Windward Mall
  Windward Mall, 46-056 Kamehameha Highway
  Kaneohe, HI 96744
  Tel: (808) 235-1143
  Website: http://www.windwardmallhawaii.com

The Hawai'i phone directory (http://www.theparadisepages. com) also has maps of all the malls and a list of stores.

These are typical American malls with branded clothing, books, music, pets, jewellery, food, etc. The food court at the ground floor of Ala Moana Center is fun and has a good variety of food. Pearlridge has a monorail and a movie theatre. Ward Centers has the Old Spaghetti Factory and the restaurant Kakaako Kitchen. Just a few blocks up Ala Moana Boulevard is the all-you-can-eat restaurant Todai. Lastly, there is shopping all over Waikīkī (such as the Royal Hawaiian Shopping Center) and Chinatown is a must-visit for food shopping and restaurants.

WHAT TO BRING FROM HOME

- Shipping: Unless a company or the military is paying to ship your car and furniture, you may want to consider selling it off because it is very expensive to ship here. Because housing is more expensive here, you will probably have to downsize your house to live here. You will have to buy less furniture than you had previously.
- Clothes: Chances are you won't need any of your warm clothes. There are a few areas that will get chilly at night in the winter months, so you will need pyjamas and blankets, but in other places, you may need only a T-shirt. Find out if your favourite chain store or shop is here and if not, buy all you need before coming (i.e. Target, organic food market, etc.)
- Memories: Of course, always bring your items that have special meaning, especially photo albums and other sentimental mementos.
- Books: You do not need to bring books unless they are mementos. They are heavy and expensive to ship. There are plenty of bookstores and libraries here. If you want to purchase books online, the US post office has a special

book rate. I bought a single used book on Amazon and it cost US$ 3.50 to ship to Hawaiʻi using the USPS Media mail rate. However, I bought something small from eBay and the minimum shipping using UPS (not USPS) was US$ 12 because it had to go by air.

- Computer: Don't forget to back up anything important on the hard drive of your computer before moving. If you ship your computer, make data backups just in case your computer gets lost, stolen or damaged. Backups can be done in various ways. One way is to copy critical data onto digital media like CDR's, and then carry the CDR's with you on the airplane. If you have an Apple computer, they have a special service where you can back up everything to their secured servers. If you have both laptop and desktop computers, copy everything to both computers and ship the desktop and carry the laptop with you on the plane. If you have less than a gigabyte of

Documents to Bring

- Bring your shipping paperwork to contact the shipping company when you arrive. They will give you a list of what was shipped—make sure you have that available in case anything goes wrong.
- Birth certificates, passports, driver's licences and social security cards. You are not required to get a Hawaiʻi driver's licence if you already have one from another state. However, you are required to get Hawaiʻi licence plates and safety sticker on your car.
- If moving from another state, you will need tax forms for that state and all W-2's from employers in that state. You will have to file a partial year tax return for both states.
- Car insurance policy—don't cancel it if you plan to buy or bring a car here; just have it transferred to a local insurance office within 30 days.
- Car registration if shipping your car.

critical files and data, you can purchase a USB zip drive; it's finger-sized and can be put in your pocket or carry-on bag on the aeroplane. Many people refuse to put their computers and zip drives through the X-ray machines at the airport. They say it doesn't hurt computers, but why take a chance? Have them manually examine your computer equipment.

- Aeroplane: When moving here, we took six huge boxes as baggage on the plane at no extra cost. If you have children, strollers are allowed all the way to the entrance of the plane. The crew will put the stroller in the baggage area under the aeroplane and when you get off the plane, it is there waiting for you at the door. There is no extra charge for this and it is not counted as baggage.
- Lastly, try to get a phone book with maps before coming or buy a detailed map with city names.

- If you are going to use a rental car, make sure you have a credit card that has rental insurance, otherwise you will have to pay extra for insurance—sometimes around US$ 15 a day. Bring the driver's licence and credit card in the name of the driver who will be the designated driver. They also charge for your spouse as an additional driver.
- Health insurance cards and names and contact information for all the doctors you have used.
- Children's vaccination records—you will need to prove all shots have been taken before your child will be allowed in school.
- Bank account numbers—savings, current, etc. Some banks require a signed notarised note before they will close an account. This is more difficult to do from Hawai'i, so try to close these accounts before leaving.

TRANSPORTATION
The Bus

Call TheBus at tel: (808) 848-5555 and get information on bus schedules, numbers and stops. Information is also available through the website at: http://www.thebus.org. The bus fare is US$ 2 for adults and US$ 1 for youths and senior citizens with reduced fare card or valid Medicare Card. Each passenger may receive one free transfer upon boarding when paying a cash fare. This transfer is valid for two hours and expires at the time stated. It can be used only once and must be presented upon boarding the bus. TheBus might be one of the great ways to get to know the island. It is easier to see various things along the way that you wouldn't notice if you drove your car. This cheap US$ 2 tour of the island is an important learning experience to better understand your new home.

The people that get on and off the bus also give you a flavour of the people of Hawai'i and the different areas they come from. The ads on the bus are for subsidised health care and planned parenthood but this doesn't accurately portray the ridership. The bus has a variety of people, but most seem to be from the clean-cut working class compared to riding the bus in California, where some of the passengers can look a little bit scary.

Autos

With the cost of petrol going up, many are looking to hybrid cars instead of petrol guzzling SUVs. A hybrid car can get up to 50 miles a gallon whereas an SUV gets 18. Hybrid cars use a variety of technology, like rechargeable batteries to supplement and sometimes replace the power of the gas engine. In Hawai'i, petrol costs are higher than on the mainland. Since Hawai'i has more sunshine than the mainland, maybe one day, cars charged with solar PV-photovoltaic panels will be the solution for Hawai'i.

Auto insurance rates are high in Hawai'i and having a large or expensive car makes it even more costly. Switching to discount insurance companies like Geico can help defray the cost, but it will also lower the level of service—additional

Transport of the past: the Oʻahu Historical Railway is great fun for the kids and an interesting historical tour for adults. Kids enjoy blowing the train's whistle after the ride is over. The railway was used to carry plantation crops and later as military equipment transport. When Pearl Harbour was attacked, the railway was temporarily closed and people who commuted on the railway couldn't get to work. There is a new controversial light rail system being built to ease the traffic problems going into town (Honolulu).

services normally included, like roadside towing, are an additional cost. If you are coming from the mainland, you can keep your existing insurance for about a month while you transfer over to a local policy. Call for rates before moving so you know which company you will be using, or if it's a local branch of the same company. Rates will vary depending on the island so get a quote from a branch on the island you will be staying.

We found that the cost of shipping a car from Colorado would be anywhere from US$ 1,500–2,000. Even if we drove it to California, it would still be US$ 1,000 or more, so we sold our car and bought a fairly new one here. A great way to compare prices is by going online. Both the Kelly Blue Book (http://www.kbb.com) and the NADA guide (http://www. nadaguides.com) can be used for comparisons. I compared the blue book value of my Toyota Camry in Colorado and Hawaiʻi and found that it wouldn't justify the shipping costs, not to mention the headaches. I also checked actual cars for sale under http://www.cars.com and found the market rate to be what the blue book stated.

I rented a car from Thrifty at the airport for a couple weeks until we found the car we liked. We ended up buying a car from one of the used car dealers next to the airport. The safety/emissions sticker had been stolen off the car so the dealer replaced it before we bought it. The dealer said these stickers are frequently stolen and the way to protect the sticker is to cut lines across it so that it can't be pulled off in one piece. Lastly, they don't send out anything in the mail telling you it's expired so check it yourself to make sure you have an up-to-date safety sticker.

Getting Towed

It's a hard lesson to learn. We had parked our car in a guest parking spot while one of our guests parked in our stall. We forgot to move our car back to our spot. The Homeowners Association (HOA) rule was to tow any car in guest parking after 2:00 am. They wasted no time and towed my car at 4:00 am. The towing company charged me US$ 200 to get my car back. It was robbery, but according to Hawai'i law, they can charge this much. It cost US$ 80 for the after hours tow and US$ 100 for the miles—to tow the car out to the end of the remote peninsula called Sand Island. There was also a minimum day charge of US$ 20 for storage, even though they only had the car for six hours! Parking is tight in Hawai'i so getting towed isn't uncommon. Be careful.

Driver's Licence

You are not required to get a Hawai'i driver's licence if you already have one from another state. However, I got one so that I could get the *kama'āina* (resident) discounts. Along with a completed application, you will need two of the following forms of identification: old driver's licence, social security card, Green Card, passport or birth certificate. The fees for Oahu are: US$ 2 for the written test, US$ 8 for a road test and US$ 18 for the card. Requirements differ across the islands as there isn't a statewide Department of Driver Licensing. See website: http://www.state.hi.us/dot/publicaffairs/driverlicense.htm for information on individual island requirements.

A driver's licence requires a written test and road test. If you have a licence from another state, you can exchange your licence for a Hawai'i one by taking the written test. They keep the driver's licence card from your old state. The new licence expires after six years on your birthday. The written test consists of 30 questions and you must get 24 questions correct. The test is available in many different foreign languages. If you are Japanese, there are 160 practice questions written in Japanese in the *Yellow Pages Japan* directory (http://www.ypj.com). My wife was able to pass 28 questions on the first try after studying the practice questions.

For further information and testing locations on all the islands, check:

http://www.state.hi.us/dot/publicaffairs/driverlicense.htm

Traffic

O'ahu has terrible traffic jams that don't always happen at regular times (like the rush hour). The traffic can be unpredictable and frequently backed up from accidents. There are several proposals on how to fix the traffic jams. In addition to a light rail solution coming in several years, Mayor Hannemann has the idea of reversing the traffic flow by creating more job opportunities in places like Kapolei on the opposite side of Pearl Harbour from Honolulu. One local politician is suggesting a tunnel running underneath and connecting the two sides of the mouth of Pearl Harbour. It would be paid for with a US$ 2 toll fee, which seems reasonable when you consider the rising cost of petrol. It probably takes US$ 2 in petrol to drive all the way around Pearl Harbour.

Car Tint

The sun has to be respected here. People here tint their windows on their cars more than even southern Californians do and for good reason. Not only does it protect your skin, it also keeps the car cooler when sitting in the sun. The law allows only a certain level of tinting and if you tint darker than allowed, you can be pulled over and fined. I called an auto tinting shop and they said for my Toyota, the limit was a darkness level of 35. They won't go darker than that because they can get fined for more than the car owner does.

If you want those pitch black windows you see on all the cars on the highway here, you will have to do it yourself or find someone willing to do it under the table. My neighbour, in typical island fashion, had his cousin do the tinting job on his Honda so he could make the tint dark black. He put the illegal tint on the side windows so that if a cop is behind him on the road, he only sees his legal level tint on the back window. Also, if you have illegal tint, you can't pass the safety check unless you know someone who will fudge it for you like my neighbour's cousin.

The auto tinting company charged US$ 140–200 for my car and another US$ 30 for a four-inch, anti-glare strip across the top of the front window. This is the only tinting allowed on the front windscreen by law. There are no regulations for SUVs and trucks so you can make the window tint (with the exception of the front window) as dark as you want, and lots of people make it pitch black. Prices start at US$ 150 and can go all the way up to US$ 400 for a clear ceramic film. Ceramic keeps out the heat like the tiles on the space shuttle. It is also claimed to cut down on UV exposure.

WHAT IS CULTURE SHOCK?

Hawai'i is part of the US, but it can feel like a foreign country and adjusting to it will be just like dealing with the culture shock of living in a foreign country. Culture shock happens when you enter into a new culture. This can happen on a small scale, like when you start a new job with the new corporate culture, or on a larger scale, like moving to a foreign country.

When you start a new job, you have to understand your new department's way of doing things, their communication style and office politics. Lots of water has gone under the bridge before you arrived. Your new ideas may be something they have heard before, perhaps even ideas that have caused conflicts in the past. You can step on a political landmine at your new job without knowing it.

Moving to Hawai'i, your stress level may be high. You have the stress of a new job, new city, new schools for the kids, making new friends, etc. The first level of shock is trying to get physically oriented. Finding a good doctor for the kids, where the good shopping is, trying to get word of mouth referrals for a good dentist, which neighbourhoods are safe, what are the good schools, what government services are available, where to get your car licence and plates, where to file your property tax exemption, etc.

The next level of culture shock is dealing with etiquette and customs—what is acceptable behaviour. This can be as small as understanding the rules of driving on the road: if you cut someone off or they let you in front of them, you should wave.

Beyond the physical orientation and learning the etiquette and customs, there is a hidden stress—one that comes from the general confusion of not knowing why people are acting strangely and why you seem to be too. You do not understand their different behaviour and complex social cues—why they act the way they do and how you are supposed to act and react.

Collisions

A thirty-something Caucasian UH grad student from the mainland lived in the UK and Germany before, but Hawai'i was the worst culture shock he had ever experienced. He adjusted to the intense culture shock by reading everything he could get his hands on about the culture. One local Chinese has had many friends come from the US and commented that their culture shock has been very intense. On the other hand, an Asian-Indian grad student said he didn't feel any culture shock here, but he also didn't get outside his little academia world. He thought Hawai'i was similar to Asia, both in the social and academic system.

Culture shock happens from cultural collisions, one person is acting in a manner appropriate to their culture and the other doing the same. They have an interaction and all of a sudden, it is like two people speaking different languages. The newcomer doesn't understand the local's behaviour. The local is either confused or offended because the newcomer doesn't realise they are acting inappropriately.

Spend more time in Hawai'i and these collisions start to add up. Newcomers can't understand what is going on, why they keep receiving negative reactions. They keep repeating the same mistake and don't understand the cause. They begin to withdraw and even get depressed. Maybe they can figure out what the problem is, but they don't understand what's below the surface: the values and beliefs of the locals.

If you are from the mainland, you say, "But I thought we are in America?" Yes, but the people of Hawai'i have amazingly managed to hold onto their heritage values and beliefs. For example, many fourth generation Asian-Americans in Hawai'i still practise Zen and Buddhism and there are many *hongwanji* (Buddhist temples) all over the island. Additionally, Hawai'i, like many Polynesian and Asians societies, value collectivism or being group-centred.

Crossing Culture

In the library, grocery store, and especially at work, we are faced with cross-cultural interaction. Some people can be warm, friendly and filled with the legendary *aloha* spirit, yet others are cold, insensitive and prejudiced against you. Until you learn the local ways, it can seem like an unpredictable society. We observe a behaviour and interpret it as being rude by our cultures standards, but as we learn more, we find out that it was actually our lack of understanding.

Learn the customs and etiquette and the do's and don'ts of the culture. Customs are unspoken and unwritten laws of the society. Also, learn the traditions and history, such as the first birthday of a child being a very important occasion in Hawai'i. Through learning history, some of the local behaviour and stereotypes can be understood.

To an extent, the Hawaiians lost their culture to the imposition of Western/American values through the quasi-colonialism of Hawai'i by the US. Many countries have been colonised and after the occupation ended, the culture was forever changed. Some post-colonial countries have tried to resurrect their previous culture. Hawai'i could not do this because they were never post-colonial—they became the 50th state of the US. There are still Hawaiians that wish to gain sovereignty, but they are not in the majority.

Additionally, the Asians came to Hawai'i in the early 1800s to work on the plantations. The plantation owners fought hard to keep the plantation workers from organising and unionising. They made the workers wear number tags and only buy from the company store. These may be a couple of historical explanations for modern-day prejudice.

Some Hawaiians continue to call for the sovereignty of the island, as seen from these banners put up along the side of a road.

One such explanation is that the locals fear for their financial security, jobs and ability to provide for their families. Some may see immigrants from the mainland and foreign countries as a threat, just like how mainland America sees Mexico and Mexican workers as an economic threat and erects the equivalent of the Berlin wall along her southern border. The difference is that the people of Hawai'i can't put up physical walls, so they put up social fences.

Coping

If we are to build a cultural bridge, it will take honest effort and work on our part. That is why many opt to stay in their cultural bubbles in an expatriate community, or in Hawai'i's case, in a racial enclave or on a military base. Adapting takes work and change on your part, because Hawai'i isn't going to change for you. However, you will get lucky and find people sympathetic to your cause and some have fluency in your own cultural behaviour. However, limiting yourself to only those kind of people still puts you in a bubble, albeit a larger one.

> If you plan on settling in Hawai'i for good, it is important to learn the local behaviour like you would a foreign language, and the better you speak the 'local' language, the smoother your journey will be.

A source for problem solving is your neighbour, someone you see succeeding in the culture the way you would like to. In Hawai'i, some of your neighbours aren't going to want to help a newcomer, but some will. A culture mentor can make a huge difference because they can usually explain better than a local why the locals act they way they do. Usually someone of the same culture as you who can explain how they learned to cope with the differences. Understand there are some who will bash the locals and others who will bash white people or foreigners. Try to avoid these people and find someone that is succeeding in the local culture without going native, someone who is proficient at behavioural switching between Hawai'i's culture and your home culture.

We need to develop new problem-solving skills and ways to cope with emotions. Reflect on your observations and experiences, both good and bad. Keep a journal. Write about

Soccer is popular and a great activity for kids and a way for parents to get involved. AYSO is a volunteer organisation where parents coach, referee, etc. It is a US$ 50 fee for the child to play for the 16-week season. The fee includes uniforms.

the things that stump you. Watch how you progress and find the answers. Many expatriates have blogs—an online journal of their experiences while they are living abroad. They also write related stories, news and commentary.

Another strategy for adjusting to the culture is to interact with the local people. Many say that to be successful in Hawai'i, you have to be involved and contribute to the local community. Newcomers like a college chancellor or an executive of a corporation may be invited to join golf country clubs or to speak at functions like charities and philanthropic events. As a regular guy, you may not get rock star treatment but you can still be involved. One person I know volunteers at the local civil defense and Red Cross. I have kids so I get involved through my children's school activities and the regional youth soccer organisation (American Youth Soccer Organization or AYSO).

It is a different experience for different people. There is the affluent executive, the prestigious academic, the university student, the military family, the working class (office worker or blue collar) family, the retiree—both wealthy ones and regular ones—and foreign immigrants. Some will be invited to balls and charity events while some will be invited to a barbecue on the front lawn of the renter next door. Some will be asked to speak at fundraisers or community events while others will be asked to help out at their kid's school craft fair sale.

One wonders where the emotional energy comes from when it's overwhelming enough just trying to make ends meet and understand this culture. It seems the more you reach out, the more they feel obligated to return the goodwill and therefore you have to find a way to make it all work through the synergy of it.

By familiarising yourself with people of your community, you let them see that you are here to stay and make your good intentions evident. It has been my experience that putting in face time alone can improve their reception. I visited the local library and used the computer frequently. After a couple months, they recognised me, and even though I never had a conversation with them, they softened up.

Overload

Feeling tired, overwhelmed, depressed and experiencing inability to do your new daily routine is normal in a new culture. You wonder why you do not have any energy and why you cannot get anything done. You are mentally, emotionally and physically adapting to your new culture all at once. Mentally you are learning the ropes at a new job, emotionally you are experiencing collisions with the new culture, and physically you are adjusting to the new climate.

Depending on who you are, you may or may not feel a spiritual high being in a new place. You may feel disconnected from your support system and ungrounded—a stranger in a strange land. Even during the honeymoon phase, you will still feel unable to function. The stimulation of new people at work and the adventure of a new place—unexplored roads, areas, shops, beaches and mountains. Your senses alive with the warm climate, sounds of birds, smells of flowers and new bugs inside and outside the house. Your strange looking neighbours speaking foreign languages and behaving oddly. Even the TV programmes are in different languages.

You are on overload: that's why you are feeling tired all the time. Depression can be a sign that you are growing and adjusting. I take depression as a sign to slow down and take care of myself. Don't fight the depression, just let it take its course like a common cold. Your body, mind and spirit are building up strength to respond to the array of new experiences. It's not a matter of trying to figure out why you are depressed any more than you try to figure out where you caught that cold. The possibilities are endless, because everything has changed. Just recognise that you need to slow down, take care of yourself until it passes.

You look at the cost of everything and wonder how you will manage, but as the months pass, you will figure it out. You figure out the simple things first, like planning your meals by the supermarket sales ads in the weekly newspapers that come free in the mail—that way you don't pay those crazy food prices.

Simply Out Of It

Sometimes you are in a new place and you don't even realise you're not 100 per cent yourself. Sometimes culture shock is really like being in shock—you don't even realise it! Maybe others who know you in your home environment can tell you that you're not completely yourself. It is times like these that accidents can happen.

Watch Out!

I have always loved riding my mountain bike. I have ridden the bike paths of Fort Collins, Denver, San Jose and even across the urban sprawl of Tokyo. For a few years before coming to Hawai'i, I had been commuting to work on my mountain bike in Colorado. The very first day I rode my bike to work here in Hawai'i, I got into an accident. We had been here two months and I had just gotten my bike from the movers and was ready to get back into my exercise routine of riding my mountain bike to work. I took the gravel road running along the Pearl Harbour waterside. After work, going down a hill, I did an end-over. I slipped on some gravel, the handlebars twisted and I flew over the handlebars onto my shoulder then my back. I blacked out for a second and then I was in a jumble on the ground.

I wandered back to work and had my co-worker take me to the emergency room. I had broken my collarbone (clavicle), and I had severe road-rash (abrasions) to my head, shoulder and elbow.

When you're experiencing culture shock, don't expect to be able to do all the things you normally did. You're not at full capacity yet. Take it slow and easy whether you think you're okay or not. Chances are you don't realise the effect moving and culture shock has had on you.

I went to the doctor for dizziness. It turns out that stress can be a big factor and cause of dizziness. If you are depressed and stressed out enough because of your culture shock, some people could experience dizziness. I went through a whole MRI and hearing tests. They didn't find anything so they just gave me some eardrops. It may have been stress or it could have just been an ear infection caused by swimming in the ocean.

Watching and Waiting For Your Blunders

By reading this book, you are arming yourself. When you spend time watching and processing, you are actually learning; and by making friends with the locals, old-timers and other newcomers, you are finding cultural mentors and people to share common experiences with and receive support from. As time passes, you learn to avoid or deal with the bad situations so that the goodwill is what keeps you in Hawai'i.

I live among Filipino-Americans and Filipino immigrants in Waipahu, and I have worked among the Japanese-Americans in Pearl City. Also, my child's schools were in the Japanese-American neighborhoods of Pearl City. As I understand the locals more, I begin to expect them to act like locals and this makes it easier for me to interact with them. I am still working on trying to understand what they expect of me, but I also know that they will always consider me as a Caucasian or mainlander, so I don't let it worry me if I sometimes act that role.

After all, being a mainland-born American is a part of my identity, and no one is saying I have to give that up. I will always wear my Velcro sandals and never completely convert to slippers. I don't think I will ever be the cliché white guy in the *aloha* shirt either. I still wear my Colorado T-shirts. So maybe I get labelled more often as a newcomer, but who's to say that doesn't have its advantages too.

Hawai'i is like an Asian culture where they only let you see what they want you to see. Be patient, watch, wait and see the lay of the land unfold before you jump to conclusions or make rash decisions.

Ethical and Moral Conflicts

According to Craig Storti in his book *Art of Crossing Cultures*, if you have an ethical or moral conflict with the local behaviour or the behaviour they expect of you, then it will continue to be a cultural incident for as long as you remain there.

It's nice to have the affirmation that there are some things about a culture that we will never accept and that it doesn't mean that we aren't being a culturally-aware, sensitive, respectful or understanding person.

For example, I have a moral conflict with taking part in toxic gossip that seems to take place more in collective cultures like Hawai'i than individualistic ones. I also refuse to worry about other peoples' perceptions about me or my work, even though perception and appearances are sometimes more important than facts in Hawai'i. Also, I don't accept the label *haole*.

On the other hand, I accept stereotypes of white mainlanders as arrogant, assertive, etc. I also accept cronyism because I can see the roots of group and family survival that came from the plantation legacy, and that it is also a part of collectivist societies such as the Asian and Hawaiian cultures. I don't like cronyism but I don't have an ethical or moral conflict with it, so I can learn to live with it, even with regards to racial preference in hiring. I think cronyism and racial preference hurt the people that do it as much as the person that suffers by it. It feeds mediocrity and stifles change.

Being Who We Are

An anthropologist must deeply integrate into the culture to get accurate observations, but it is not necessary to go native. The problem is that some immigrants choose to go native instead of becoming bicultural. They change who they are in order to fit in and in the process lose their identities. As immigrants, we must integrate and assimilate. To be able to do this, we have to step outside the ways that we are used to back home and step into the ways of Hawai'i. The goal is to assimilate the good of both our home culture and Hawai'i, and in the process make something better of ourselves. It is important not to lose ourselves by surrendering who we are to become a local—besides they already have enough locals in Hawai'i! Instead, we are a bicultural bridge, and those that come into contact with us may learn something through us.

Crossing cultures will cause you to question your identity because you do not have any of the positive reinforcement you had in your home culture. You will also be faced with prejudice and conflicting values. The new culture will tell you different things than the culture you grew up in. It's important to understand and reaffirm what our personal values are.

Speaking the local behavioural language doesn't mean you have to change your personal beliefs and values. This is where a lot of the resistance to adapt to the culture arises. We get confused into thinking we have to value the same things as locals to be successful in the culture. We get the impression that we have to think like the locals if we want to get along, but really we just need to communicate and behave like them. We can respect and communicate in local ways and not lose our identity. Our values and beliefs remain intact and we bridge the cultural divide with our skill in switching to acceptable behaviour. Our skill in communicating and interacting using local ways is all we need.

Sometimes, the people of Hawai'i seem to expect immigrants to assimilate or go away. I subscribe to the Canadian government's way of thinking: that we should be a mosaic of cultures, heritages and languages. We should enjoy and cherish the differences instead of fearing or avoiding them. Because of the many interracial marriages in Hawai'i, the mosaic is changing so fast that it may look more like a kaleidoscope with racial lines and colours changing all the time.

What's Your Motivation For Being Here?

You may get puzzled looks and questions like "why did you come here?" And "are you planning on staying?" Despite the dubious nature of these questions, it may be something to put some thought into.

Don't move to Hawai'i expecting it to put some new life into your marriage or jump-start a failing career. Culture shock and the stress of moving may only put more pressure on these areas.

We came here because we felt it was a better fit for our multi-ethnic family, with better part-time work opportunities for my wife. It also had a combination of Japanese and American cultures for our bilingual children to grow up in.

Faith is the Key to Living Anywhere

I read a manual on how to cope with stress, which suggested exercising and talking about my emotions with others. However, in my experience, the real answer to the stress of culture shock and the most important source of peace and well-being was the Lord Jesus Christ. I believe that you will see a miraculous transformation in yourself and your circumstances if you place your life in His hands. I came back to the Lord and the church while living in Hawai'i. In my book, *Discovering the Water of Life*, I go into the details of my Christian experience in Hawai'i.

Twenty-five years ago, Pastor Ralph Moore came to Hawai'i and planted the first Hope Chapel. He reports there are over 700 daughter and granddaughter churches that have sprung up in Hawai'i, Asia and elsewhere from his church in Kaneohe (http://www.hopechapel.com). I am a member of Hope Chapel West Oahu (in Waikele), which is one of the daughter churches (http://www.hcwo.com). If you are looking for spirit-filled worship and sermons, I recommend either Hope Chapel or New Hope (http://www.enewhope.org).

One of the most popular pastors on the radio in Hawai'i is Wayne Cordeiro, who also founded the New Hope churches in Hawai'i. There are several Christian radio stations in Hawai'i: FM95.5, 103.5, 105.5; AM760, 1040.

Feeling Like a Foreigner With No Upside

A mainlander moving to Hawai'i can experience the same culture shock of living in a foreign country without any upside. In a foreign country, you're given a lot of leeway if you don't know the local culture. You can say or do the wrong thing and people understand you're not from there. In Hawai'i, you don't get that kind of leeway. If you don't act according to local ways and understand the local culture, you sometimes get the 'stink eye' (the local equivalent of the evil eye), and are ignored or treated rudely.

In a foreign country, you have people who want to get to know you because you are from somewhere else; sometimes you are the centre of attention. In Hawai'i, they assume they know all there is to know about the mainland and some aren't particularly interested in or proud to share the unique aspects of the local culture. It can seem that they think the less they share with you, the faster you'll go back home. So you're on your own.

One of the benefits of being in a foreign country is that you have a group of other fellow foreigners and immigrant services to rely on. Where this is true for foreign immigrants to Hawai'i, mainlanders don't have this support net and must make it on their own.

All the leeway that you are given as a foreigner in a foreign country is not given in Hawai'i. There are no stimulating cultural exchanges. People who want to share and teach you about their culture and the local culture in Hawai'i are rare.

Despite this, you will still experience an upside. You will have vivid inspirations and insights into yourself, your culture, others and their culture, just as if you were in a foreign country (or if an immigrant, you really are in a foreign country!).

One of the beauties of living in a different culture is the ability to learn from it. I challenge you to find one aspect of the new culture's values that might be worth considering adding to or changing your values to. The attraction of Hawai'i to many mainland immigrants is that they want a change and often see something in Hawai'i's values that they want.

A New Perspective

Living in a foreign country, you will get a new perspective on your own country's culture. The same is true in Hawai'i. You see the history that was missing in school, the effects of colonialism, and you ask why the Native Hawaiians haven't gotten special legal status like the Native Americans did long ago.

If you come from mainland America, you will see the American behaviour from a new vantage point. Much like living in Asia, living in Hawai'i will make you realise how arrogant some Americans can be. You may also see the American's lack of concern for the others and placing their self-interest above the good of the group, family or community.

If you come from a developing country—as many refugees come to Hawai'i from Vietnam, Laos or Myanmar, etc.—you will see both Hawai'i and mainland America from a different vantage point too. You may think how superficial and wasteful Americans can be with their petrol guzzling SUVs and obsessive consumerism.

As a foreign immigrant, you may be surprised by the violence on TV. One Asian-Indian immigrant wondered how he would keep his children from viewing it when even the cartoons are full of it. You may be shocked at the materialism of the people of Hawai'i and Americans, and the competition and greed that leads to disharmony and poverty in so many aspects of life. You may be shocked by the disparity of wealth—million-dollar condos next to thousands of homeless on the beach.

Whether you are from the mainland or from another country, you will be challenged in new ways and have a chance to grow more. You will adopt some of the behaviour and values of Hawai'i and try to lose some of those that you grew up with in your home culture. Of course, this is a matter of how open you are to letting Hawai'i or any new place change you.

Some go native, hate their home country's ways and people, and lose their identity in the local culture. Or you could be like the guy in my German class who was stationed in Munich, Germany, and said he only left the base once in the four years that he was stationed there. Let's hope that you think like the Hawaiian Buddhists and find the middle way.

Ready For Visitors

Eventually, you will have family members that want to visit you. And you will be in the position of explaining the local culture. What will you say? How can you explain something that took you a year or more to understand yourself? If you are like me, you love culture. Talking about culture is fascinating, and I could spend hours sharing and debating about it.

Perhaps the one way to approach this is to start out with your observations of what is different from where you came from. And then everything else you have learned about the local culture. But the joy is telling them what you have learned about your own culture. Values, beliefs and behaviour you used to hold but from the vantage point of your new culture have decided they no longer fit you. Or maybe there are some things you never really understood or questioned about your culture that you have found some answers to.

In some ways, your identity has been broken down but in other ways, it has been reaffirmed in a way your own culture never could. Things like realising that the world doesn't revolve around your home country. That other countries may be economically poorer and yet vastly richer in culture and social wealth. Their outlook on life and way of life may be superior to your home culture. You have had to unlearn many things your culture has taught you which you have found to be untrue. You learn history written in other places that are missing from what you learned about the world.

Learning More
We don't learn about Polynesian history or culture in mainland USA. Times are changing and so are the history books and things like the history of the American Indians are being added. So the lapse of our culture may only be a temporary one, but it is still a shortcoming of our home culture. Another example is one Canadian living in Hawai'i who said it was shameful that she can tell you where the 50 states are but Americans can't tell her where the ten Canadian provinces are.

You can try to explain some of the shortcomings of your home culture to your visiting relatives but they may just look at you like you have gone native with no intention of coming back. You have to realise they have no frame of reference to understand your little personal paradigm shift.

Third Culture Kids
Whether you are from a foreign country or the mainland, you will be raising your kids in a foreign culture. You will be teaching them your culture and they will be learning the local culture outside the home. They will end up being a mix

of both cultures: yours and Hawai'i's. This is called a third culture kid. They may come home speaking the local accent or even pidgin. They will have a strong sense of the role groups play in this society and have a better understanding of local ways than you will.

It also depends on the schools your children are in. If they go to a private school, they may get a social education similar to the mainland. If they go to public schools, it depends on the area you are in. Filipinos have the highest number of children in the schools today but that also depends on the area you live in. On one side of us is Pearl City, and the public elementary Momilani has more than half Japanese-Americans students. In Waikele, it's more than half Filipinos. My child went to both schools and I saw the different behaviour she was learning in these schools. She was quieter but learning a lot when she was in the Japanese school and more talkative and testing boundaries when she went to the elementary school in Waikele.

It depends on the child's personality whether they enjoy change and new cultures or desire to stay in one place with friends and roots. I attended a seminar on Global Nomads at the university and found there were people who enjoyed growing up abroad and others that hated it the whole time.

One American middle-aged man said he went to an elementary school in Japan and hated leaving Japan as a child. On the other hand, an American middle-aged woman who was a military brat hated moving around and losing her friends. Her father wasn't sympathetic and told her to be happy that she had the opportunity to see the world.

The third culture psychology literature talks about problems of identity with these children. They don't fit in with either their parents' culture or the culture they have been living in. They have mixed the two together and become a third culture. Children like these need roots and support. My Japanese language teacher sent her kids over to Japan every summer after the school year in Colorado finished to attend public school because the school year in Japan ended in August. Her children, through learning Japanese and making school friends they saw every year, grew roots in Japan too. Her solution was to make sure they always had roots in both countries so they wouldn't have an identity crisis or feelings of loss.

FOOD AND ENTERTAINING

CHAPTER 6

'There is a local adage that, like most adages,
has a grain of truth. It is this: recent transplants
from the mainland go to parties mainly to socialise.
Locals, a term that can encompass individuals of
any ethnic group, go to parties mainly to eat.'
—Floyd Takeuchi, 'Feelings on Food Rooted in Culture',
7 May 1989, *Honolulu Star Bulletin*

GRINDS

In Hawai'i, *grinds* (food) is the cornerstone of socialising and community. Hawaiian, Japanese, Chinese, Filipino, Korean, Vietnamese and other ethnic food make up the mixture of local food and restaurants. If there is anything missing, it's probably some really great Mexican restaurants.

Rice rules in Hawai'i and comes with the everyday food and on plate lunches. At KFC, you can buy a chicken rice bowl and at A&W, you can get your fast food with a side of rice. When you order a plate lunch, mini means one scoop of rice and regular is two scoops and usually twice the meat. McDonald's serves spam on the side for breakfast, *saimin* (noodle soup with fishcake) for lunch, and pineapple and taro pies for dessert.

There are several supermarkets: Safeway, Foodland, Daiei, Times, etc. Step inside the supermarkets and get ready to see new food everywhere. Packaged foods from Japan, seafood in the deli that you've never seen, lots of local grown produce such as avocados, papayas, mangoes, pineapples, etc. Snacks are also big. There are all kinds of snacks like dried, thinly sliced or shredded squid and octopus. This is the Japanese equivalent of beef jerky. They put *ling ling* (Chinese word *li hing mui*) powder on everything from pineapple to dried plums. It gives plums a salty-sour taste.

Lunch wagons are everywhere and serve the popular hot plate lunches. At lunch wagons, you can find food like

Hawaiian food from the Highway Inn in Waipahu on O'ahu. Combo meals consist of *pipi kaula*, *lomi salmon* and *haupia* (from left to right on the top of plate). Meals also come with a choice of (clockwise from upper left): *kalua* pig, beef stew, *lau lau*, and a side of either rice or *poi*.

fried *mahimahi* (dolphin fish), BBQ beef, chicken *katsu* (pork or chicken deep fried cutlet) or even *teppanyaki* (a Japanese dish of meat or fish fried with vegetables on a hot plate) for about US$ 6. Some are on the beach while others are in front of supermarkets like Daiei. If you work downtown, you may find even find steak, *lau lau* (meat steamed in taro leaves), and lobster at one of the corner lunch wagons.

Fine dining is big time in Hawai'i because of tourism. For the refined dining, you can have a romantic sunset dinner with a prime rib and crab leg buffet, including live entertainment, for anywhere from US$ 32–55 in Waikīkī hotels like the Sheraton, Moana Surfrider and Royal Hawaiian. Children between the ages of five and 12 pay about half the

Even Iron Chefs Hiroyuki Sakai from Japan and Masaharu Morimoto from New York have come to Hawai'i for cooking demonstrations and food competitions. For famous local chefs and fine dining, try Sam Choy's or Roy's. They make some original creations that fuse Hawaiian, local and international elements into extravagant dishes.

For Thanksgiving dinner, we went to the Surf Room at the Royal Hawaiian. It was a pricey US$ 50 each for the special Thanksgiving buffet. In addition to the regular seafood buffet, they had turkey and a cranberry sauce made with strawberries, mashed potatoes and gravy and two kinds of pumpkin pie. In proper Thanksgiving tradition, we filled up until we could eat no more. However, the best part of the Royal Hawaiian is the architecture, its history and the beach.

price of adults. There are also *kama'āina* discounts which are about US$ 4–6 off the regular price of the buffet. The Kaiulani doesn't have a *kama'āina* discount but one kid eats free with each paying adult. Some have a dress code requiring a collared shirt and long pants for gentlemen; and no shorts or beach wear is allowed for ladies. There are also breakfast buffets that range from US$ 18–28, with kids' meals going for about half that price.

BBQ HAWAIIAN-STYLE

The people of Hawai'i love to barbecue out in the parks, on the beach, in their front yards, at potlucks, basically everywhere. One man from Hilo says he will roll down his window on the way home from work as he approaches his neighbourhood and there is always someone charcoal grilling something. People are friendly and they will invite you over to have a bite. He smells his way around to who's

got the best meat cooking on the grill and makes his way over to say hello.

Meat is expensive in Hawai'i, but sometimes you can get it cheap and already barbecued. The Times supermarket chain runs an ongoing takeaway barbecue special. The huge grills are smoking up the parking lot with the crisp and juicy smells of sirloin steak, chicken, salmon and even pot roast. My wife says you can't even buy sirloin as cheap as they are selling it for in their takeaway barbecue meals.

The more locals on the beach, the more barbecues you will see. Not only are people living on the beach but they are cooking as well. The local family will take their mini charcoal griller to the beach with them. They set up camp for a long day with a portable DVD movie player, foldable lounge chairs, umbrella and an ice chest. They plop on the sand or at a picnic table and fire up the meat; the smoke gives the beach a friendly, homey feel.

Barbecue Delights

The local barbecue has a Hawaiian twist, not only will you find corn, garlic mashed potatoes, rice and salad, but also rice balls filled with tuna or other meats, and *manapua*—a Chinese dough ball stuffed with *char-sui* pork or other meats. These are some of the foods you will find accompanying the barbecue delights.

If it starts to rain, they just pull it over to the covered picnic tables and the feast continues without a hitch.

POTLUCKS

Lots of people will have a potluck in their front garage or their back porch. Since everyone would have to take off their shoes to go in the house, it is easier to have people walk around to the back of the house to the back porch instead of walking through the house. One guy had the toilet built right off the back porch. Which was great because people didn't go walking through the house.

These are the things you might find at a potluck: garlic chicken, noodles and ham, *poke* (raw fish with seasoning or relish), *futomaki* (thick sushi rolls) with Japanese pickles, cookies, rice crispy treats, brownies, hot dogs and *spam musubi* (like Hawaiian/Asian hot dog), *musubi* (rice ball), cupcakes, brownies, *lumpia* (egg roll), chicken quarters, rice casserole, pig and cabbage, noodles, rice (they just bring the whole rice cooker and plop it on the table) and chilli (sometimes from Zippy's).

> When visiting someone's house, even if it isn't a potluck, bring something for the host like fruit or something you made. And when offered food, always take some, even if just a little.

Don't put your plate on the floor or the ground during a potluck—a swarm of ants will overtake it before you know it.

BLOGS AND 'FLOGS'

People are passionate about food and express it online. There are several web forums and 'flogs' (blogs dedicated to food) on food in Hawai'i. Unlike the newspapers' restaurant review sections, flogs aren't slanted by advertisers and offer a wider variety of cuisine. You can find discussions on which restaurants are good, pictures of the food and also the interior of the restaurants, and even some recipes. There are even podcast (audio) interviews about food. You can also learn interesting news like why the milk in Hawai'i seems to go bad so fast: because half of the milk in Hawai'i comes from the mainland and it takes a week

The author eating some of his favourite plate lunches: *loco moco*—two hamburger patties, two over-easy eggs and gravy on rice (right); *mochiko* chicken—fried chicken made with *mochi* rice flour on a bed of cabbage (left). Plate lunches come with two scoops of rice and macaroni salad.

to get here. It is the same with eggs, so you should only buy products with the island fresh logos because they are made in Hawai'i.

Forums on Food in Hawai'i

- Start at http://forums.egullet.org/ then go to eGullet Forums > Restaurants, Cuisine, and Travel > United States > Hawai'i
- Start at http://www.hawaiithreads.com then go to HawaiiThreads > Kaukau Korner

Flogs from people throughout the islands:

- http://onokinegrindz.typepad.com/
- http://maona.net/
- http://kaukautime.blogspot.com/
- http://musicinkitchen.blogspot.com/
- http://www.bigislandgrinds.com

Commercial sites:

- http://www.hawaiidiner.com/

FOOD OF ALL KINDS

'Ono means 'tasty and delicious' in Hawaiian. Here is what is *'onoliscious* in Hawai'i:

A Sample of Everyday Hawaiian Food	
Pipi kaula	Literally 'beef rope'. Thick chunks of soft beef jerky
Lau lau	Means 'wrapping', and *lau* means 'leaf' in Hawaiian. *Kālua* pig, meat or butterfish steamed in taro (karo) leaves
Stew	Beef, tripe, or *na'au pua'a* (pig intestine)
Baked *mahimahi*	White fish or dolphin fish (not related to the dolphin mammal) with firm, white meat and a delicate flavour
Pickled onions	Raw onions with salt
Raw squid with *kukui* (candlenut)	
Squid, chicken, or *tako* (octopus) *lū'au*	The meat is baked with young taro tops and coconut cream
Miso (*zuke*) butterfish	A local fish pickled or marinated with *miso*, a paste made from fermented soya beans and barley or rice malt
Chili water	Hot sauce for anything
Pipi pūlehu	Broiled beef
Taro (karo)	A starchy root with a potato consistency. Taro bread and pancakes are popular

A Sample of Lū'au Food

Kalua pig / *pua'a* in the *imu*	Literally 'pig baked in the ground oven'. Baked pork sometimes served with cabbage
Hulihuli chicken	Barbecued chicken cooked with *hulihuli* sauce (made with pure Hawaiian brown sugar cane along with soy sauce, fresh ginger and more)
Lomilomi salad / *lomi 'ahi* / *lomi* salmon	Raw tuna or salmon mixed with tomatoes, onions and seasoning
Limu	Raw seaweed
Taro rolls	Delicious, soft, purple, dinner rolls

Hulihuli (*huli* means 'turn over' in Hawaiian) barbecued chicken on a rod is cooked up everywhere in Hawai'i, like next to the road in Hale'iwa on the North Shore or downtown Honolulu in front of Safeway. This is some *'ono* chicken great for taking to the beach or the park.

A Sample of Lū'au Food

Breadfruit	A large green fruit that looks like green cantaloupes growing on trees. Baked and smashed to eat
Chicken with long rice noodle	
Uhi	Yam
'Uala / 'Uwala	Sweet potato
Poi	Mashed taro root. There is a proper way to eat *poi*, which involves dipping the first two fingers in the bowl. The hand is then twisted on the way to the mouth to scoop the drippings into the mouth. Some people eat it with *lomilomi* salad on top
Kūlolo	Taro and coconut cream pudding
Haupia	Coconut pudding also used on top of cakes

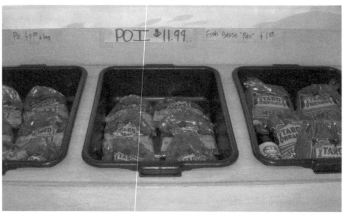

The traditional Hawaiian food *poi* is made from mashed taro root and sold at this local market.

Fish Names	
I'a	Means 'fish'
Shibi	Yellowfin tuna
'Ahi	Bigeye tuna
Ahu	Bonito tuna
Mahimahi	White fish or dolphin fish
Ono	Mackerel
He'e	Octopus
A'u	Swordfish, marlin, sailfish

Food from the Philippines	
Halo-halo	This popular Filipino dessert is a mix of crushed ice, tropical fruits, sweet red beans, coconut milk and topped with ice cream
Lumpia	Egg roll; also banana *lumpia* dessert
Bagoong	Fermented fish or shrimp sauce
Pancit noodles	Thin rice noodle
Paksiw	*Paksiw* is cooking with a sour base, usually vinegar. A common dish of such style is *paksiw na tilapia*
Sinigang	Milkfish
Pork or chicken *adobo*	Considered the national dish of the Philippines and is very popular in Hawai'i. It is meat cooked in soy sauce, vinegar, garlic and bay leaves
Longganisa sausage	Pinoy-style sausage
Pig feet soup with rice	

Food from the Philippines	
Pinakbet	Pork crackling, okra, *ampalaya* (bitter gourd) and aubergine
Chicken papaya	

Food from Korea	
Kal bi	Korean barbecue short ribs
Tae gu	Spicy squid
Kimchi or *kim chee*	A spicy side dish of Korean cabbage or radish pickled with salt, sugar, garlic, ginger and chilli pepper
Mandoo guk	Dumpling soup
Bulgogi	Grilled steak

Food from Japan	
Musubi	This rice ball is found everywhere from 7-Elevens to supermarkets
Bento	Box lunch
Kamaboko	Fishcake, popular at New Year and also in *saimin*
Sashimi	Raw fish, like *sushi* without the rice underneath
Tofu	White soybean curd
Ume boshi	Pickled plum
Senbei	Rice crackers
Mochi	Soft rice pounded into a taffy consistency and sometimes stuffed with sweet bean paste
Curry	With beef, chicken or pork

Food from Japan

Nishime	Vegetables and seaweed boiled well in soy sauce
Shoyu pork	Pork cooked with soy sauce (Okinawa style)
Katsu	Pork or chicken deep fried cutlet
Zaru soba	Cold/chilled buckwheat noodles
Hiyashi somen	Cold/chilled thin wheat noodles
Okazu	Side dish. There are many *okazuyas* tucked away in corners of shopping centres throughout the islands. These takeaway counters have a variety of Japanese side dishes. You can make your own *bento* or snack by picking from the various noodle and fried delicacies
Tempura	Vegetables, shrimp, and other foods deep-fried in batter
Gobo	Burdock
Namasu	Raw fish or vegetables cut up small and soaked in vinegar
Takuan	Pickled radish
Nitsuke butterfish	Fish boiled well in soy sauce
Inari sushi	Rice in a blanket of fried tofu
Norimaki	Seaweed roll

Food from China	
Crack seed	The local name for a variety of flavoured snacks and candy, especially, the ones with the *li hing mui* (plum) powder. My wife's favourite is the Enjoy brand Premium Red Li Hing Mui. Native Japanese love this snack because it is similar to their *ume*, a preserved/pickled plum
Char siu	Red-coloured meats, usually pork
Dim sum	Dumplings filled with meat or seafood
Manapua	Baked or steamed dough ball filled with meat or seafood
Chow fun	Thick rice noodle like *udon*

Food from Portugal	
Portuguese sausage	A mild, thick, red sausage sliced up and served at breakfast with eggs, with lunch or on a *pupu* platter
Malasadas	Portuguese doughnut

YET MORE KINDS OF FOOD
Food from the Mixture of Ethnic Groups

- Spam *musubi*
  This has become an icon of Hawai'i. Spam is short for spiced ham. During the war, meat didn't come to Hawai'i so spam became popular. On the mainland, spam is stigmatised as something you eat if you are poor and might be embarrassed to have around the house. Forget that notion here, because everybody eats it and

Crack seeds or *li hing mui* is the name of a local snack obsession. It is a variety of candy and snacks from dried plums and mango to many different flavours of dried *ika* (Japanese for squid)—many covered with the popular *li hing mui* powder. Other favourites are *norimaki* (Japanese for seaweed rolls), shredded *tako* (Japanese for octopus), and a crunchy *arare* and *senbei* (Japanese rice crackers).

loves it. The spam *musubi* is an example of the fusion of American and Japanese food. It is a long slice of spam wrapped to a square of cooked rice with a strip of seaweed. Spam isn't just for *musubi*. It's sometimes substituted for the pork meat in fried rice and put in a variety of other dishes.

- *Poke*
  Raw fish with seasoning or relish. This is a big seller and all the supermarkets have several varieties in the deli or seafood department. During holidays like the

Lomilomi salmon US$ 4.99/lb, *ahi shoyu* (tuna and soy sauce) *poke* US$ 4.99/lb, *madako* (Japanese for octopus without any sauce) *poke* US$ 8.99/lb, *ahi limu* (tuna and seaweed) *poke* US$ 6.99/lb and shrimp *poke* US$ 7.99/lb. *Poke* is said to have first been eaten by the ancient Hawaiians on fishing trips. On the canoe, they would cut up the fish and eat it with salt. *Sushi* and *sashimi* lovers are sure to enjoy all the different varieties of *poke* in Hawai'i.

New Year, they sell loads of *poke*. During the Superbowl, its not chips and beer, its *poke* and beer! Be aware that *sashimi* and *poke* are expensive at New Year. Some different types of *poke* include *'ahi* or *ahu* (Hawaiian for tuna), *tako* (Japanese for octopus), crab, shrimp and mussel. In addition to spices, it is mixed with sesame seeds or *limu* (seaweed). There is even raw crab, *kimchi*, and Cajun spice kinds of poke. You can find fried poke—day-old raw poke fried into a sort of soft fish jerky—at the *okazuya* shops.

- Shave Ice

  This is a treat from Japan. *Kakigori* means 'shaved ice' in Japanese. The pidgin pronunciation is 'shave ice' and not 'shaved ice'. This is better than a 'sno-cone'. The ice is shaved to a snow-like softness. A popular shaved ice is a rainbow of three flavours of syrup striped across the top. Guava, pineapple, lychee, coconut, tamarind and papaya are some of the unique flavours available in Hawai'i. Another twist on this treat is ice-cream or *azuki*—Japanese sweet red bean paste—on the bottom.

Local Grinds—Everyday Food

Plate lunch	Two scoops of rice, macaroni salad and a main dish of meat. Available everywhere, at lunch wagons, fast food restaurants like Zippy's, L&L Drive-In, Loco Moco, etc. There is a long list of main dishes found on a plate lunch, such as fried fish, *mochiko* chicken, chili and hot dog, *teriyaki* beef, etc.
Pūpū platters	Appetiser or main course platters with a mix of any of the following: *teriyaki* beef, *mahimahi*, spam, chicken *katsu*, shrimp patty, breaded shrimp, Portuguese sausage, hot dog, egg rolls, spare ribs, etc.
Loco moco	Rice, hamburger patty, egg and gravy
Saimin	Noodle soup with *kamaboko* (fishcake)
Hulihuli chicken	Barbecued on a rod over charcoal fire; *huli* means 'turn over' in Hawaiian
Squid *lū'au*	The green soupy stuff in the stirofoam cups. Native Japanese love this because it has a taste of squid innards—a Japanese delicacy

Shoyu chicken	*Shoyu* is Japanese for 'soy sauce'
Mochiko	Flour made from *mochi*
Spam *katsu* curry rice	
Pork tofu	

Oxtail soup with grated ginger (*shoga* in Japanese) and rice is a popular local dish. There is a technique to eating it: Put the ginger in a small side dish with *shoyu* (soy sauce). Then dip the meat in the sauce or just spoonfuls into the side dish and eat. Once the soup bowl is half full, dump all the rice in and eat it like rice soup.

Receipe for Mochiko Chicken

Ingredients:

6 eggs

2 cups of *shoyu* (soy sauce)

2 cups of *mochiko* flour

2 cups of cornflour

2 cups of sugar

2 crushed garlic cloves (depending on preference)

Instructions:

- Mix wet ingredients together and then add dry ingredients to form a smooth batter.
- Cut 6–8 chicken thighs into halves (no skin or bones) and coat with batter.
- Fry until golden brown.

ENJOYING HAWAI'I

CHAPTER 7

THERE IS NO "ALL SQUIDS DAY" AND NO DAY OFF SCHOOL!

'Ye weary ones that are sick of the labour and care, and the bewildering turmoil of the great world, and sigh for a land where ye may fold your tired hands and slumber your lives peacefully away, pack up your carpet sacks and go to Kailua! A week there ought to cure the saddest of you all.'
—Mark Twain, *Letters From Hawai'i*

FESTIVALS

One of the great ways to spend a Saturday is at one of the many festivals around the islands. If there is one reason to come into Honolulu, it would have to be for the festivals. Many of them are held at Kapi'olani Park in Honolulu, such as the Okinawan, Korean and Thai festivals. These festivals have ethnic music and performances at the Kapi'olani Park Bandstand. Others like the Pan-Pacific Matsuri have parades along Waikīkī beach.

The Japanese Cultural Center of Hawai'i has its own festival, and so does the Kaua'i Japanese Cultural Society (called the Matsuri Kaua'i). These festivals have martial arts demonstrations and cultural arts demonstrations such as learning how to wear a *kimono*. There are also classes in calligraphy, tea ceremony rituals, martial arts, etc. The Pan-Pacific and Japanese Cultural Center festivals have *mochi* pounding—the Japanese tradition of pounding rice into gooey taffy and stuffing it with sweet bean paste. The *mochi* is free and made by volunteers from the local Buddhist temple. Parking is always hard to find in the metered parking lot next to Kapi'olani Park.

The Pineapple Festival is in the middle of May and held at the Wahiawa District Park (next to the Botanical Gardens). Wahiawa provides a taste of a rural and more friendly part of O'ahu. The pace is slower and people aren't crowding each other, like at the festivals at Kapi'olani Park

Taiko (drum) players pound out Japanese rhythms at the Kapi'olani Park Bandstand (actually a huge gazebo).

in downtown Waikīkī. On the trolley, an old lady moved to another seat so that my wife and I could sit down with our kids. Wahiawa is right next to Schofield Barracks, so the military guys help out with traffic control into the entrance of the park.

The kids can ride all the rides with a special five-dollar armband. Xtreme Fun Rentals Inc is the company that runs the kids rides at many festivals and the owner is from Wahiawa. He made the special armband especially for this festival. Meadow Gold Dairy has free yoghurt and cottage cheese and Dole Plantation has free pineapple chunks covered in spicy *ling ling* powder. There is a pineapple toss game for the kids. The festival is over at 4:00 pm and all the pineapples are given away. Parking near the park is difficult to find, so most people park at the high school up the road and take the trolley shuttle. The trolley and parking are free. The trolley takes you on a small tour of the town before dropping off at the festival. On the narrated tour, you will hear some of the history of Wahiawa and see some of the old plantation areas and houses.

The Taste of Mililani

One of the festivals we like is the Taste of Mililani. This festival is better than the many Honolulu Kapi‘olani Park festivals. The parking is right next to the Mililani District Park and it's free. It isn't as crowded as the Korean or Okinawan festival, so there are no long queues for food and lots of seating.

This festival has food from local restaurants, rides for the kids and many tents filled with different crafts, food and other items for sale. There is a small stage with live entertainment where a youth group dances to Hawaiian music in front of drummers on a stage. The audience eat at tables under tents. There's always something for the kids: T-shirts from the YMCA, *keiki* IDs or water bottles from the Lutheran church, all free of charge.

The granddaddy of all festivals is the summer-long Bon Odori. In Japanese, *bon* is 'festival of the dead' and *odori* is 'dance'. This festival is great for culture lovers. Based on a thousand-year-old tradition brought over from Japan, it is the Buddhist practice of remembering and honouring their dead ancestors. During this festival, many participants—not only the Japanese—wear a *yukata* or *hapi* coat (traditional Japanese summer dress) and dance in a circle around a tower.

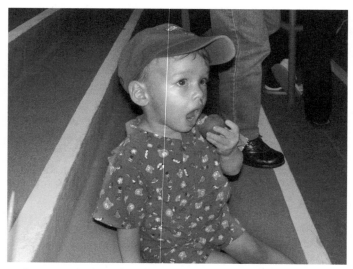

Andagi—a popular festival food with the kids—is a ball-shaped, deep-fried doughnut originally from Okinawa.

In the tower, musicians play traditional Japanese music. Bon Odoris are held every weekend through the summer at different *hongwanji* throughout the islands. Here you can eat *andagi*, a ball-shaped, deep-fried doughnut originally from Okinawa. You can also tour the inside of the *hongwanji* and meet the members.

Festivals in Hawai'i

There are festivals throughout the year. Most festival dates vary each year, so it's best to check the local weekly newspapers that come free in the mail for the exact dates. There are way too many to list, so here is a sampling of some festivals both big and small:

- Bon Dances (June through August): statewide.
- Pan-Pacific Festival/Matsuri in Hawai'i: this festival is held in Waikīkī and celebrates both the Japanese and Hawaiian culture. It is a three-day event in the middle of June with a parade, marathon, party and other activities. It appears to be geared to the Japanese tourists and other tourists who are interested in Japanese culture. Find out more at the website: http://www.pan-pacific-festival.com
- King Kamehameha Day Parade (11 June): a state holiday, celebrated with a parade and other festivities.
- Annual Lantern Floating event on Memorial Day (last Monday of May): held at the Magic Island at Ala Moana Beach Park. Everyone makes their own lanterns and floats them out to sea in the Buddhist Obon tradition. Find out more at: http://www.lanternfloatinghawaii.com
- American Indian Pow Wow Festival (June): held at Kapi'olani Park.
- Maui Film Festival.
- Big Island Queen Lili'uokalani Long Distance Outrigger Canoe Race (September).
- Merry Monarch Festival (April): held in Hilo on the Big Island with *hula* contests.
- Statewide Aloha Festival Week: held on each of the islands throughout September to December with royal pageantry, *hula* and Hawaiian arts and crafts.
- Prince Lot Hula Festival (July): held at Moanalua Park on O'ahu.
- Annual Talk Story Festival: held at Ala Moana Park in the summer.

HOLIDAYS

The fireworks on New Year's Eve blast through the neighbourhoods. People stay at home and set off rounds of 1,000 firecrackers at a time. There were so many fireworks in my neighbourhood that we couldn't see down the road through all the smoke for a couple hours. It was still a smoky haze the next morning.

It is no surprise, with all the military in Hawai'i, that the 4th of July is a big event. The 4th of July isn't as crazy in the neighbourhoods, because everyone goes to see one of the several shows on the island. From Leeward, it is possible to see a few shows at once. There are several spots, like at the parks, where you can see Pearl Harbour and beyond. We went to the Waikele Outlets parking lot. From there, you can see the Ala Moana, Aloha Tower and Pearl Harbour all at once. They started at 8:30 pm, 8:40 pm and 8:30 pm respectively.

The Ala Moana mall closes off their top level of parking so that people can sit up there and watch the fireworks at Magic Island. The Ala Moana show is crowded and parking is so hard to get that many people camp out overnight. There are also fireworks at Kailua Beach Park and Kāne'ohe Bayfest. Schofield Barracks is open to military and civilians alike to watch the army base's fireworks show. Parking is free but the food stand prices are high. There are hordes of people that go to the Schofield Barracks show. On Maui, there are shows at Lahaina and Wailea; on Kaua'i, at the Vidinha stadium; and on the Big Island, there are several shows at Coconut island in Hilo and King shops in Waikoloa and others.

Public Holidays and Other Holidays

- New Year's Day / Makahiki Hou (1 January): the first day in January is a public holiday.
- Martin Luther King Jr Day: the third Monday in January is a public holiday.
- Chinese New Year Day (January or February, depending on the lunar calendar): celebrated in Chinatown.
- Valentine's Day (14 February).
- Presidents' Day / La Pelekikena: the third Monday in February is a public holiday.

- Girl's Day (3 March).
- Saint Patrick's Day (17 March).
- Prince Jonah Kūhīo Kalaniana'ole Day / La Kūhīo (26 March): birthday of the nephew of Queen Lili'uokalani and republican delegate to congress.
- Good Friday and Easter Sunday / Pō'alima Hemolele and Ka La i ala hou ai ka Haku (March or April): the Friday preceding Easter Sunday is a public holiday.
- Lei Day (1 May): the Hawaiian version of May Day.
- Boy's Day (5 May): the flying of the carp, fish-shaped streamer outside the home. Called *koi nobori* in Japanese tradition.
- Memorial Day / La Kau Pau: the last Monday in May is a public holiday.
- King Kamehameha Day / La Kamehameha (11 June):the founder of the kingdom of Hawai'i is commemorated with a parade. A public holiday.
- American Independence Day (4 July): public holiday.

Halloween is celebrated in Hawai'i just like on the mainland USA. These kindergarten children are on a field trip to a pumpkin patch outside Kapolei on O'ahu. They will take a pumpkin home, carve a face on the front and display it in front of their house for the trick-or-treaters that will visit their home on Halloween night.

- Admission Day / La Ho 'Ōkomo 'Ana (21 August): commemorates Hawai'i becoming a state on 21 August 1959. The third Friday in August is a public holiday.
- Labour Day / La Limahana (September): the first Monday in September is a public holiday.
- Discovers Day (Columbus Day) / La Ho 'ike (October): Captain Cook was the first non-Polynesian to discover Hawai'i. The name has been altered since Christopher Columbus' discovery did not affect Hawai'i, and even though Cook's discovery fell on another day.
- General Election Day (November): the first Tuesday in November following the first Monday of even-numbered years is a public holiday. State and local government elections as well as presidential and congressional elections in the appropriate years are held on this day.
- Veterans' Day / La Koa Kahiko (11 November): a public holiday.
- Thanksgiving Day / Lā Ho'omaika'i (November): the fourth Thursday in November is a public holiday. Many places declare the day after Thanksgiving Day (Friday) as an off day too. This is one of the biggest Christmas shopping days of the year.
- Christmas / Kalikimaka (25 December): a public holiday.

Resident Discount

Kama'āina (KAH-mah-EYE'-nah) means child of the land and one who has lived in Hawai'i a long time. There seems to be a little bit of controversy over who can be called this so I just ask for the Hawai'i resident discount and they understand what I mean. They usually ask for my Hawai'i driver's licence as proof. My Colorado driver licence actually had eight years left before it expired but I traded it in for a Hawaiian licence that only lasts seven years because I wanted to get the discounts.

The other way to get discounts is to get a Hawai'i ID that costs US$ 15 (US$ 10 for seniors). You will need to show your original social security card and birth certificate. Non-US citizens will need to show their original social security card and alien resident card or passport. The state ID office (http://www.Hawaii.gov/hcjdc/sid.htm) is open from 8:00 am to 2:00 pm, Monday through Friday, except on state holidays. It is located in Honolulu at 465 South King Street at the corner of Punchbowl Street in Room 102.

You can get resident discounts at places like Hanauma Bay, Polynesian Culture Center, Hawai'i Nature Center and Sea Life Park. Even the parking is discounted by a dollar at Sea Life Park. With a local ID, there are also discounts on greens fees at some golf courses. Most hotels (Sheraton, Aston, Ohana, etc.) and many condo rentals have *kama'āina* discounts. You can also get discounts on Hawai'i vacation packages, including air, hotel and car.

THE BEACH

You will know the difference between someone living here and a tourist on the beach. The people who live here respect the sun, and even though they spend the entire day at the beach, it's always under the shade of trees or umbrellas. On the other hand, the tourists can be spotted as the glaring white beached seals laying out fully exposed to the sun's harmful rays, all for the purpose of going home looking like lobsters so their friends will ask them where they got that suntan in the dead of winter. When going to any beach, don't forget your sunglasses, sunscreen and umbrellas.

There are beautiful beaches on all the islands and some are popular with tourists but others are secluded. The Bellows Beach next to Bellows Air Force is open to civilians on the weekends (Friday noon to Sunday midnight). It's a beautiful beach right below the famous Lanikai beach and isn't crowded.

One can tell the change of the seasons by the shift of the ocean waves. The North Shore has the highest waves on the island and a huge surfer community. However, as the seasons change, the waves become higher on the east and west coasts. Summer is a great time to take the kids to the North Shore. There are many beaches along the northern side of the island and the waves are smaller and safe for the kids.

Tour guides tell people that Ko'olina resort will be the next Waikīkī. Ko'olina is a posh resort on the south-west tip of the O'ahu island. It is past Kapolei on H-1, an exit on the right side with a well-groomed landscape and many palm trees. The condos in Ko'olina go for US$ 700,000 and have beach and golf access within walking distance. In contrast to Waikīkī, there is only one hotel resort—a Marriott hotel. Marriot also has a huge tower of timeshares on one of the lagoons and is building another one right next to it. Just like Waikīkī, the beaches are man-made lagoons and all the sand was brought in. There are four crescent-shaped lagoons that have a low rock barrier that keeps the waves from crashing in. These are great beaches for the kids. There is no charge for parking but you will need a day parking pass that is picked up at the

A great activity for the kids is to see the turtles on the North Shore. Please don't touch the turtles.

security gate on the way in. There is also a boat marina, a lū'au restaurant and wedding chapels on the beach. The last lagoon has the most parking (about 100 spots) and also has a little market which sells sandwiches on the marina.

There are many golf clubs throughout the islands, and even if you don't play golf, it's a nice spot to eat lunch. The Ko'olina golf club has the famous Roy's restaurant. This chain has restaurants throughout the US, Japan and even in Guam. If you want more than a view of a golf course, you can head out to Mākaha. The Mākaha golf resort has a restaurant overlooking the golf course with a view of the ocean. Also worth visiting is the Kāne'aki *heiau* (ancient Hawaiian temple) up the street from the Mākaha golf resort. The *heiau* was built after 1545, underwent six alterations and restoration was started in 1940 with the supervision of the Bishop Museum staff. Tradition says that in 1795, Kamehameha ordered the *heiau* to be transformed into a war *heiau* (from an agriculture one) to insure his final conquest of Kauai (Kaeha Point nearby points directly at that island). It is considered one of the best preserved *heiau* on O'ahu. The *heiau* is open from 11:00 am–2:00 pm, Monday through Saturday.

BEACH CABINS

There are several ways to stay on the beach in a cabin. Camp Erdman is a wonderful YMCA camp at the far end of the North Shore past the Dillingham Airfield. They have programs for school groups, families and others, which include ropes courses, campfires and mountain hiking. They also have an incredible stretch of unpopulated beach. For college students on break or anyone who loves working vacations, great short-term job opportunities are available.

Another facility along the North Shore a little closer in is the Salvation Army camp. Our church holds its men's retreats at this camp, located right on the beach. The cabins are rough, so pitching a tent (if you don't mind listening to the ocean waves) is recommended.

There are also cabins available for the military and civilian employees at Bellows Air Force Station in Kaneohe. A range of cabins, from nice to roughing it, are all located on the beach with a large sand play area for the kids. This beach is open to the public on the weekends. Information on cabin rates and job opportunities can be found on their website: http://www.bellowsafs.com.

BASE ACTIVITIES

All activities require a military or Department of Defence (DOD) civilian employee ID. Many bases have bowling alleys that are great for kids' birthday parties. Hickam Air Force base has a nice beach for kids. Movie rentals at base libraries are free, as opposed to paying a dollar at the state libraries. There are also no late fees on books or DVDs. Visit the website for DOD base libraries at http://dodhawaiilibraries.org/uhtbin/webcat.

Catching a show at base movie theatres are also inexpensive. The Scholfield Barracks costs $4 for adults (12 and up) and $2 for children (under 11). Pearl Harbor Navy Base costs $3 for adults (12 and up) and $1.50 for children (6–11), while admission is free for those under five.

MOUNTAIN BIKING

If you look around, you can find some bike paths. There is a dirt bike path behind Central O'ahu Park. There is a paved path that stretches all the way through the centre of Waipi'o.

Unlike the bike paths in Colorado and California, there are no high speed bikers frequently whizzing by so this path is perfect for young children weaving along on training wheels.

Another path starts at the Aloha Stadium and ends at Waipahu Depot Road next to the fire station and police training centre in Waipahu. This path winds along the edge of Pearl Harbour waterfront and through Pearl City.

Bike Safety

Put your bike on the front of the bus to head out for some exercise. Don't forget to get your bike when you get off the bus. Recently, a flaw was found with the U-shaped bike locks with the circular key. If you take a Bic ballpoint pen case and jam it in the circular lock and twist is around, you can open the lock. This is a very popular lock that is available at all the chain superstores (Kmart, Wal-Mart, etc.), so the problem hasn't been fixed and people are still buying these locks, unaware of the problem.

One of the sights along the way is the 'mothball fleet'—the navy's harbour parking lot of old ships in Waipahu. For you diehards, this is where the fun begins. Across Waipahu Depot Road is a bridge that is blocked by cement barriers. Carry your bike over the barriers and pipes on the bridge. Follow the dirt road to another bridge where you must carry your bike. Past that bridge, you will find a paved bike trail. This paved trail goes from lower Waipahu all the way to Renton Road in Eva.

For the more technical mountain biker, there are some trails on the highway side of Mililani near Kīpapa Gulch. You take Ka Uka Boulevard across the H2 highway and up Mililani Cemetery Road. There is a point along this road where bikers take off on small paths.

THINGS TO DO

In Hawai'i, there are movie theatres, concert halls, museums, sporting events, Waikīkī showrooms, and, on top of all that, hundreds of tourist attractions and sightseeing spots. For the kids, there is the circus, Sea Life Park, Hawaiian Waters Park, O'ahu train, turtle watching, whale watching and Chinatown. Sports that can be enjoyed are golf, swimming, hiking, surfing, etc. You can even ice skate at the Ice Palace on O'ahu or ski on top of Mauna Kea on the Big Island

The Bishop Museum has Kama'āina discounts and a new Science Adventure Center (with a gigantic volcano) for the kids. The Bishop Museum Press had an artwork contest and my daughter won the grand prize of museum passes and a collection of children's books.

during the winter. Many communities have public pools and
swimming lessons for community members. Central O'ahu
Park has brand new tennis courts that are free to use and a
brand new community pool.

The Hawai'i Data Book has a long list of the most popular
attractions by numbers of people visiting. Here are a few
recommended attractions from the list:

O'ahu

- Bishop Museum
  1525 Bernice Street
  Honolulu, HI 96817
  Tel: (808) 847-3511
  Website: http://www.bishopmuseum.org
- Byodo-In Temple
  47-200 Kahekili Highway
  Kane'ohe, HI 96744-4562
  Tel: (808) 239-8811
- Halawa Xeriscape Garden
  99-1268 Iwaena Street
  'Aiea, HI 96701
  Tel: (808) 748-5041
- Hawai'i Children's Discovery Center
  111 Ohe Street
  Honolulu, HI 96813
  Tel : (808) 524-5437
  Website: http://www.discoverycenterhawaii.org
- 'Iolani Palace
  364 S King Street
  Honolulu, HI 96813
  Tel: (808) 538-1471
  Website: http://www.iolanipalace.org
- Queen Emma Summer Palace
  2913 Pali Highway
  Honolulu, HI 96817-1417
  Tel: (808) 595-316
- Tropic Lighting Museum
  Building 361, Wai'anae Avenue
  Schofield Barracks

Tel: (808) 655-0438
- Hawai'i's Plantation Village
94-695 Waipahu Street
Waipahu, HI 96797-2601
Tel: (808) 677-0110
Website: http://www.hawaiiplantationvillage.org/

Big Island
- Ellison S Onizuka Space Center
Keahole-Kona International Airport, Kailua-Kona
Tel: (808) 329-3441
- Hawai'i Volcanoes National Park
P O Box 52
Hawai'i National Park
HI 96718-0052
Tel: (808) 985-6000
Website: http://www.nps.gov/havo/home.htm
- Parker Ranch
67-1435 Mamalahoa Highway
Kamuela, HI 96743
Tel: (808) 885-7311
Website: http://www.parkerranch.com/
- Volcano Art Center
P O Box 129
Volcano, HI 96785
Tel: (808) 967-8222
Website: http://www.volcanoartcenter.org/

Maui
- Hana Cultural Center
4974 Uakea Street
Hana, Maui, HI 96713
Tel: (808) 248-8622
Website: http://www.hookele.com/hccm
- Lahaina
648 Wharf Street
Lahaina, Maui, HI 96761
Tel: (808) 667-9175
Website: http://www.visitlahaina.com/

- Bailey House Museum
  2375-A Main Street
  Wailuku
  Tel : (808) 244-3326
  Website: http://www.mauimuseum.org/
- Whalers Village
  2435 Ka'anapali Parkway
  Lahaina, HI 96761
  Tel: (808) 661-4567
  Website: http://www.whalersvillage.com
- Maui Tropical Plantation
  1670 Honoapiilani Highway
  Wailuku, HI 96793
  Tel: 808-244-7643
  Website: http://www.mauitropicalplantation.com/

Kaua'i

- Wai'oli Mission House
  Kuhio Highway
  Kauai, HI 96766
  Tel: (808) 245-3202
  Website: http://www.hawaiimuseums.org/mc/iskauai_
  waioli.htm
- Kōke'e Natural Historical Museum
  Mile Marker 15 Kokee Road
  Kekaha, Kaua'i, HI 96752
  Tel: (808) 335-9975
  Website: http://www.kokee.org/
- Kīlauea National Wildlife Refuge
  Kilauea Lighthouse Road
  Kilauea, HI 96754
  Tel: (808) 828-1413

Moloka'i

- Kalaupapa Settlement
  106 Pauahi Street
  Kalaupapa, HI 96742
  Tel: (808) 567-6928

LEARNING THE LANGUAGE

CHAPTER 8

THERE'S NOTHING WRONG IN HERE. HE SHOULD BE ABLE TO LEARN THE LANGUAGE

'The Hawaiian uneasiness with compliments,
a feeling that praise invites the blessing to be
rescinded."Pupuka keia keiki"—"this baby is ugly"—
might have been a familiar introduction to a new baby
in the old days. For example, (Hawaiian Kapuna)
Keli'ia'a said, "How many times have you heard folks say,
'Eh, you some ugly, braddah!' as a friendly greeting." '
—'Comparing Cultural Differences Results in Common Bonds'
Wade Shirkey, *The Honolulu Advertiser*, 14 May 1999

SIX MONTHS BEFORE MOVING, I vacationed here with my wife and kids. We experienced the wonderful customer service as tourists but we wanted to get a real sense of the local people so we drove out to Leeward and Central O'ahu.

At the Daiei supermarket fish counter, there were varieties of fish I had never seen. The guy behind the counter looked at me.

I pointed at a red fillet of fish that kind of looked like tuna, "What is this?"

"*Ahu.*"

"Is it like tuna?"

He pointed over his shoulder at the wall. There were several trophy fish mounted on the wall.

He pointed to a big one at the end, "That one."

I remembered that tuna was a huge fish and he was pointing to the biggest fish on the wall.

I asked again, "Isn't that tuna?"

He smirked, "*Ahu,* is the Hawaiian name."

Learning Hawaiian will not only give you language skills but might also save you some face. It is your job to learn the culture, not theirs to teach it to you. Learning the language gives you a valuable window into the culture—you learn the minds of the people. However, if you don't have time to learn the Hawaiian language, don't worry. You can still communicate with the locals by learning some frequently used words from Hawaiian and other languages.

Opened to public, this huge maze is found at the Dole Plantation. The Dole company is one of the world's major producers of pineapples and other fruit.

Visitors enter the USS Arizona Memorial, which marks the resting place of the sailors killed on the USS *Arizona* during the attack on Pearl Harbor in 1941.

Hawai'i is known for its high level of volcanic activity, as seen here from the lava flow at the Kilauea Volcano on Big Island

Surrounded by the city of Honolulu, Punchbowl Crater was used by early Hawaiians as a sacrificial ground, and today serves as the site of the National Memorial Cemetery of the Pacific.

The enormous waves generated off the coast of Hawai'i make it one of the most exciting and challenging surfing spots in the world.

THE HAWAIIAN LANGUAGE
—ALPHABET AND PRONUNCIATION

Hawaiian is a dialect of the Polynesian language, so there are similarities with other Polynesian languages such as Tahitian, Marquesan, Maoris, Samoan, etc. The early Christian missionaries converted the Hawaiian language into writing. The alphabet has twelve letters: the five vowels and seven consonants—**h**, **k**, **l**, **m**, **n**, **p**, **w**. In some words, the letter **w** is pronounced like a 'v'.

Hawaiian language also uses an *'okina* (glottal stop) that is an audible release of air, almost like a quick pause. The pause is similar to the one in 'uh-oh' or 'oh-oh'. The *'okina* is considered another consonant, so treat it like a letter when pronouncing words. Look in the Hawaiian dictionary and you will see that the *'okina* is a very frequent consonant in many words in the Hawaiian language. The character used for this is a left single quotation mark or reverse apostrophe ('). The word Hawai'i has an *'okina* in it, so don't be surprised when you hear people pronouncing it the proper way.

With the increasing revival of the Hawaiian language, we are bound to see more of it in everyday life. Part of the revival is the proper use of the language and this includes writing it with the *'okina* (glottal stop) and *kahakō* (macron). The *kahakō* is a line over the vowels: **ā**, **ē**, **ī**, **ō**, **ū**. Vowels with a *kahakō* are stressed and pronounced slightly longer.

When looking around, you will see the *'okina* is written differently in many places as ` or ' or ´ and the *kahakō* is sometimes used or just left out. The Hawaiian dictionary uses traditional ' for the *'okina*. You will find some books use ' and others use ` for the *'okina*, and of those, some use the *kahakō*. Newspapers frequently use ' and less frequently the *kahakō*. Street names on street signs in Hawai'i have both the *'okina* with a ' and the *kahakō* (i.e. **ā**, **ē**, **ī**, **ō**, **ū**).

Five vowels sounds:

a	*ah about*
e	*eh get*
i	*ee bee*
o	*oh bone*
u	*oo boo*

Similar to learning Japanese, when vowels are side by side, it is easier to remember the sound of the vowel combinations, then pronouncing each individual vowel.

For example:

oi	as in *boy*
ia	*ee yah* (two sounds in quick succession)
io	*yo*
iu	*you*
ei	as in *lei*
ae	*aye*
ai	as in *my*, Lahaina as 'Lah-HAI-na'
ao	as in *now*
au	Maui as 'MOW-ee'

Both **ao** and **au** have similar pronounciation but rise to their 'o' or 'u'.

- For the rising 'u':
  Kaua'i—Kau-(W)AH-'-ee
  Don't forget the 'uh-oh' glottal stop.
- For the rising 'o':
  Makawao—MA-ka-WOW (town on the island of Maui)

When pronouncing the words, not only do you need to remember the glottal stop and long vowels, you must also remember the accents. In the Hawaiian dictionary, the accent is made with periods. Accents fall after vowels. Long vowels take precedence over accents.

If you are coming from Japan or have studied Japanese, the pronunciation of Hawaiian may come easier to you. Hawaiian is similar to Japanese in that each consonant is tied to a vowel, but vowels can also stand alone. This makes it easier to pronounce because you break up each word into vowel-consonant pairs. For example, with repeating words, this is easy to do: the word *hulihuli* becomes 'hu-li-hu-li'.

The Hawaiian dictionary also breaks up words by accent to make them easier to pronounce. For example, the name of Queen Ka'ahumanu (wife of Kamehameha I) has been used for street names and building names. In the dictionary, it is accented 'Ka.'ahu.manu'. Break up a word according to this accent and it makes it easier to say. Another frequently spoken name is Queen Lili'uokalani (the last monarch of the Hawaiian kingdom), which is pronounced 'Liliʻu.o.ka.lani'.

The best method for pronouncing Hawaiian words is to break them up into their vowel-consonant pairs and by accent. Now try Kamehameha. The dictionary accents it like this: 'Kameha.meha'. Or one with a double vowel pair: Kalākaua is 'Kala.kaua'—'Kala kow a'. When you can say these words correctly, you know you are on your way to pronouncing Hawaiian.

Computers and the Hawaiian Language

Nowadays, Mac and PC computers allow you to type the accent marks for characters of the Hawaiian alphabet. For example, on Mac computers under system preferences in the international icon, you can select Hawaiian from the list of foreign languages. This allows you to type Hawaiian language using a regular keyboard. For ā, ē, ī, ō, ū, press the option key in combination with the vowel. For the glottal stop ʻ, you don't need to press the option key, just the ʻ key.

However, many websites use ' and ` and not the reverse apostrophe (ʻ) or the macron (i.e. ā, ē, ī, ō, ū) because some older web browsers and search engines don't have Hawaiian language support and because it is tedious to write the html coding for these Hawaiian characters. Hawaiian language supporters are trying to get the state and city governments to use the proper spelling of Hawaiian words—using the ʻokina (glottal stop) and kahakō (macron)—on their websites.

A great online Hawaiian dictionary that uses the ʻokina and kahakō is on the Ulukau Hawaiian Electronic Library located at:
http://www.wehewehe.org

Many Hawaiian words are onomatopoeic. Many words are also repeated. Some are for repeated action. Examples of these include:

Ahiahi	Evening
ʻAuʻau	Bathe

Ha'iha'i	Talk back and forth
Hilahila	Embarrassed, shy, ashamed
Hoehoe	Paddle constantly
Holoholo	To go for a walk or ride
Honihoni	Kiss repeatedly or smell
Huihui	Mix, mingle
Hulihuli	Turn repeatedly, as in *hulihuli* barbecue chicken
Kilakila	Majestic, imposing
Makemake	Want, desire
Nahenahe	Gentle, sweet, soft
Onaona	Fragrant, aroma, alluring
Pokepoke	To chop
Wehewehe	To explain
Wikiwiki	Hurry, quick. *Wiki* is a Hawaiian language word that has entered the English vocabulary. According to the Wikipedia, a *wiki* is a group of web pages that allows users to add content, as on an Internet forum, but also allows others (often completely unrestricted) to edit the content.

Many place names (cities, roads, hotels, condominiums) in Hawai'i have meanings:

Honolulu	Protected bay
Waikīkī	Spouting water
Waikele	Still water with silt
Ala Moana	Seaway

Lumi'au'au (Street)	Bathroom
Lumi'aina (Street)	Dining room
Kaulana	Famous
'Ilikai	Surface of the sea
Ho'omaka	To begin
Kailua	Two seas
Ala Wai	Way of water
Kīlauea	Rising cloud of smoke
Lanikai	Heavenly ocean
Mauna Loa	Long mountain
Mauna Kea	White mountain
Puna	Coral
Waipi'o	Arching water
Kapi'olani	Heavenly arch
Wailua	Two waters
Waimea	Reddish waters
Mililani	To praise or give thanks

Some examples of Hawaiian personal names are: Noelani (heavenly mist), Puanani (beautiful flower), Momi (pearl or precious one), Leilani (heavenly *lei*) and last names such as Kāne (after the Hawaiian god of creation, sun and fertility).

There are two ways to make your name into a Hawaiian one: either by sound or by meaning. My first name, Russell, by sound is Lukela in Hawaiian. We gave our children Japanese first names and American middle names. My daughter's name, Minami, means beautiful wave in Japanese so her Hawaiian name is Nanikai (literally 'beautiful wave').

American names are harder because you have to find out what your name means first then translate it into Hawaiian. My name, Brent, means steep

Interest in the Hawaiian language

The author of the book *Hawaiian Street Names* gave a presentation on publishing at the Kapolei library. When promoting his book he noticed that only Caucasians and Hawaiians bought it.

Moanalua Dog Park is one of the first 'bark parks' in Honolulu. *Īlio hau'oli pāka* literally means 'dog happy park'. Dogs were brought to Hawai'i by the Polynesians and also eaten as food. Some considered dogs a spiritual *'aumakua*.

hill, so according to one book, a Hawaiian equivalent of that might be Kahakea.

My son's name, Kouhei (a common name in Japan), means peaceful sailing or smooth sailing in Japanese. His Hawaiian name would be Maluholo.

LOCAL ENGLISH ACCENT AND PIDGIN

I was surprised by the English accent here in Hawai'i. After being an English teacher in Japan, I had become accustomed to non-native speakers' English pronunciation and accent. I had travelled around Asia to countries like Taiwan, Thailand and Singapore, and had gotten so good that I could tell you what country an Asian was from by their English accent.

The locals in Hawai'i are obviously native English speakers, but the accent and word usage made it difficult to for me to understand. It is a bit more than another regional American accent like in New York or in southern USA. It is sort of a surfer accent with the dragging of words, with some sentences ending with 'yah' and 'brah'.

Pidgin English or Hawaiian Creole English was a language used by the plantation workers, and it is still used today. Pidgin was the formation of a shared language between the many non-native English speakers of Hawai'i. Creole is a mother tongue language that evolves after the pidgin stage, with many native-born speakers. Some consider it pidgin English, others Hawaiian Creole. There are books you can learn pidgin from and even a class at the University of Hawai'i.

Pidgin English

There is the local English accent and then there is pidgin English. One day, the electricians came in and starting saying something between themselves that sounded like English but I couldn't understand a word of it. Then one of them smiled and said something to me. I smiled back, not having any clue what he just said because he was speaking pidgin English.

However, pidgin isn't a matter of education. It is more a local way to identify with other locals. People who speak pidgin also speak regular English. Half the population of Hawai'i knows how to speak pidgin. English aside, that's more speakers than Hawaiian, Japanese, Filipino or any other language.

Drop letters, syllables, words; change the order and run words together to make pidgin. Pidgin mixes mainly English words, but many words also come from the Hawaiian, Japanese, Chinese and Portuguese languages. To understand pidgin, you may need to study some Hawaiian or at least the Hawaiian words listed in the glossary.

Some Japanese Words

- *Issei*: a first generation Japanese immigrant to another country
- *Nisei*: a second generation Japanese immigrant to another country
- *Sansei*: a third generation Japanese immigrant to another country
- *Kibei*: a second generation Japanese from Hawai'i educated in Japan
- *Bachi*: It serves you right! Divine punishment. Sort of like bad karma—do something bad and it will return to punish you

Island with many languages: Japanese words on a memorial stone at the Hawai'i Okinawa Center.

Some locals think it's fun to speak pidgin and it feels familiar and friendly to them. They may even speak it to newcomers—don't bother to pretend to understand what they are saying to you, they will just have more 'fun' with you. It isn't necessary to learn pidgin and locals may look at you weirdly if you try to speak it. Pidgin is their way of keeping their local identity. However, let's have some 'fun' and try to figure it out.

Pidgin English	Translation
Brah	Pal
Bruddah	Brother
Tutu	Granny
Sista	Sister
Hapa (originally *hapa-haole*)	Meaning half-white or sometimes mixed ethnicity
Da	The
Dat	That
An den?	And then?

Pidgin English	Translation
K den	Okay
Doz	Those
Befo	Before
Mas	Must
Ax	Ask
Grind	Eat
Grinds	Food
Kaukau	Food
Cockaroach	Steal
Kakio	Cuts and scratches
Stink eye	Dirty look
Ass right	That's right
Lolo	Stupid
Boddah	Bother
Shaka	Hello, goodbye, thank you, right on, hang loose—the thumb-and-pinkie salute—a greeting that symbolises pride and local identity
Tita	Local girl (sometimes tough looking)
Moke	Local guy (sometimes tough looking)
Zori	Rubber thong/slippers
Shishi	Urinate (from the Japanese word oshiko)
Janken po	Rock, scissor, paper (a hand/finger game)
Coastie	Coast guard
Kain, kine	Kind
Any kine	Any kind
All kine (kain)	All kinds of
Chicken skin	Goose bumps

Pidgin English	Translation
Da kine	Anything to which you are referring
Bumbye	By and by, later on
Shoots	Alright
Neva	Never
Town	Honolulu
Townie	Someone who grew up in Honolulu
Yobo	A Korean person
Shibai	Lies or bullshit
Babooze	Dumb
Boss	A mess, messy

Pidgin Phrases	Translation
Can!	Yes, that is OK!
Can-not, No can	Not possible
Wha fo?	Why?
Make quick	Be quick
No act	Stop or don't do something
What fo you talk like dat?	Why do you talk like that?
Wassamatta you?	What's the matter with you?
Brok da mout!	Delicious!
Hybolic	Intellectual/pompous words
Howzit brah?	How ya doin, pal?
Cheapes wan	Cheapest one
Hele on	Let's go (*hele* is Hawaiian for 'to go')
Wa lie beef?	Wanna fight? You want trouble?
Bigga dolla	More money

Pidgin Phrases	Translation
Talk story	Shoot the breeze, chew the fat
Talk stink	Say nasty things about someone
Kau kau time	Time to eat
Mo betta	Is better, good going
Buckaloose	Get out of control
Geeve um	Go for it
He fo do 'um	He is the one to do it
No make li' dat	Don't act like that

Pidgin Today

Lois-Ann Yamanaka, a local author, took a writing class in college. She tried to avoid writing in pidgin but her instructor told her she should write in pidgin because that was her writing 'voice'. She is popular for her short novels which she writes entirely in pidgin English. Some say she is more popular on the mainland than in Hawai'i because her novel is said to have a racist characterisation of a Filipino character. Along with the revival of ethnic culture, there seems to be a revival of pride in pidgin. A popular book in the local bookstores is a set of *Pidgin to Da Max* books.

Broke da mouth: pidgen English is also commonly used in advertising.

STYLE SWITCHING

People who speak two languages sometimes have different personalities when they use the different languages. When speaking another language, there is more to it than a set of words. There are many mannerisms, ways of initiating conversation and even topics of conversation that typify another language. For example, when the Japanese try to speak English, they find themselves having to move their mouths and lips more, use hand gestures, make eye contact, etc.

One lady grew up here but was also married to a mainlander. When she spoke to me, it was different from when she spoke to a local. She changed her accent and even the topics of conversation she used. She was switching styles like someone who spoke two different languages but she was still speaking English. In Hawai'i, it is still English, but there are different accents, expressions and topics of conversation, even if they aren't speaking in pidgin English.

WORKING IN HAWAI'I

CHAPTER 9

'I am always telling our federal agencies
and contractors that if they bring work to Hawai'i,
they need to hire Hawai'i residents.'
—Hawai'i Senator Daniel Akaka

THE ECONOMY

The original trade with the Western world was in sandalwood (used for chests and incense) and whaling later supported the economy of Hawai'i. Eventually, whales grew scarce and petroleum was discovered, which replaced the need for oil from whale fat.

In the last hundred years, sugar and pineapple plantations first drove the economy, then later military spending and finally tourism. Plantations and military spending are still a part of the economy, but tourism tops the chart.

In 2005, according to the state's Department of Labor and Industrial Relations, the unemployment rate stood at 2.8 per cent, down from 3.3 per cent in 2004, 3.9 per cent in 2003 and 4.1 per cent in 2002. According to *The Honolulu Advertiser*, unemployment in March 2005 (at 2.8 per cent) was the lowest since 'the Japanese economic bubble was powering Hawaii's economy 14 years ago.'

The Honolulu Advertiser also explains that the current economy is fueled by 'robust real estate and construction market and growing tourism sector' with the majority of the new jobs coming from the service sector. And according to the Department of Labor and Industrial Relations, 2005's increase in jobs were fueled by construction, trade, transportation and utilities.

Tourism is the main economy of Hawai'i and a big source of jobs. Tourism increases and decreases as a result of many forces. It declined because of war (Desert Storm), threat of disease (SARS) and threat of terrorism (9/11). The Japanese stopped coming during all of these events. Yet, tourism increased because of natural disasters at tourist spots on the mainland (Hurricane Katrina) as more Americans started coming to Hawai'i.

Look in the newspaper classifieds and there are plenty of jobs. Walking around Waikele Outlets and other shopping areas, there are signs on many retail stores and restaurants seeking employees. The problem is that none of these jobs pay a living wage.

One study conducted in the 1990s claimed that a family in Hawai'i could receive up to US$ 36,000 worth of welfare benefits (including food stamps, health insurance, etc.) This study was flawed and inaccurate, but it does give you an indication of the gap between welfare and the living wage jobs in Hawai'i. The retail and restaurant jobs pay less than this (average US$ 10 an hour). If welfare is an indication of poverty, then these are poverty level jobs. On the other hand, Hawai'i is a 'feminine values' society, so that may explain why it has higher levels of welfare benefits.

About 585,300 people are employed in Hawai'i; that's around 50 per cent of the population. To say that half the people here are working is surprising, when you consider that there are many retirees and children. Although Hawai'i currently has the lowest unemployment rate in the nation, families are still struggling. Many people hold down more than one job.

There was a time in Hawai'i, maybe 20 years ago, when only those who wanted bigger houses and a more expensive lifestyle went to the mainland. People came to Hawai'i to take it easy instead of worrying about getting ahead. But now, people are moving to the mainland because it's difficult to make ends meet in Hawai'i. Every year, thousands of people move to the mainland to work and live.

Governor Linda Lingle said, "Good schools, good jobs, good government. These are not unreasonable demands. But sadly, some of our people have already lost heart and have left Hawai'i to look for these things elsewhere."

COLLECTIVISM AND RACIAL PREFERENCE

In 1970, American sociologist Frederick Samuels, for his book *The Japanese and Haoles of Honolulu*, did a survey and found one of the top complaints about prejudice was preferential hiring. Both Japanese and whites complained that the other had a tendency to hire people of the same race. Even more interesting was the acknowledgment by both Japanese and whites that preferential hiring was being done by their own kind. However, Samuels concluded that the lack of good jobs is the primary basis for prejudice. This appears to be still true today, but some say it's not a matter of race but of who you know.

Everyone from the ranks of the unemployed and lowly paid service sector are competing for the better jobs. They are not joking when they say it's hard to get a living wage job here. It's no surprise that residents of Hawai‘i resent immigrants from the mainland or other countries coming in and taking the good jobs, so they try to hire someone local first. This goes back to the plantation days when people had to stick together and be loyal to their group to survive. Collectivist value loyalty to the group.

Favouritism in the Workplace

The Bishop Museum has a daily show in the main exhibition hall. One man sings ancient songs in Hawaiian while a couple of girls dance the *hula* to the music. After he finishes his songs, he introduces his nephew who helps with the show. He also introduces the two *hula* dancers as his nieces. He is proud because he got them jobs at the museum and he explains that his brother's family has him over every third Sunday for dinner and thanks him profusely for getting them jobs. This is the way people in a collectivist society like Hawai‘i find jobs, and this is also why it makes it so hard for newcomers to get jobs. There are no cries of nepotism or favouritism in the hiring process. Instead this man is morally obligated to help out his extended family and could never think of saying no.

If you are a newcomer from the mainland, locals think you can always go back to the mainland if it doesn't work out here. Some locals feel they do not have the option of going to the mainland to live and work. It is difficult to leave their families and it will be difficult for them to get jobs here if they want to return to Hawai'i. Also, they may take vacations to the mainland and they see how Asian-Americans are stereotyped and feel the prejudice. Lastly, it is difficult because they are used to being on the top of the pecking order in Hawai'i and on the mainland, that would be reversed. There is one phenomenon of the mainland called the Bamboo Ceiling. Like the glass ceiling for minorities, Asian-Americans on the mainland are finding it hard to move up.

PUTTING COCONUTS ON THE TABLE
According to a lady working at the unemployment office, a lot of jobs do not get advertised and are through word of mouth. For these jobs, you need to know someone. Do not be fooled by the 2.8 per cent unemployment rate, it means nothing here because there are so many people who already have a job but are applying for a better job. Many people are working part-time or on contract, hoping to eventually find something better.

There are people who grew up in Hawai'i but are presently living on the mainland who are trying to get work here so they can move back to Hawai'i. Many people from the mainland also want to live in Hawai'i and apply for jobs here. The temporary employment agency Manpower, to avoid getting so many applicants from the mainland, requires that applicants be available for an in-person interview within 48 hours. Many companies mention in their job advertisements that they will not pay relocation costs. The State of Hawai'i only allows residents of Hawai'i to apply for state civil service jobs (but interestingly enough, they also allow former residents to apply), with a few exceptions such as police officers and life guards.

Some people say to succeed here, you need to bring or start your own business. The Pacific Gateway Center offers immigrants small business loans and helps them start their own businesses. There is also a local organisation called the Service Corps of Retired Executives (SCORE, website: http://www.hawaiiscore.org) that has retired businesspeople who volunteer to help and consult entrepreneurs on starting and running their own businesses.

Lastly, it's not what you know, it's who you know and how you will fit in. In a collectivist society, what's important is how you will fit into the group and the best way to find that out is by talking with others. Recommendations are more important than your qualifications or how well you do in an interview. Of course, I was able to get a job in Hawai'i but this shocked a lot of locals who couldn't believe I got a university job without knowing anyone.

How I Got My Job

I had been applying to jobs in Hawai'i for a year and got an interview with the University of Hawai'i at Hilo and another one for a Colorado State University position located at Schofield Barracks. I was over-qualified for both jobs and they ended up hiring someone who already lived in Hawai'i.

After that, I applied to Leeward Community College for a job in December and was told I wasn't qualified because I didn't have the right Bachelors degree. I appealed the decision stating that the job requirements in the ad didn't require a specific degree. HR found me eligible a week later and forwarded my resume to the hiring committee.

A month and a half later, the hiring manager contacted me to set up an interview. I had the interview in March on the phone with a committee of five: two Japanese, one Chinese, one Caucasian and one *hapa* (half Caucasian and Japanese). I continued to email my interest in the position several times until I was made an offer in June. I started in August.

The salary was 25 per cent lower than my mainland salary (I had the exact same position at Colorado State University). I requested a higher rate but they couldn't raise the salary because it was based on the position classification and the number of years of work experience.

JOB ASSISTANCE

If you come to Hawai'i without a job, you can use the facilities provided by the State of Hawaii's Workforce Development Department (WDD). Register at one of their several locations and they will contact you if they have anything that fits you. At the WDD office, there are computers with Internet access for you to use in your job hunt. There are also free services like a printer, fax machine and copier. The WDD counsellors give great advice about the job search in Hawai'i. They tend to

WE'D LIKE TO HIRE YOU. WE JUST HAVE TO GET REFERENCES FROM YOUR FRIENDS AND RELATIVES ALREADY WITH THE ORGANISATION.

be better than the temp agencies because they aren't trying to sell you on the jobs they have; they are just there to help you.

Contractors in Hawai'i

This is the list that the WDD counsellor gave me of federal contractors that have positions in Hawai'i.

- ACS
  Website: http://www.acs-inc.com/career/index.html
- AECOM Combat Service Support
  Website: http://www.aecom-gsi.com
- Anteon Corporation
  Website: http://www.anteon.com/careers/careers.htm
- Alliant Techsystems Inc
  Website: http://www.atk.com/homepage
- BAE Systems
  Website: http://www.baesystems.com/careers
- Boeing
  Website:http://www.boeing.com
- Booz Allen Hamilton
  Website: http://boozallen.com

(Continued on the next page)

(Continued from previous page)

- CACI International Inc
  Website: http://www.caci.com/job/search.shtml
- Computer Sciences Corporation
  Website: http://careers.csc.com
- Dyncorp
  Website: http://recruiting.dyncorp.com
- General Dynamics
  Website: http://www.generaldynamics.com
- GTSI
  Website: http://www.gtsi.com
- Halliburton
  Website: http://www.halliburton.com/careers/index.jsp
- Honeywell
  Website: http://www.honeywell.com
- ITT Industries
  Website: http://www.itt.com/careers
- Lockheed Martin Corporation
  Website: http://www.lockheedmartin.com
- Mantech Internatioinal Corporation
  Website: http://www.mantech.com
- Northrup Grunman Corporation
  Website: http://www.northgrum.com
- Quantum Research International
  Website: http://www.quantum-intl.com/careers.htm
- Raytheon Corporation
  Website: http://www.raytheon.com
- Resource Consultants Inc
  Website: http://www.resourceconsultants.com
- RS Information Systems
  Website: http://www.rsis.com
- The Systex Group
  Website: http://www.sytexgroup.com/careers.htm
- TITAN
  Website: http://www.titan.com

(Continued on the next page)

(Continued from previous page)

- SAIC
  Website: http://www.saic.com/career
- United Technologies Corporation
  Website: http://www.utcjobs.com
- Vinnell Corporation
  Website: http://www.vinnell.com
- Wackenhut
  Website: http://www.wackenhut.com
- MPRI
  Website: http://www.mpri.com
- KBR
  Website: http://www.kbr.com
- Actus Lend Lease
  Website: http://www.actuslendlease.com

One WDD counsellor specialises in helping veterans find jobs. With a security clearance, it's a cinch to land a great paying job. For those who aren't veterans and without a security clearance, there are still other avenues. The veteran counsellor has a list of companies who contract with the military. You can contact these companies directly to find out about contract positions available on the many military bases. According to the veteran counsellor, this can be a much easier way to get a position than through the regular federal employment process, and the contract positions pay better.

Hawai'i Workforce Informer, powered by the Department of Labor and Industrial Relations, has information on top jobs in Hawai'i at http://www.hiwi.org/. They have a list of sectors with the most projected job openings in Hawai'i. It's a list of high turnover or low-paid jobs like waiters, maids, retail sales, cooks, groundskeepers, cashiers and clerks. Each of these jobs has from a thousand to several hundred annual job openings.

On the other hand, Hawai'i's fastest growing jobs are computer (networking, programming, etc); health and medical (counselling, nursing, etc); trades (carpenter, electrician, etc); and business (PR, sales, etc), but most of these have under a hundred annual job openings. The Workforce Informer website has the following jobs listed as both the fastest growing and most projected job openings up to the year 2012:

- elementary and secondary school teachers and teacher assistants
- sailors and marine oilers
- special education teachers in preschool, kindergarten and elementary schools
- self-enrichment education teachers
- vocational education teachers (post-secondary)
- carpenters
- education administrators in elementary and secondary schools
- childcare workers
- construction labourers
- biological science teachers (post-secondary)
- educational, vocational and school counsellors
- correctional officers and jailers
- transportation attendants, excluding flight attendants and baggage porters
- captains, mates and pilots of water vessels
- business teachers (post-secondary)
- combined food preparation and serving workers, including fast food

Many jobs like retail sales, tourism, airport, wedding, etc. look for people who are bilingual in Japanese and English because there are so many customers from Japan. The Japanese customers seem to prefer native Japanese speakers so therefore the employers do too. There is a large pool of Japanese-speaking people in Hawai'i, so they may get first shot at a job that doesn't require a native speaker. The Japanese newspaper *Nikkan Sun* has lots of jobs listed every week in Japanese. One interesting job is working as a preacher at one of the local chapels doing marriage ceremonies in Japanese for Japanese tourists.

VOLUNTEER WORK

Aloha United Way (AUW) maintains a website (http://www.auw.org) with hundreds of volunteer opportunities available in Hawai'i. It is the biggest contact point for volunteer jobs in Hawai'i and is located at http://search.volunteerhawaii.org/volunteer. You can also call tel: 211 and they can search for opportunities for you. There are also several volunteer opportunities for immigrants and also for helping immigrants.

BUSINESS ATTIRE

Some locals show up late at work wearing a US$ 4 pair of Locals, Surfah or Old Navy slippers. They have on their Bermuda shorts and usually a T-shirt with something written on it relating to Hawai'i, such as a local surf shop, restaurant, etc. You may blend in if you're dressed like this and it's not a professional business environment.

Business and office attire could be considered the equivalent of the mainland's 'business casual' with the twist of an *aloha* shirt. In downtown, you see businessmen and people who work at the university don their *aloha* shirts. Instead of suits, these men have a whole wardrobes full of *aloha* shirts. Typical business attire is a silk *aloha* shirt (you don't wear ties with *aloha* shirts), slacks with a belt, loafers and socks. For women, it is also business casual—no suits, just slacks and blouse or a dress. Fabrics such as rayon are more light and comfortable in the heat.

During the welcoming ceremony for you at your new job, you may be given a *lei*. They will give a hug and touch your cheek with theirs in the traditional Hawaiian fashion. You may wonder how long you are supposed to wear the *lei*. Typically, people wear them all day and go home with them. It also gives other people a chance to recognise your special day or achievement. You will also find out there are different kinds of *leis* for men and women, maybe a *kukui nut lei* for a guy and a fragrant flower for a woman. It is typical for politicians and other people to wear an *aloha* shirt and a *lei* for a picture in the newspaper.

LOCAL WAYS AT WORK AND BUSINESS

Sometimes, high-level positions are filled with people from mainland. However, even a CEO or a university president from the mainland can stumble on local ways. Former president of UH, Evan Dobelle, didn't stay long in his position before being ousted by the Board of Regents. Some 'stink' that it was cultural differences that caused his failure.

The *Star Bulletin* had several commentaries on where he failed:

Paul Costello, a former vice president for Dobelle, said that Dobelle 'rubs some of the establishment the wrong way. Maybe he talks too loudly or is too brash, blunders into local sacred ground or doesn't pay appropriate homage.'

Political columnist Richard Borreca, wrote: '[Dobelle] equates the nods and positive replies as approval, not factoring in the polite local style 'yes' meaning 'yes, I understand you' rather than 'yes, I agree with you'.'

On the other hand, one local man wrote an editorial letter to *The Honolulu Advertiser*: 'Nobody's held accountable; we bring people in (from the mainland) to solve our problems, then we kick them out.' He felt that the people of Hawai'i needed to become aware of this fact and take responsibility for doing this.

One reporter wrote in *The Honolulu Advertiser*: 'While Honolulu has long been as cosmopolitan as any large city on the Mainland, an intense localism still defines many social and business relationships, and Dobelle's East Coast confidence sometimes came across as arrogance.'

CRONYISM IN POLITICS

The incident of firing the president of UH, Evan Dobelle, again brought to question Hawai'i politics and cronyism. UH Vice President Costello claimed that the new governor used her political appointees on the Board of Regents to oust Dobelle because he had endorsed her opponent in the election for governor. Some say he showed the level of his arrogance in doing so.

One man wrote to the *Honolulu Star Bulletin*: 'We can't wait to get back to sodden, old-crony mediocrity? When Dobelle was hired, I wondered how long such a man would be tolerated by the old guard.'

Ironically, Dobelle was accused of cronyism when he hired many of his friends from the mainland for top positions and paid them more than their predecessors.

An article on 26 April 1999 in *The Honolulu Advertiser* stated:

Mediocrity

In the Hawaiian proverb 'Crabs In The Bucket', one crab tries to climb out of the bucket then the other crabs grab on him and pull him back down into the bucket. In an article in *The Chronicle of Higher Education*, Mr Dobelle said the people in Hawai'i had clawed and pulled each other into a trap of sustained mediocrity just like the crabs in the bucket.

'The plantation solidarity that brought Hawaii's races together also is credited with creating an 'old boy' network of cronyism that pervades politics, state government and the job market today.'

However, it isn't all an old boy network and Governor Lingle as an example of a mainlander immigrant breaking in. She is a Caucasian originally from Saint Louis, Missouri, who moved to Hawai'i when she was 12 with her family. She got her degree in California and moved back to Hawai'i. She worked her way up as a politician from Maui County Council to the position of mayor of Maui County to the seat of the governor of Hawai'i in 2002.

DO'S AND DON'TS IN THE WORKPLACE

Locals use 'talk story' to build a rapport before getting down to business. Even Governor Lingle has a weekly 'talk story' radio show. In a business setting, participate in talk story and let others do it, even if it seems like that is all they are doing. That same secretary or co-worker will come through when there is work to be done—sometimes by calling all these different people that they have been talking story with because they have built a rapport with them through their constant chats.

Go to the *'ohana* picnics for work, family or school, and it's OK to arrive on Hawaiian time. It is especially important to attend a baby *lū'au* and a high school graduation. It is looked on as very bad if you do not attend at least some of these events that are part of your *'ohana*. People sometimes make up excuses such as an aunt who died on another island to get out of *'ohana* events like graduations. But this is believed to creates bad *bachi*.

Hawaiian time sometimes applies to the workplace too. Some departments expect you to follow the clock while others are more flexible. You can have two different departments across the hall from each other—one department has a person watching TV at his desk, and the other department has someone else constantly working overtime.

Pa'a ka waha, nana ka maka; hana ka lima (literal translation: shut the mouth; observe with the eyes; work with the hands) from Mary Kawena Pukui's *'Olelo No'eau: Hawaiian Proverbs and Poetical Sayings* means that one learns by listening, observing and doing. Whether you're adjusting to a new job in Hawai'i or Hawai'i's culture in general, people will expect you to keep quiet while you learn the lay of the land. It is important to understand everyone's opinions and abilities before making a suggestion or offering a solution.

According to UH Professor of Management and Industrial Relations, Richard Brislin, people in Hawai'i attach their self-esteem to their opinions. If you attack their opinion, you attack them personally.

In the workplace, find out everyone's position or opinion then make sure your solution takes into consideration those viewpoints. You can even run your proposal past individuals beforehand. Build consensus and understanding outside of meetings and group discussions.

Don't talk stink. It's a small town mentality and people talk stink as much as they talk story—so reputation is more important. On the mainland, it's easy to do things like job-hop and not get a bad reputation in your field, but people here talk. Be careful not to burn any bridges. Even on O'ahu where there are three-quarter of a million people, it's still a small town atmosphere.

With locals, communication tends to be indirect, in an effort

Hard work is a value ingrained in the locals of Hawai'i. The plantations involved long hours of work for little pay. Later, immigrants came to Hawai'i and struggled with working long hours at tough jobs. Descendants of these immigrants grew up in households with strong work ethics. Many people today hold down more than one job in order to make ends meet. They work hard but when they go home, they get back on Hawaiian time and live the island pace.

to maintain harmony and prevent anyone from losing face. Therefore, when working with them, it is important to understand that sometimes a suggestion should be treated as a direct request.

Bring food for the break room. There is always something in the break room someone has brought from their last trip, off the tree in their yard, or bought in bulk from the superstore (like candy, etc).

If it's work related, appearances are sometimes more important than facts. You may have to appear to be busy even if you are taking a break. I took walks on my breaks but my supervisor told me that people were getting the impression that I didn't have any work to do. Pay attention to how you appear or are perceived by others.

Kōkua or helpfulness is seen in the many fundraisers that are announced at your child's school or in the emails you receive from your co-workers at work. If you can help out, do so.

Locals all agree that it's not what you know, it's who you know. This results in cronyism in business and politics and everyday life like getting a job or finding a house. There is a system of returning favours and taking care of one's own.

Adjusting to the Hawaiian Work Environment

My neighbour is a mechanic on contract to the military. He has had to learn how to overlook the cronyism and low pay at work and to live on Hawaiian time.

He has extensive experience from the military and holds a security clearance. He thinks that he had gotten the job because they couldn't refuse him. All his co-workers are cousins and nephews of someone who works there.

He says he is one of the top paid mechanics there and makes US$ 25 an hour. His co-workers all have more than one job, because they don't want to live in a town house anymore and bought houses.

When he was looking for a job and doing job interviews, the interviewers always showed up late. It also frustrated him that all his co-workers were in a laid-back 'mode' and nothing got done. It drove him nuts. He still hasn't really gotten used to Hawaiian time after living here for eight years. It is more of a personality clash than a culture clash—he just likes to be a scheduled person. But nevertheless, he is slowly learning how to overlook the cronyism, low pay and to live on Hawaiian time.

BEING ACCEPTED

When Costello, vice president at UH, first arrived, he was told by long-timers to get some *aloha* shirts, to try to learn the local language like the word 'howzit', and that if he didn't go crazy in two years, he'll stay for a lifetime. They also told him the joke about the 'crabs in the bucket'. Costello felt as if those who lived in Hawai'i were in on the joke and these warnings were recycled for each newcomer. On his leaving after three years as vice president at UH, he commented on what was it like to live in Hawai'i: 'As an outsider, one is never truly accepted.'

A Caucasian from Colorado who has been living here for many years said that Hawai'i is open to all individuals to enter—giving and listening and not taking or talking. Locals feel hesitant about opening up to newcomers because a newcomer is an unknown. It's the fear of the unknown. The locals do not know where the newcomers are from and about their background. They are hesitant to talk about things that might be considered offensive, i.e. race. You must build a rapport, a relationship, and then they will open up to you and even talk about things like race.

A local born Japanese-American said that newcomers need to put in the effort and time and show that you're going to be around and things will turn around. You will be accepted and always be a part of the group and protected by the group. Don't go native, but if they see you eating at a local restaurant and they've seen you around, they will think you are alright. You have to pay your dues, put in the time and they will come around. One day, their attitude will flip and suddenly you are one of them and it doesn't change after that; you are accepted as part of the group.

FAST FACTS
ABOUT HAWAI'I

CHAPTER 10

'Growing up local means being colour blind. We recognise
different ethnicities, but sharing similar *chop suey* cultural
experiences gives us the illusion of being one.'
— Nadine Kam, *Honolulu Star Bulletin Weekend Edition*
17 June 2005

Official Name
State of Hawai'i

State Nickname
Aloha State

Capital
Honolulu

Flag
Hawai'i's state flag is the flag of the kingdom of Hawai'i made around 1816. The Union Jack of Great Britain is in the upper left hand corner. Originally, a British flag was given to Hawai'i to signify the islands as a protectorate of Great Britain. It is believed that this is the reason for the inclusion of the Union Jack in Hawai'i's flag. Eight horizontal stripes in white, red and blue (in that order from top to bottom) represent the eight main islands

State Anthem/Song
Hawai'i Ponoi (Hawai'i's Own); music by Henri Berger and lyrics by Kalākaua

State Motto
Ua mau ke ea o ka aina i ka pono (The life of the land is perpetuated in righteousness)

State Bird
Nene (rare goose native to Hawai'i)

State Mammal
Humpback whale

State Tree
Kukui (candlenut)

State Flower
Hibiscus

Time
Greenwich Mean Time minus 10 hours (GMT–1000). Unlike the rest of the United States, Hawai'i does not observe daylight savings

Telephone Codes
Country code: 1
Area code: 808

Land
The Hawaiian islands are located in the North Pacific Ocean, off the west coast of the United States. They are made up of eight main islands, which are actually the tops of submerged volcanoes, of which Kīlauea and Mauna Loa are still active

Area
total: 28,311.2 sq km (10,931 sq miles)
land: 16,635.5 sq km (6,423 sq miles)
water: 11,675.7 sq km (4,508 sq miles)

Highest Point
Mauna Kea (4,205 m / 13,796 ft)

Major Rivers
Wailuku River located on the island of Hawai'i and Anahulu River on the island of O'ahu

Climate
Mainly tropical with mild temperatures throughout the year

Natural Resources
Fish, flowers, pineapples, stone, sugar cane

Population
1,211,537 (as of April 2000)

Ethnic Groups
2000 census: Asian (41.6 per cent), Caucasian (24.3 per cent), mixed heritage (21.4 per cent), Native Hawaiian (6.6 per cent), African American (1.8 per cent), Pacific Islander (1.3 per cent) and Native American and Alaskan Native (0.3 per cent)

Religion
2000 census: Christianity (68 per cent), agnostic (18 per cent), Buddhist (9 per cent), others (5 per cent)

Official Languages
English and Hawaiian

Main Islands
Hawai'i	Big Island / Orchid Isle, Kaho'olawe
Kaua'i	Garden Isle
Lāna'i	Pineapple Island
Maui	Valley Isle
Moloka'i	Friendly Isle
Ni'ihau	Forbidden Island / The Distant Isle
O'ahu	Gathering Place

Government Structure
Federal government with three branches (executive, legislative and judicial) as provided for in the Constitution of Hawai'i

Currency
US dollar (USD or US$)

Gross Domestic Product (GDP)
US$ 50 billion (2004)

Agricultural Products
Livestock, macadamia nuts, pineapples and sugar cane

Industries
Clothing, food processing as well as clay, glass, metal and stone products

Exports
Coffee, flowers and nursery stock, livestock, macadamia nuts and sugar cane

Imports
Being an island community, Hawai'i has to import almost everything. Hawai'i imports petroleum, machines, fruits and vegetables, fish, cars (many from Japan) and consumer goods. Japan is Hawai'i's biggest foreign import and export trading partner

Airports
A total of 15 on the islands, with international airports at Honolulu, Hilo and Kona.

FAMOUS PEOPLE
Daniel K Akaka
The first US senator of Native Hawaiian ancestry and the only Chinese-American member of the Senate. He has served as Hawai'i's senator since 1990.

Akebono Taro (born Chad Rowan)
Born in Hawai'i, Akebono became the first non-Japanese wrestler ever to reach *yokozuna*, the highest rank in *sumo*, on 27 January 1993. Akebono means 'sunrise' in Japanese.

Princess Bernice Pauahi Bishop
The great-granddaughter and the last surviving descendant of King Kamehameha I. She and her husband, Charles R

Bishop, helped establish the Kamehameha Schools in 1887, and created the Bishop Museum in Honolulu in 1889.

George Ariyoshi
Elected state governor of Hawai'i from 1974 to 1986. He was the first Japanese-American to be elected governor of a state in the United States.

Tia Carrere
Born Althea Rae Duhinio Janairo Carrere, with Filipino, Chinese and Spanish heritage. She is a singer and actress and is famous for her role as Cassandra in the feature film *Wayne's World* and appearances in *Playboy* magazine.

Steve Case
Born and raised in Hawai'i and graduated from the prestigious Punahou School. He is the former chairman and CEO of America Online.

Samuel N Castle
A missionary to Hawai'i in 1836. He founded the Castle & Cooke Corporation in 1851. From the corporation, a trust fund was built that is now the Samuel N and Mary Castle Foundation.

Benjamin J Cayetano
Hawai'i's first Filipino-American governor. He is the first Filipino-American to serve as a state governor in the United States. He was elected for two terms and served from 1994–2002.

Hiram L Fong
A republican United States senator from 1959–1977. He was the first Asian-American and Chinese-American US senator.

Princess Victoria Ka'iulani
Heir to the throne of the kingdom of Hawai'i who died at an early age. Some Native Hawaiians believe that Ka'iulani died

of a broken heart, having suffered many losses in her life (e.g the overthrow of Hawaiian monarchy in 1893).

Father Damien

Born in Belgium and a missionary in Hawai'i from 1864, he is famous for dedicating his life to helping the victims of leprosy (Hansen's Disease) in the leper colony on the island of Moloka'i.

Don Ho

Born as Donald Ho Tai Loy, he was a famous Hawaiian musician and entertainer of mixed Chinese, Hawaiian, Portuguese, Dutch and German descent. He got his start at Duke's, the club owned by Duke Kahanamoku.

Daniel K Inouye

Currently US senator for Hawai'i and was first elected in 1962. He has been serving as US senator for over 44 years.

Duke Paoa Kahanamoku ('The Big Kahuna')

Generally regarded as the inventor of the modern sport of surfing. He was also a 1912 Olympic medalist swimmer and an ambassador of surfing and possibly the most famous Native Hawaiian.

Israel Kamakawiwo'ole

A Native Hawaiian entertainer and singer that died in 1997. He was a huge man that sang while playing the *ukulele*. His album *Alone In IZ World* is considered one of the most popular Hawaiian music albums of all time.

Konishiki Yasokichi (born Salevaa Atisanoe)

A Hawaiian-born Samoan, he is the first foreign-born champion, or *ozeki*, in the Japanese sport of *sumo*. *Ozeki* is the second highest rank in the sport.

Ellison Onizuka

An American astronaut from Kealakekua, Kona, who died during the destruction of the Space Shuttle Challenger.

Bette Midler
A famous actress and entertainer. She was born in Honolulu and is of Jewish decent. She majored in drama at the University of Hawai'i.

Musashimaru Koyo
Born as Fiamalu Penitani in Samoa and grown up in Hawai'i, he was the second foreign-born *sumo* wrestler in history to reach the rank of *yokozuna* in Japan.

Kelly Preston
Born in Honolulu and a graduate of Punahou School, she is an actress and has starred in movies such as *Jerry Maguire*. She is married to John Travolta.

Harold Sakata
Born and raised in Holualoa, he is of Japanese descent and was famous for his villain role in the James Bond film *Goldfinger*.

James Shigeta
Born in Hawai'i of Japanese descent, he is an actor and has appeared in movies such as *Diehard*.

Claus Spreckels
A major industrialist in Hawai'i during the kingdom, republican and territorial periods of the islands' history. He was a land developer and powerful in the sugar industry.

Jasmine Trias
Born and raised in Mililani and the daughter of Filipino immigrants, she is a singer and a former American Idol finalist.

John Waihee
Governor of Hawai'i from 1986 to 1994, he was the first American of Native Hawaiian descent to be elected governor of a state in the United States.

Don Stroud
Grew up in Waikīkī and has starred in Clint Eastwood and James Bond movies.

Michelle Wie
Considered a golf prodigy, she was born and raised in Hawai'i and graduated from Punahou School. She became a golf professional at the age of 16.

Frank Delima
A popular comedian from Hawai'i of Portuguese descent, he is known for his comedic caricature of various ethnic groups.

ACRONYMS
AYP   Annual Yearly Progress of public schools that is used for a passing or failing standards by the Hawai'i Department of Education
AYSO   All Volunteer Youth Soccer Organization
AJA   Americans of Japanese Ancestry

CULTURE QUIZ

SITUATION 1

What do you wear to a job interview in Hawai'i?

A Suit and tie.
B T-shirt and shorts.
C Slacks and *aloha* shirt.
D Swimsuit and slippers.

Comments

C This is the correct answer. It is the same as the business attire, which is business casual. A typical example of this is a pair of slacks, socks and loafers with a pressed *aloha* shirt tucked in with a belt.

SITUATION 2

How do you get rid of a giant centipede?

A Step on it.
B Pick it up with long barbecue tongs.
C Throw some dirty clothes on it.
D Move out.

Comments

A They can wrap around your shoe and bite you.
B This works OK if they aren't moving too fast.
C Covering them with something like dirty clothes makes them think they are safe and they stop moving. Grab the pile of clothes and throw it outside.
D Sometimes you can't help feeling this way.

SITUATION 3

You are the IT guy and someone asks in passing where the scanner that used to be in the lab last semester has gone to. You:

A Tell them you don't know because you are new and you weren't here last semester.
B Tell them you will put it on your to-do list.
C Go beg around for a scanner and set it up.
D Tell them you will look into it and let the other people in your department know that someone was looking for a scanner.

Comments

A This won't work because communication is indirect so you should take offhand suggestions as formal requests.
B This depends on how quickly you follow up.
C This is the *maikai* answer. The local concept of excellence and going the extra mile.
D Passing the buck doesn't work.

SITUATION 4

It is your first day on the job and you notice that everything they do in the department is either backward or outdated compared to where you came from. You:

Ⓐ Create a detailed plan for change and present it at the next meeting.
Ⓑ Explain to people the better way to do things as you encounter whatever is wrong.
Ⓒ Explain to your boss the improvements you see possible.
Ⓓ Keep quiet.
Ⓔ Laugh at them hoping they will get the joke.
Ⓕ Take your co-workers out to lunch and gossip about the problems at work.
Ⓖ After work, get your co-workers or boss drunk and cut loose with the brutal truth.
Ⓗ Write a guidebook explaining how backwards Hawaiian business is.
Ⓘ Ask people to explain how they think things should be done, then give them feedback on how you think it should be done.

Comments

Ⓓ is the only answer. You only show your arrogance by telling them what needs to be changed when you are new. Take the time to get a feel for how things are done and try doing it their way first. Later, slowly introduce your suggestions to individuals or your boss. But be careful you aren't criticising others' opinions because they tend to attach their self-esteem to their opinions.

SITUATION 5

The AJA librarian makes you wait an inordinate amount of time, and even waits on someone that came after you. You:

Ⓐ Get passive-aggressive and when it's finally your turn and ask her a million questions.
Ⓑ Be assertive and tell her it is your turn.
Ⓒ Slip her a buck or two.
Ⓓ Take it in stride and be patient
Ⓔ Give her the stink eye until she realises you're not to be toyed with.

Comments

Ⓐ The answers or attitude you may get will only infuriate you more.

Ⓑ Being assertive is an act of aggression here.

Ⓒ This isn't a third world country and people don't use bribes here.

Ⓓ This is the best answer. Locals value being in control and losing yours doesn't help. Be patient and courteous. Put in the face time of coming to the library a few times. After they start to recognise you and know you won't lose your cool, they will soften up.

Ⓔ This won't get you anywhere. You probably aren't doing it right anyway.

SITUATION 6

You work for a community college and your Japanese manager wants to have a meeting everyday at the end of the day right before the time to go home. This is a similar situation to what you would encounter in Japan. It seems like a ploy to try to get you to work more hours because these meetings always go past regular office hours. None of your Japanese co-workers claim overtime for these meetings even though union regulations require it. What do you do?

Ⓐ Object.

Ⓑ Claim the overtime pay for extra hours worked.

Ⓒ Just go along to get along.

Ⓓ Go over his head and complain to his boss.

Comments

Ⓒ. Making an effort and working hard are especially important to the Japanese. Also, building working relationships and team-building are as important as the work to be done. This meeting is an important after-hours team-building time. If no one else claims overtime even though they are supposed to, you should probably go along with the crowd. Remember this is a collectivist society and the nail that sticks out gets hammered down. Also, for some locals, there is a give and take—work extra hard some days and be compensated when there are times with less work to be done. Lastly, people are used to working hard and long hours (without complaining) and have more than one job to be able to afford to live here.

SITUATION 7

One local man had his wedding ring fixed by a local Japanese-American jeweller. The ring looked ruined after the jeweller was finished. He demanded for the jeweller to fix it, but the jeweller put up his defences and held his ground saying nothing was wrong with it. So the man, having grown up here, knew that the harder you push, the harder they push back. He took a different approach. He started to cry. The jeweller came from behind the counter, rushed to his side and consoled him. He told him he would have the ring fixed. Why did this work?

A He was afraid that he would lose face in front of his other customers.

B You can push and they will push back but if you are humble and ask for help, they will go out of their way for you.

C He valued this customer's business.

D The jeweller was forced to act or be considered insensitive by others.

Comments

Although **A** and **D** may have played small role in his turning around, **B** is probably the best answer. If you criticise their work or opinion, locals will take it personally and put up their defences. He was successful by turning the situation around and appearing to need help. Appealing to a local's emotions tends to bring about better results.

SITUATION 8

What do you do if you cut off someone in traffic?

A Flick your cigarette at them.

B Flip them off.

C Wave in the rear view mirror.
D Wave a *shaka* hand sign out the side window.

Comments
Either **C** or **D** is correct.

SITUATION 9
You love to walk around outside during your breaks at work. Why should you be careful?
A You might get in an accident and have to claim worker's compensation.
B You might run into someone who wants to give you more work.
C People might think you have nothing to do.
D If you get dirty, you will have to go home and change your clothes.

Comments
C is the correct answer. Appearances are more important than facts here. Find a way to de-stress outside of the watchful eyes of others.

DO'S AND DON'TS

DO'S

- Realise that Hawaiian time is different from Western time. Not only is it a relaxed pace, it has a different set of priorities. And sometimes punctuality is not one of them. Some say Hawaiian time means always being late. Others say that it's not a matter of planning on being late but that you will always be forgiven if you show up late. You usually don't need an excuse if you are late, but many locals mumble something about traffic.
- When visiting someone's home, it is good to bring a small gift like a dessert. Some ethnic groups value this tradition more than others. Many observe this tradition if they haven't seen someone in a long time or if they are visiting someone on another island.
- Bring food for any occasion. Food is the cornerstone of socialising in Hawai'i.
- Be generous when you bring something to a potluck or even a snack for your kids' team. People notice how generous you are, so do like the locals do—go overboard, but without being a show-off.
- When communicating with people at work or talking with people at a store, take a long breath, relax, be patient, take the time to be understood and understand them.
- When leaving a gathering like a small potluck, shake everyone's hand and/or give them a hug at the same time with a touch to the cheek with the nose.
- Thank everyone for the major events but sometimes even for the small things. Authors have a long list of people they thank in their acknowledgements. People send thank you notes.
- Consider the small things. If you receive a *lei*, wear it all day. Learn how to use chopsticks because they are as common as silverware here. And take off your shoes before entering the house.
- Listen more and talk less. Here, being assertive is considered pushy and will quickly be rewarded with the

'stink eye'—a hostile disapproving stare. Locals value self-depreciation and humility.

- Ask for help. You may be trying to fix something and are having trouble, and everyone just holds back and watches. But as soon as you give up and ask help, they jump right in and help you out. People don't want to butt into your business. They feel it's not their place to intrude, unless invited.
- Show face. If you are invited to participate in potlucks, fundraisers, etc., make sure you show your face at a few of these events.

DON'TS

- Don't hold back. Join the PTA, HOA, a humanitarian organisation or something. There is an expectation of group involvement and giving back to the community. This is an excellent way for the newcomer to learn the culture and make local friends.
- Don't be a show-off and don't stick out. In Japan, the nail that sticks out gets hammered down. It is often the same here; kids bragging at school will get teased. This also means not being loud and aggressive.
- Don't talk stink (talk bad about people). People are more sensitive here; they also gossip more and everyone knows someone.
- Don't forget to reciprocate. If you help yourself to food provided, then bring and share food at other times.
- Don't honk your horn even when waiting behind another car when the light has been green for a while.
- Don't speak up in a way that shows off your expertise. Teach what you know through doing instead of telling.
- Don't be afraid to make mistakes.
- Don't be afraid to laugh at yourself and be yourself.
- Don't be afraid to make local friends.

Himakamaka means 'self-righteous' in Hawaiian. Sometimes, locals see newcomers as *himakamaka*. Also, locals may have an inferiority complex in thinking that people from the mainland or other countries are more educated than they are. They put up their defences when they see a newcomer because they are afraid the newcomer might blurt out something they do not understand. Don't talk down to locals and try to understand there is a different local vocabulary and topics of conversation. Be sensitive to their self-esteem and saving their face.

GLOSSARY

Below is a list of the frequently used vocabulary, place names and phrases for the Hawaiian language:

PEOPLE

Hawaiian	English
Tūtū	Granny
Pēpē	Baby
Wahine	Girl, female, wife
Hapa	Half white or mixed blood
Kama'āina	Person of the land, long-time resident, native
'Ohana	Family or the group you are part of
'Ohana nui	Extended family
Mea Aloha	Beloved one
Malihini	Newly arrived, newcomer
Kāne	Male, man, husband
Keiki	Child
Paniolo	Cowboy
Kanaka	Commoner, formerly used by Westerners for Native Hawaiians but still used in Hawaiian language and for Hawaiians among locals.
Pākē	China or Chinese person
Makua	Parent
Makua kāne	Father, uncle
Makuahine	Mother
Hānai	Adopted
Ali'i	Ruler
Kupuna	Ancestor or grandparents
Kupuna kāne	Grandfather

Hawaiian	English
Kupuna wahine	Grandmother
Kahu	Guardian
Huna	Secret
Akua	God
Kahiko	Old, ancient
Hoa pili	Close friend
Aikāne	Friend
Ipo	Sweetheart

ADJECTIVES

Hawaiian	English
Maika'i	Good, excellence, beautiful, handsome
Maika'i loa	Very good
Maika'i hana	Good work
Akamai	Clever or smart
'Eleu	Quick, energetic, active
Nani, u'i	Beautiful
Hau'oli	Happy
Pilikia	Trouble
Kāpulu	Messy, careless
Huhū	Angry, upset
Pupule	Crazy
Ho'omalimali	Sweet talk, flattery
Lōlō	Dumb, stupid, crazy
Kapakahi	Crooked
Kolohe	Naughty
Manini	Stingy
Honi	Kiss
Hou	New
'Ae	Yes
Pilau	Spoiled, dirty

Hawaiian	English
Pololei	Correct
Hoihoi	Interesting
Maha'oi	Forward, brazen, bold

BODY RELATED

Hawaiian	English
Po'o	Head
'Ōkole	Butt
'Ōpū	Stomach
Piko	Navel
Ola	Life, health
Ma'i	Sick
Hāpai	Pregnant
Lomilomi	Massage
'Au'au	Take a bath
Mu'umu'u	Loose gown, full-length dress

NATURE

Hawaiian	English
Kukui	Candlenut tree. The oily nuts inside were burned for lights in ancient times
Koa	Native hardwood forest tree; Hawaiian mahogany used in furniture and *ukuleles*; brave; goddess of the *hula*
Kapa, Tapa	Bark cloth made out of the paper bark of mulberry trees
Pua	Flower
Paka lōlō	Marijuana

Hawaiian	English
Pāhoehoe	Smooth, ropey lava
Pōhaku	Stone
One	Sand
Wai	Water
Ua	Rain
Ahi	Fire
Lā	Sun
Lani	Sky, heaven, royal
Hōkū	Star
Honua	Earth, world
Makani	Wind, break wind
Ānuenue	Rainbow
Ao	Cloud
Wailele	Waterfall
Pō	Night
Noe	Mist
Manō	Shark
Manu	Bird
Ipu	Gourd
Pulelehua	Butterfly
Pōpoki	Cat
'Īlio	Dog
Honu	Turtle

GEOGRAPHY

Hawaiian	English
Uka	Towards the shore or inland
Mauka	Mountains or towards the mountains
Makai	Coast or towards the ocean (*kai*)

Hawaiian	English
Koʻolau	Windward side of the islands
Kona	Leeward or south side of the islands
Moana	Ocean
Mauna	Mountain
Waena	Middle, central
Pali	Cliff
Ala	Path, road
Lae	Cape
Ahupuaʻa	A pie-shaped piece of land falling in the valley between mountains ridges and running out to the ocean
Ana	Cave
Awa	Harbour, port
Hono	Bay
Kua	Ridge, gulch
Kula, papa	Plain, field
Moku	Island, district
Olo, puʻu	Hill
Puna	Spring of water

FOOD

Hawaiian	English
Lilikoʻi	Passion fruit, grown in Hawaiʻi and used in desserts
Pūpū	finger food, appetiser
Lūʻau	Hawaiian feast

Hawaiian	English
Taro / Karo	Edible root and major food source of ancient Hawaiians
Poi	Taro pounded into a paste
Imu	Barbecue fire pit or underground oven used to cook things like *kālua* pig
Kālua	Baked in the *imu*
Pua'a kālua	*Kālua* pig
'Ono	Delicious
'Oki	Cut
Mā'ana	Full
I'a	Fish
Niu	Coconut
Limu	Seaweed
Hala kahiki	Pineapple
I'a maka	Raw fish
'Ōpae	Shrimp
Kupa, Kai	Soup
Kō	Sugar, sugar cane
Kī	Tea
Kope	Coffee
Pia	Beer
'Ulu	Breadfruit
Ipu	Watermelon
Pipi	Beef

HOME AND WORK

Hawaiian	English
Hale	House, building
Lānai	Porch, veranda or walkway
Puka	Hole, door

Hawaiian	English
'Ōpala	Trash
Lua	Pit, crater, toilet
Hana	Work, occupation
Hui	Organisation, club
'Ōlelo	Word, language, also name of one of the television stations
Pau	Done, finished
Kālā	Money
Puke	Book
Luna	Boss, overseer
Manawa	Time
'Apōpō	Tomorrow

ANCIENT HAWAI'I, HAWAIIAN ANIMISM AND SPIRITUALITY

Hawaiian	English
Kāhili	Staff held by royalty with feathers at the top that looks like a huge feather duster
Pahu	Drum
Wa'a	Canoe
Kākau	Tattoo, Tatau is the Tahitian word
Mōlī	Tattoo needle traditionally made out of bone
Kane	Creator god
Pele	Volcano goddess
Lono	God of earth, storm and fertility, the one that Captian Cook was mistaken for; news
Kū	God of nature and war
Kanaloa	God of ocean and death

Hawaiian	English
Hina	Goddess of moon
Laka	Goddess of hula
Uli	Goddess of sorcery, healing
Māui	God of adventure
'Uhane	Soul, spirit
Mana	Spiritual power; to have authority
Moe'uhane	Dream
Mele	Song, poem
Oli	Chant
Hula	Type of Hawaiian dance
Kahuna	Master, expert, priest
'Aumakua	Spirit of ancestral gods
Kapu	Keep out; set of rules and prohibitions
Kumu	Teacher, source
Heiau	Ancient Hawaiian temple
'Awa	Drink made from kava root that induces an altered state, used by the *kahuna* in ceremonies
Lōkahi	Unity, harmony
Noa	Freedom
Aloha	Love, compassion, hello, goodbye
Mālama	Take care of, preserve, serve, care for
Pono	Moral, good, order, right
Ho'oponopono	Put in order, a family conference to talk out problems to reach a fair solution also, including prayer and confession
Kalikiano	Christian

Hawaiian	English
Makahiki	Year, also annual celebration now called Aloha Week

NUMBERS

Hawaiian	English
Kahi	One, first
Lua	Two, second
Kolu	Three, third
Hā	Four, fourth
Lima	Five, fifth
Ono	Six, sixth
Hiku	Seven, seventh
Walu	Eight, eighth
Iwa	Nine, ninth
Umi	Ten, tenth

COLOURS

Hawaiian	English
'Ele'ele	Black
Uli, polū	Blue
Ke'oke'o, kea	White
'Ula'ula, mea	Red, reddish; symbol of royalty and sacred Polynesia
Māku'e	Brown
'Ahinahina	Gray
'Ōma'oma'o	Green
'Alani	Orange
'Akala	Pink
Poni	Purple
Melemele	Yellow

EVERYDAY PHRASES

Hawaiian	English
E 'olu'olu oe	Please
He mea iki	You're welcome
Pehea 'oe? Maika'i nō?	How are you?
Maika'i no au, mahalo	I'm fine, thank you
O wai ko'u inoa?	What is your name?
O Brent ko'u inoa	My name is Brent
Aia i hea 'oe e noho nei?	Where do you live?
Ke noho nei au ma Waikele	I live in Waikele
Waikele no ka 'oi	Waikele is the best
Aloha kakahiaka	Good morning
Aloha ahiahi	Good evening
Aloha awakea	Good day
Pau hana	Work finished
Hana hou	Do it again
Hele mai	Come here
Hele aku	Go away
Hele pēlā!	Get out! Go away!
E ha mau leo	Be quiet
Pehea ho'i	Who knows?
Aoia	That's it
E hele 'oe e 'au 'au	Go take a bath
E holoi i kou lima	Wash your hands

COMMON PHRASES IN LETTERS AND EMAILS

Hawaiian	English
Mahalo ā nui	Many thanks. You will see aloha *mahalo nui* at the end of letters or emails
Mahalo nui loa	Thank you very much
Aloha 'ohana	Greetings family, group

Hawaiian	English
Please Kōkua	Please help out. This one is frequently seen on letters or emails looking for donations of time or money to a worthy cause
Me ke aloha	With love
Me ke aloha pumehana	With warmest regards
A hui hoa ka ua	Goodbye until we meet again

OTHERS

Hawaiian	English
Mele kalikimaka	Merry Christmas, a borrowed word from English
Hou ʻoli la hānau	Happy birthday
Hou ʻoli makahiki hou	Happy new year
ʻŌkole ma luna	Bottoms up, a toast
E komo mai	Welcome, come in
Kipa hou mai	Come and visit again
Aloha au ia ʻoe	I love you
Aloha ke akua	Aloha is God; God is love
Hawaiʻi Neʻi	This Hawaiʻi, our beloved Hawaiʻi
Aloha ʻāina	Love for the land
Ua mau ke ea o ka aina i ka pono	The life of the land is perpetuated in righteousness (state motto)

RESOURCE GUIDE

As soon as you get your phone line set up, Hawaiian Telcom will send out a new phone book to you. Lots of general and frequently called numbers can be found in the front of the telephone directory. You can also visit a local Hawai'i telephone directory online at http://www.theparadisepages.com. It has several guides with general numbers for just about everything. There is also a *Yellow Pages* Japanese telephone directory in Hawai'i at http://www.ypj.com.

IMPORTANT NUMBERS

- Emergency (ambulance, fire, police)
  Tel: 911
  There are operators who speak other languages who can assist you.
- Weather forecast
  Tel: (808) 973-4380
- Aloha United Way 211
  Tel: 211
  A service line for the community that can link you up with the appropriate resources and contacts to assist your specific needs
- US Citizenship and Immigration Services
  Tel: 1-800-375-5283
  Website: http://www.uscis.gov
- US Customs and Borders Protection
  Tel: (1-202) 354-1000
  Website: http://www.cbp.gov
- US Post Office
  Website: http://www.usps.com
  1-800-275-8777
- Directory Assistance
  Tel: 1411

HOSPITALS

- Castle Medical Center
  Tel: (808) 263-5500

- Department of Health (Hawai'i State Hospital)
  Tel: (808) 247-2191
- Kahuku Hospital
  Tel: (808) 293-9221
- Kaiser Permanente
  Tel: (808) 432-0000
  Website: http://www.kp.org
- Kapi'olani Medical Center
  Tel: (808) 486-6000
- Queen's Medical Center
  Tel: (808) 538-9011
  Website: http://www.queens.org
- Saint Francis Medical Center
  Tel: (808) 547-6011
- Straub Clinic & Hospital
  Website: http://www.straubhealth.com
  Tel: (808) 522-4000
  Straub has several clinics in different areas.
- Wahiawa General Hospital
  Tel: (808) 621-8411

DENTAL
- Hawai'i Dental Association
  Tel: (808) 593-7956
  Website: http://www.hawaiidentalassociation.net
  Provides emergency dental services and dentist referrals.

CHILDCARE
- PATCH
  Tel: (808) 839-1988
  Website: http://www.patch-hi.org

UTILITIES
- Oceanic Cable
  Tel: (808) 625-8100
  Website: http://www.oceanic.com
- Hawaiian Electric Company [HECO]
  Tel: (808) 543-7771
  Website: http://www.heco.com

- The Gas Company
  Tel: (808) 535-5933
  Website: http://www.hawaiigas.com
- Hawaiian Telcom
  Tel: (808) 643-3456
  Website: http://www.hawaiiantel.com
- Honolulu Board of Water Supply
  Tel: (808) 532-6510
  Website: http://www.hbws.org

TRANSPORTATION
- TheBus
  Tel: (808) 848-5555
  Website: http://www.thebus.org/
- Drivers License Information
  Tel: (808) 532-7700
  Website: http://www.honolulu.gov/csd/vehicle/dlicense.htm

COMMUNICATIONS
When making local and international phone calls, inner-island calls are unlimited with basic phone service, but those between islands cost extra. How you dial an international number may depend on your long distance provider. For long distance providers like AT&T, you dial 011- country code and then the number. The country code for Japan is 81 so you would dial 011-81 first then the number. For calling other states within the USA, you need to dial 1 then the area code. For Colorado, it would be 1-970 then the number. See the front of the phone book for a listing of country codes and area codes.

EMBASSIES
- Australia
  1000 Bishop Street, Penthouse
  Honolulu, HI 96813
  Tel: (808) 524-5050
- Austria
  1314 South King Street, Suite 1260

Honolulu, HI 96814
Tel: (808) 923-8585

- Bangladesh
3785 Old Pali Road
Honolulu, HI 96817
Tel: (808) 595-3370
- Belgium
707 Richards Street, Suite 600
Honolulu, HI 96813
Tel: (808) 535-1440
- Brazil
345 Queen Sreet, Suite 400
Honolulu, HI 96713
Tel: (808) 235-0571
- Chile
2240 Kuhio Avenue, Apartment 3804
Honolulu, HI 96815
Tel: (808) 550-4985
- Cook Islands
5313 Oio Drive
Honolulu, HI 96821
Tel: (808) 373-1315
- Denmark
285 Sand Island Access Road
Honolulu, HI 96819
Tel: (808) 844-2028
- Federated States of Micronesia
3049 Ualena Street, Suite 910
Honolulu, HI 96819
Tel: (808) 836-4775
- Finland
1650 Ala Moana Boulevard, Suite 813
Honolulu, HI 96815
Tel: (808) 943-2640
- France
1099 Alakea Street, Suite 1800
Honolulu, HI 96813
Tel: (808) 547-5852

- Germany
  252 Paoa Place, Suite 4-1
  Honolulu, HI 96815
  Tel: (808) 946-3819
- Hungary
  6710 Hawai'i Kai Drive, Suite 1110
  Honolulu, HI 96825
  Tel: (808) 377-3637
- India
  P O Box 10905
  Honolulu, HI 96816
  Tel: (808) 732-7692
- Italy
  735 Bishop Street, Suite 201
  Honolulu, HI 96813
  Tel: (808) 531-2277
- Japan
  1742 Nu'uanu Avenue
  Honolulu, HI 96817
  Tel: (808) 543-3111
- Kiribati
  95 Nakolo Place, Suite 265
  Honolulu, HI 96819
  Tel: (808) 834-6775
- Korea
  2756 Pali Highway
  Honolulu, HI 96817
  Tel: (808) 595-6109
- Malaysia
  999 Bishop Street, Suite 805
  Honolulu, HI 96813
  Tel: (808) 525-7702
- Marshall Islands
  1888 Lusitana Street, Suite 301
  Honolulu, HI 96813
  Tel: (808) 545-7767
- Mexico
  P O Box 88152

Honolulu, HI 96830
Tel: (808) 945-2291
- Netherlands
  745 Fort Street Mall, Suite 702
  Honolulu, HI 96813
  Tel: (808) 531-6897
- New Zealand
  900 Richards Street, Suite 414
  Honolulu, HI 96813
  Tel: (808) 595-2200, (808) 543-7900
- Norway
  4215 Kilauea Avenue
  Honolulu, HI 96816
  Tel: (808) 732-2926
- Palau
  1154 Fort Street Mall, Suite 300
  Honolulu, HI 96813
  Tel: (808) 524-5414
- Philippines
  2433 Pali Highway
  Honolulu, HI 96817
  Tel: (808) 595-6316
- Poland
  2825 South King Street, Suite 2701
  Honolulu, HI 96826
  Tel: (808) 955-4488
- Portugal
  P O Box 240778
  Honolulu, HI 96824
  Tel: (808) 377-9201
- Russia
  4117 Kahala Avenue
  Honolulu, HI 96816
  Tel: (808) 737-5248
- San Marino
  4615 Kahala Avenue
  Honolulu, HI 96816
  Tel: (808) 923-2468

- Slovenia
  900 Fort Street Mall, Suite 1450
  Honolulu, HI 96813
  Tel: (808) 544-3203
- Spain
  P O Box 240778
  Honolulu, HI 96824
  Tel: (808) 377-9201
- Sri Lanka
  60 North Beretania Street, Suite 410
  Honolulu, HI 96817
  Tel: (808) 524-6738
- Sweden
  Pacific Guardian Center
  737 Bishop Street, Suite 2600
  Honolulu, HI 96813
  Tel: (808) 528-4777
- Switzerland
  4231 Papu Circle
  Honolulu, HI 96816
  Tel: (808) 737-5297
- Taipei Economic and Cultural Office
  2746 Pali Highway
  Honolulu, HI 96817
  Tel: (808) 595-6347
- Thailand
  1287 Kalani Street, Suite 103
  Honolulu, HI 96817
  Tel: (808) 845-7332
- Tonga
  738 Kaheka Street, Suite 306B
  Honolulu, HI 96814
  Tel: (808) 953-2449
- Uruguay
  1833 Kalakaua Avenue, Suite 710
  Honolulu, HI 96815
  Tel: (808) 955-8641

EDUCATION
Public Schools:
- Department of Education
  Website: http://www.doe.k12.hi.us/
- School Status and Improvement Reports (SSIR)
  Website: http://arch.k12.hi.us/school/ssir/default.html

Private Schools:
- Hawai'i Association of Independent Schools (HAIS)
  Website: http://www.hais.org/

Universities and Colleges
- Brigham Young University Hawai'i (Lā'ie)
  Tel (808) 293-3211
  Website: http://www.byuh.edu/
- Chaminade University (Honolulu)
  Tel: (808) 735-4711
  Website: http://www.chaminade.edu/
- Hawai'i Pacific University (Honolulu)
  Tel: (808) 544-0200
  Website: http://www.hpu.edu/
  The following are all part of the University of Hawai'i
  system at website: http://www.hawaii.edu/
- University of Hawai'i (Mānoa)
  Tel: (808) 956-8111
  Website: http://www.manoa.hawaii.edu/
- University of Hawai'i (Hilo)
  Tel: (808) 974-7414
  Website: http://www.hilo.hawaii.edu/
- University of Hawai'i (West O'ahu)
  Tel: (808) 454-4700
  Website: http://www.westoahu.hawaii.edu/
- Hawai'i Community College
  Tel: (808) 974-7611
  Website: http://www.hawaii.hawaii.edu/
- Honolulu Community College
  Tel: (808) 845-9211
  Website: http://www.honolulu.hawaii.edu/

- Kapi'olani Community College
  Tel: (808) 734-9000
  Website: http://www.kapiolani.hawaii.edu/
- Kaua'i Community College
  Tel: (808) 245-8311
  Website: http://www.kauai.hawaii.edu/
- Leeward Community College
  Tel: (808) 455-0011
  Website: http://www.lcc.hawaii.edu/
- Maui Community College
  Tei: (808) 984-3500
  Website: http://www.maui.hawaii.edu/
- Windward Community College
  Tel: (808) 235-7400
  Website: http://www.windward.hawaii.edu/

EXPAT CLUBS
- Honolulu Newcomers Club
  Tel: (808) 944-3310
  Website: http://www.newcomersclub.com/hi.html

VOLUNTEER ORGANISATIONS
- Pacific Gateway Center
  Tel: (808) 845-3918
  Website: http://www.pacificgateway.org/
- Helping Hands Hawai'i
  Tel: (808) 536-7234
  Website: http://www.helpinghandshawaii.org/
- Aloha United Way
  Tel: 211
  Website: http://www.auw.org

NEWSPAPERS
- *Honolulu Star Bulletin*
  Website: http://www.starbulletin.com
- *The Honolulu Advertiser*
  Website: http://www.honoluluadvertiser.com
- *Kaua'i Garden Island News*
  Website: http://www.kauaiworld.com

- *Hawaii Reporter*
  Website: http://www.hawaiireporter.com
  Online Hawai'i business news based in Kailua.
  Free weekly newspapers that come in your mailbox are
  Mid Week and *Island Weekly.*

Magazines
- *Pacific Business News*
  Website: http://www.bizjournals.com/pacific/
- *Honolulu Weekly* (entertainment guide)
  Website: http://www.honoluluweekly.com
  Other magazines include *Honolulu Magazine*, *Island Business*, *Honolulu Weekly* and *Island Lifestyle* (alternative gay and lesbian).

TELEVISION
- KBFD
  Website: http://www.kbfd.com/eng/
  Korean and other Asian language programmes.
- KIKU
  Website: http://www.kikutv.com
  Japanese, Cantonese, Mandarin, Filipino, Korean, Vietnamese, English language programmes.
- KHLU
  Website: http://www.univision.com
  Website and programmes in Spanish.

RADIO
Popular foreign language radio stations include AM, 940 KJPN (Japanese), 1210 KZOO (Japanese), 1270 KNDI (Filipino) and 1540 KREA (Korean).

BUSINESS
- Chamber of Commerce of Hawai'i
  Tel: (808) 545-4300
  Website: http://www.cochawaii.com/
- The Hawai'i Island Chamber of Commerce
  Website: http://www.hicc.biz
  Tel: (808) 935-7178

- Honolulu Japanese Chamber of Commerce
  Tel: (808) 949-5531
  Website: http://www.honolulujapanesechamber.org/
- SCORE (business information and counselling centre)
  Tel: (808) 532-8232, (808) 522-8132
  Website: http://www.score.org
- The Department of Business, Economic Development
  and Tourism
  Tel: (808) 586-2423
  Website: http://www.hawaii.gov/dbedt/

USEFUL LINKS AND RESOURCES
Language
- Hawaiian Dictionary Online
  Website: http://www.wehewehe.org
- Pidgin English Dictionary
  Website: http://www.e-hawaii.com/fun/pidgin/default.asp

Interpreter
- Bilingual Access Line
  Tel: (808) 526-9724
  A 24-hour referral service for interpreters of Cantonese,
  Ilocano, Korean, Japanese, Lao, Mandarin, Tagalog,
  Tongan, Samoan, Vietnamese and other languages.

Library
- State Public Library
  Website: http://www.librarieshawaii.org/
- University of Hawai'i
  Website: http://uhmanoa.lib.hawaii.edu/

Hawai'i Forums and Blogs
- Website: http://hawaii.metblogs.com
- Website: http://www.hawaiithreads.com

Government
- Website: http://www.hawaii.gov
- Website: http://www.co.honolulu.hi.us/menu/government
- Website: http://www.honolulupropertytax.com

Government Information on Living in Hawai'i

- Website: http://pahoehoe.ehawaii.gov/portal/community/ newcomer.html
- Website: http://www.ehawaiigov.org/living/html/ housing.html
- Website: http://www.ehawaiigov.org/education/html/ index.html

Animal Quarantine Information

- Website: http://www.hawaiiag.org/hdoa/ai_aqs_info.htm

Job Search Resources

- Hawai'i State Portal
  Website: http://www.hawaii.gov/portal/employment/index. html
- Hawai'i State Jobs
  Website: http://www.ehawaiigov.org/statejobs
- Hawai'i City and County Job Information
  Website: http://www.ehawaiigov.org/working/html/ resources.html
- American's Job Bank Hawai'i
  Website: http://www.ajb.dni.us/hi/
- State of Hawai'i's Workforce Development Job Bank
  Website: http://web0.dlir.state.hi.us/
- Hawai'i Workforce Informer
  Website: http://www.hiwi.org
- All University of Hawai'i system (includes community colleges) jobs
  Website: http://workatuh.hawaii.edu
- Military base NAF jobs in Hawai'i
  Website: http://www.nafjobs.com
  Employment agencies can be found in the phone book and in the online phone book, here are a few:
- ALTRES
  Website: http://www.altres.com
- Adecco
  Website: http://www.adecco-hawaii.com
- CTA
  Website: http://www.cta.net

Real Estate Multiple Listing Service (MLS)
- Honolulu Board of Realtors
  Website: http://www.hicentral.com

Phone Directories
- The Paradise Yellow Pages
  Website: http://www.theparadisepages.com
- Superpages
  Website: http://www.superpages.com
- Yellow Pages Japan in USA
  Website: http://www.ypj.com(Japanese)

Military
- Military in Hawai'i
  Website: http://www.yourmilitaryinhawaii.com

OTHER RACES
Hawaiian
- Uluka: The Hawaiian Electronic Library
  Website: http://ulukau.org/english.php

Chinese
- Chinese Chamber of Commerce in Hawai'i
  Website: http://www.ccchi.org
- Chinatown
  Website: http://www.chinatownhi.com

Filipino
- Filipino Community Center (FILCOM)
  Website: http://www.filcom.org
- Filipino Chamber of Commerce in Hawai'i
  Tel: (808) 792-8876

Japanese
- Japanese Cultural Center of Hawai'i
  Website: http://www.jcch.com
- Honolulu Japanese Chamber of Commerce
  Website: http://www.honolulujapanesechamber.org

Portuguese
- Hawai'i Island Portuguese Chamber
  Website: http://www.hipcc.org

Korean
- Korean Chamber of Commerce in Hawai'i
  Website: http://www.hkccweb.org

Vietnamese
- Vietnamese American Chamber of Commerce in Hawai'i
  Website: http://www.vacch.org/

FURTHER READING

HISTORY

Mark Twain's Letters from Hawai'i. Mark Twain. Honolulu, HI: University Press of Hawai'i, 1975.
- A great look at Hawai'i through Twain's eyes. It shows the effects the Western world and missionaries had on Hawai'i by the mid-1800s.

Dream of Islands: Voyages of Self-Discovery in the South Seas. Gavan Daws. Honolulu, HI: Mutual Publishing, 1980.

Shoal of Time: History of the Hawaiian Islands. Gavan Daws. Toronto: Macmillan, 1968.

Yesterday in Hawai'i : A Voyage Through Time. Scott C S Stone. Waipahu, HI: Island Heritage Publishing, 2003.
- A nice pictorial history of Hawai'i from early Polynesia to the present.

Travels in Hawai'i. Robert Louis Stevenson. Honolulu, HI: University Press of Hawai'i, 1991.

HAWAIIAN CULTURE

Nānā I Ke Kumu (Look to the Source) Volume 1 and 2. Mary Kawena Pukui, E W Haertig and Catherine A Lee. Honolulu, HI: Hui Hānai (Queen Liliokalani Children's Center),1983.
- A source book of Hawaiian cultural practices and beliefs.

The Need for Hawaii: Guide to Hawaiian Cultural and Kahuna Values. Patrick Ka'ano'i. Honolulu, HI: Ka'ano'i Productions, 1992.

Ku kanaka, Stand Tall: A Search for Hawaiian Values. George S Kanahele. Honolulu, HI: University of Hawai'i Press, 1993.

LANGUAGE

Pidgin Grammar: An Introduction to the Creole Language of Hawai'i. Kent Sakoda and Jeff Siegel, Honolulu, HI: Bess Press, 2003.

Hawaiian Dictionary. Mary Kawena Pukui. Honolulu: University of Hawai'i Press, 1981.

Hawaiian Dictionary: Hawaiian-English, English-Hawaiian. Mary Kawena Pukui and Samuel H Elbert. Honolulu, HI : University of Hawai'i Press, 1986.

LOCAL CULTURE
People and Cultures of Hawaii: A Psychocultural Profile. John F McDermott. Honolulu, HI: University of Hawai'i Press, 1980.
- This book was originally written for psychologists as an approach to counselling people in Hawai'i using different approaches for each culture—Hawaiian, Caucasian, Chinese, Japanese, Portuguese, Okinawan, Korean, Filipino, Samoan, Vietnamese and Hmong (Laos). It has been written for a more general audience and is helpful in understanding the values, beliefs and motivations of each culture.

Fairly Lucky You Live in Hawai'i!: Cultural Pluralism in the Fiftieth State. Richard L Rapson. Lanham, MD: University Press of America, 1980.
- Personal reflections on life in Hawai'i written by UH Professor of History and long-time resident of Hawai'i.

Mainland Haole: The White Experience in Hawai'i. Elvi Whittaker. New York, NY: Columbia University Press, 1986.
- A Canadian anthropologist's academic research on whites living in Hawai'i. Looks at racism and stereotypes aimed at and coming from Caucasians.

The Japanese and the Haoles of Honolulu. Frederick Samuels. New Haven, CT: College and University Press, 1970.
- A University of New Hampshire sociologist's academic research on the relations between the Japanese and Caucasians in Hawai'i. Since his study, there is a new generation of Japanese and Caucasians in Hawai'i, but they may still retain some of same values of the previous generation used in the study.

GENERAL INFO ON HAWAII
Price of Paradise (Volume 1 & 2). Randall W Roth. Honolulu, HI: Mutual Publishing, 1992.

Hawai'i Data Book: A Statistical Reference to Hawai'i's Social, Economic and Political Trends. Robert Schmitt. Honolulu, HI: Mutual Publishing, 2002.

OTHER USEFUL BOOKS
Beyond Paradise: Encounters in Hawai'i Where the Tour Bus Never Runs. Peter S Adler. Woodbridge, CT: Ox Bow Press, 1993.

Art of Crossing Cultures. Craig Storti. Yarmouth, ME: Intercultural Press, 2001.
- This is an excellent resource for understanding and overcoming culture shock.

CultureShock! USA. Esther Wanning. London, UK and Singapore: Marshall Cavendish Editions, 2005.

CultureShock! Japan. P Sean Bramble. London, UK and Singapore: Marshall Cavendish Editions, 2005.

CultureShock! Philippines. Alfredo Roces and Grace Roces. London, UK and Singapore: Marshall Cavendish Editions, 2006.

CultureShock! Korea. Sonja Vegdahl and Ben Seunghwa Hur. London, UK and Singapore: Marshall Cavendish Editions, 2005.

ABOUT THE AUTHOR

Brent Massey is an author and publisher (http://www. JetlagPress.com). He loves being abroad and has travelled throughout Asia and Europe, visiting countries such as Italy, Germany, France, Netherlands, Switzerland, Taiwan, Thailand, Singapore and Myanmar. Married to a Japanese woman, Brent isn't a stranger to crossing cultural boundaries. Having lived in Japan for three years, he experienced culture shock in Japan, and reverse culture shock upon returning to the US. In 2003, Brent was awarded the prestigious Monbusho Research Scholarship by the Japanese government.

Brent moved from his hometown in Colorado to Hawai'i In the summer of 2004. In Hawai'i, he was surprised to experience culture shock (again!), and thus saw the need for a book in helping newcomers understand and adapt to the unique customs of Hawai'i, which is heavily influenced by Asian culture—especially that of Japan. He is especially excited and enthusiastic about *CultureShock! Hawai'i* because there is so much cross-cultural information that the public has yet to read about living in Hawai'i.

After residing in Hawai'i for a few years, Brent recommitted his life to the Lord. His book *Discovering the Water of Life* is a personal account of rediscovering his faith in the Lord while living in Hawai'i.

Brent can be contacted at brentmassey@yahoo.com or brentmassey@brentmassey.com. You can also visit his website at http://www.BrentMassey.com.

INDEX

Titles in the CultureShock! series:

Argentina	Great Britain	Russia
Australia	Greece	San Francisco
Austria	Hawaii	Saudi Arabia
Bahrain	Hong Kong	Scotland
Beijing	Hungary	Sri Lanka
Belgium	India	Shanghai
Berlin	Ireland	Singapore
Bolivia	Italy	South Africa
Borneo	Jakarta	Spain
Bulgaria	Japan	Sri Lanka
Brazil	Korea	Sweden
Cambodia	Laos	Switzerland
Canada	London	Syria
Chicago	Malaysia	Taiwan
Chile	Mauritius	Thailand
China	Morocco	Tokyo
Costa Rica	Munich	Travel Safe
Cuba	Myanmar	Turkey
Czech Republic	Netherlands	United Arab
Denmark	New Zealand	Emirates
Ecuador	Norway	USA
Egypt	Pakistan	Vancouver
Finland	Paris	Venezuela
France	Philippines	
Germany	Portugal	

For more information about any of these titles, please contact any of our Marshall Cavendish offices around the world (listed on page ii) or visit our website at:

www.marshallcavendish.com/genref